The

This book is to be returned on or before
the last date stamped below.

LIBREX

The
New
Reckoning

*Capitalism, States
and Citizens*

David Marquand

Polity Press

Copyright © David Marquand 1997

The right of David Marquand to be identified as author of this work has been asserted in accordance with the Copyright, Designs and Patents Act 1988.

First published in 1997 by Polity Press in association with Blackwell Publishers Ltd.

Editorial office:
Polity Press
65 Bridge Street
Cambridge CB2 1UR, UK

Marketing and production:
Blackwell Publishers Ltd
108 Cowley Road
Oxford OX4 1JF, UK

Published in the USA by
Blackwell Publishers Inc.
Commerce Place
350 Main Street
Malden, MA 02148, USA

ISBN 0–7456–1744–1
ISBN 0–7456–1745–X (pbk)

A CIP catalogue record for this book is available from the British Library and has been applied for from the Library of Congress.

Typeset in Palatino 10.5 pt on 12 leading
by Photoprint, Torquay, Devon.
Printed in Great Britain by T. J. International, Padstow, Cornwall.

This book is printed on acid-free paper.

Contents

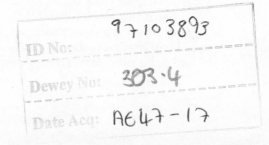

Acknowledgements

The authors and publishers wish to thank the following for permission to use the material contained in the chapters listed below:

The editors of *Archives Européennes de Sociologie* for chapter 2 (first published as 'Civic Republicans and Liberal Individualists: The Case of Britain' in *Archives Européennes de Sociologie (European Journal of Sociology)*, vol. XXXII, no. 2, 1991); the editors of *Political Studies* for chapter 3 (first published in *Political Studies*, Special Issue, 1993, vol. XLI); Macmillan Publishers Ltd for chapter 4 (first published in M. Sumner and G. Zis (eds), *European Monetary Union: Progress and Prospects*, Macmillan, London, 1982); the editors of *The Political Quarterly* for chapter 6 (first published as 'Nations, Regions and Europe' in Bernard Crick (ed.), *National Identities: The Constitution of the United Kingdom*, Blackwell, Oxford, 1991) (*The Political Quarterly*, fifth issue for 1991); Polity Press for chapter 7 (first published as 'Reinventing Federalism: Europe and the Left' in David Milliband (ed.), *Reinventing the Left*, Polity Press, Cambridge, 1994); the National Library of Wales for chapter 8 (first published as *History Derailed? The Route to 1979*, Welsh Political Archive Lecture, National Library of Wales, Aberystwyth, 1990); Routledge for chapter 9 (first published in Paul Heelas and Paul Morris (eds), *The Values of the Enterprise Culture: The Moral Debate*, Routledge, London, 1992); the editors of *The Political Quarterly* for chapter 10 (first published as 'The Twilight of the British State? Henry Dubb versus Sceptred Awe', *Political Quarterly*, April 1993, vol. 64, no. 2); Polity Press for chapter 11 (first published in Anthony Barnett, Caroline Ellis and Paul Hirst (eds), *Debating the Constitution: New Perspectives on Constitutional Change*, Polity, Cambridge, 1993); and the Economic and Social Research Council for chapter 12 (first published as *The State in Context: Travails of an Ancien Régime*, Economic and Social Research Council, 1995). Chapter 1 was written specially for this book; chapter 4 is based on a paper delivered to the Political Thought Conference in January 1992, but it has been substantially revised to bring it up to date.

Every effort has been made to trace copyright holders but if any have been inadvertently overlooked the publishers will be pleased to make the necessary arrangement at the first opportunity.

• CHAPTER ONE •

Journey to an Unknown Destination

I

We live, we are told incessantly, in a new world, on which old theories have no purchase. Globalization is dissolving national frontiers and dethroning nation-states. Jobs for life have disappeared; social classes have merged; the labour force has been feminized; the family has been transformed; old elites have been toppled; and old traditions have lost legitimacy. In economies, cultures and polities, a new individualism is carrying all before it, and the very notion of a collective social project has lost all resonance.

If this book has a single message it is that the right response to this chorus is, 'Up to a point, Lord Copper'. No one can dispute that the economic, political and cultural climate of the 1990s differs radically from that of the Keynesian 'golden age'[1] in which I grew up. Even the far from golden 1970s and 1980s, which swept me from the political moorings to which I had been attached for most of my life, now seem part of a different epoch. There is no way of knowing whether a collective social project, comparable to the creation of the Keynesian welfare state in the post-war period, would still be feasible. What is certain is that no one in any western democracy – no one with any realistic hope of power, at any rate – is proposing to embark on one. In later chapters I explore some of the causes and consequences of these differences. I try to tease out the reasons why some elites have lost authority and why some hitherto unquestioned traditions are now in contention; and I examine the effects of the progressive individuation that now affects all western societies. One recurrent topic is the cultural and economic mutation which has undermined the social compromises that ushered in the golden age; another is the impact of global economic change on European nation-states in general and on the British state in particular. But if change is one of the themes of this book, another is continuity. For there is a paradox in the current global transformation which the fashionable amnesia ignores. The dynamic driving it is new only in the foreshortened perspective of the last fifty years. In the perspective of the last two hundred, it is not new at all.

The post-war golden age, we can now see, was a short-lived aberration from the norm of the preceding 200 years. It had a variegated ancestry. Its intellectual progenitors included social imperialists, social Christians and social liberals as well as democratic socialists. The interests that helped to bring it into being included farmers, corporate managers and a wide range of professional groups as well as the labour movement. The path towards it was eased, among victors and vanquished alike, by the memory of wartime sacrifices and the ethos of wartime solidarity. The forms of economic regulation that sustained it were ideally suited to manufacturing mass production. But it was also the product of a conscious decision on the part of post-war western governments and elites to find an alternative to the economic order which had failed so catastrophically between the wars, and in doing so to overcome the internal and external threat of Soviet communism. For, in the early post-war years, memories of the inter-war catastrophes were fresh and the Soviet model alluring – in continental Europe, even if not in Britain. Capitalism was on the defensive, intellectually, politically and, above all, morally. It recovered quite quickly, but only by undergoing an unexpected, indeed astonishing, mutation. For the capitalism that recovered was not the capitalism of Ricardo, Herbert Spencer or even Herbert Hoover. It was the tamed welfare capitalism of the New Deal and the Marshall Plan,[2] of Keynes, Monnet and the architects of the German social-market economy. And one of the reasons why property owners and the parties that represented their interests were willing to see capitalism tamed is that they knew they were engaged in a worldwide contest with the Soviet model, in which they needed the support – or at least the acquiescence – of their own working classes. Tamed capitalism was the serendipitous product of a delicate social balance, between East and West as well as within the western bloc, embodied in hard-won compromises. It turned out to be enormously more productive than the untamed capitalism of the past or, of course, than its Soviet rival. But its tamers did not know that they were constructing the most successful wealth-creating machine in human history. Their motives were essentially social and political, not economic.

Now the wheel has come full circle. The balance which made the golden age possible has broken down. The command economies of the east have imploded and the ideology which legitimized them has been discredited. As a result, the internal and external challenges to the capitalist market economy posed by powerful communist parties, an apparently strong and expansionist Soviet bloc and, most of all, a rival vision of society embodied in real-world institutions, have vanished. So has the associated challenge of organized labour. Individual workers still exist, but as isolated social atoms facing capital on their own. The working class, in the sense of a self-conscious social interest that shares a common identity and a common vocation, is little more than a memory. The ameliorative pressures of the non-communist left have faded too. The ethics of democratic socialism still resonate, but its economics are as discredited as the closely related economics of the eastern bloc. The fate of the revisionist social democracy of Hugh Gaitskell or Willy Brandt – the social democracy which sought to equalize life chances by redistributing the fiscal dividend of growth; the social democracy to which I was converted while reading Anthony Crosland's *The Future of Socialism* during a summer holiday after my university Finals – is more complex. Social-democratic parties still embody a solidaristic vision and still represent the underdog; in most (though not all) western countries they do their best to defend the welfare state against cost-cutters, marketizers and privatizers. But in the crucial domain of the political economy, they no longer challenge the dominant free-market paradigm.[3]

The result is that capitalism is off the leash. Not surprisingly, it is behaving much as it did before its tamers put it on the leash during the extraordinary burst of institutional creativity that followed the Second World War. To be sure, its behaviour is not all of a piece. This is still a world of multiple capitalisms, marked by sharp variations of structure, culture and performance. The compromises of the post-war period were much more firmly embedded in the so-called 'Rhenish' capitalisms of central Europe than in those of the English-speaking world, and although their impress on 'Rhenish' economies is weakening, it is still much

stronger than on Anglophone ones.[4] Running through these
variations, however, is a common theme. The heaving, masterless,
community-destroying global economy of the 1990s may be a long
way away from its benign and stable predecessor of the 1950s and
1960s, but it is uncomfortably close to that of the nineteenth
century and even to that of the inter-war period. Keynes may be
dead, but Marx, Malthus and Ricardo have had a new lease of life.
The tamed welfare capitalism that Keynes helped to make possible
may have vanished, but the untamed capitalism of today is
uncannily reminiscent of much earlier phases in the creature's life
cycle.

Partly as cause and partly as consequence, a heavy deflationary
bias now bears down on economic activity through all the peaks
and troughs of the business cycle. The fundamental Keynesian
(and Marxist) paradox of wasted resources in the midst of
unsatisfied needs has returned. So has that old faithful of Marxian
wage theory, the 'industrial reserve army' of the unemployed. In
Britain and the United States, where capitalism's untaming has
gone farthest, two other half-forgotten props of Marxist eschatology – the immiseration of the proletariat and the proletarianization
of widening swathes of the bourgeoisie – have returned as well. In
advanced industrial societies, one of the central themes of the
golden age was 'embourgeoisement': the spread to the working
class of the job security, career ladders and lifestyles which had
formerly been the prerogatives of the middle class. Now the
engines have gone into reverse. Adjusted for inflation, average
weekly earnings of American 'production and non-supervisory
workers', comprising 80 per cent of the working population, fell by
18 per cent between 1973 and 1995. By contrast, the real annual pay
of corporate chief executives increased by 19 per cent between 1979
and 1989, and by 66 per cent after taxes.[5] In Britain, the average
real income of the bottom tenth of the population fell by 14 per
cent between 1979 and 1991, while that of the richest tenth rose by
50 per cent.[6] As Felix Rohatyn, senior partner of the Wall Street
bankers Lazard Frères recently explained, the United States has
seen 'a huge transfer of wealth from lower-skilled, middle-class
American workers to the owners of capital assets and to a new
technological aristocracy'.[7] The equivalent British transfer has been
somewhat less huge, but only somewhat.

That is only the beginning of the story. As in industrial-
revolution Britain, the social, cultural and psychic impact of
untamed capitalism goes deeper than its impact on the distribution

of resources. As well as putting money in working-class pockets, the 'embourgeoisement' of the golden age put security, stability and thereby self respect into working-class lives. As Harold Perkin has argued, the *leitmotiv*, not just of the golden age, but of the century from around 1880 to around 1980, was the growth of a professional society based on skill, expertise, meritocratic advancement and the enhancement of human capital. Professional qualifications, professional standards and professional expectations spread to a widening range of occupations, manual as well as white-collar. So did the professional virtues of commitment, service and deferred gratification, and, with them, the dignities of professional life.[8] Here too, the engines have gone into reverse. The de-casualization of labour, which a generation of trade-union leaders saw as its life's work, has given way to its re-casualization – and in what used to be the middle class as well as in the working class. Downsizing, delayering, outsourcing and re-engineering haunt the suburbs as well as the inner cities, mocking the commitments and hollowing out the institutions which were once the lodestars of the salariat. No doubt, these processes must end eventually. Delayering cannot continue when there are no layers left, and even the leanest companies need a core of committed employees. But whatever happens in future, the wounded identities and fractured communities which the re-casualization of the last decade has left in its train will still be with us.

Capitalism has turned back on its tracks in less familiar ways as well. In most of western Europe, the great achievement of the second half of the nineteenth century and the first half of the twentieth was the creation of a public domain, ring-fenced from the pressures of the market place, in which citizenship rights rather than market power governed the allocation of social goods. Now privatization is narrowing the scope of this public domain, while marketization is twisting it out of shape – restricting the scope of democratic citizenship, devaluing the ethic of public service and undermining the whole notion of the public good. Of course, there have been gains as well as losses. Joseph Schumpeter was right to think that 'creative destruction' is the hallmark of capitalism. The gales of change which have swept through the global economy in the last ten years *have* been creative as well as destructive. They have stimulated extraordinary feats of enterprise and innovation, leading to remarkable productivity gains; the rewards have gone to the resourceful and adventurous, as well as to the ruthless and the merely lucky. The trouble is that capitalism's untaming has given destruction too much scope: that the gains made by a few have gone hand in hand with mounting insecurity, dwindling commitment and spreading anomie among the rest. If the emblematic figure of the 1960s was the affluent worker, today's are the redundant middle manager, the driven contract worker and the excluded, antisocial, inner-city youth. All of these portend a desertification of the culture that threatens to choke the springs of mutual loyalty and trust on which free societies – and, for that matter, market economies[9] – depend.

Unrecognized by the market fundamentalists of the right or even the market converts of the left, the 1990s are painfully relearning the painfully acquired wisdom of the founders of the mixed economy: while classical socialism is a delusive will-o'-the-wisp, unbridled market capitalism is economically wasteful and socially destructive. But, as that formulation implies, there is nothing new in this. What *is* new is that the bridles constructed in the first forty years of the century, and applied after 1945, have now disintegrated; and that no successors are in sight.

II

This book was written as the pains of relearning began to bite. Most of the chapters were first published in the early or mid-1990s; the earliest dates from 1982. In different ways, they all have to do with the relationship between capitalisms, states and nations: with the disputed territory where the sphere of market exchanges intersects with the spheres of citizenship and identity. They reflect a set of preoccupations which have come to seem more and more urgent as the implications of capitalism's return to the past have sunk in. In this bewildering new world, which is at the same time an all too familiar old world, how can the values of social solidarity and democratic citizenship be realized? Granted that socialism, as traditionally understood, is no longer with us, does it have something to say to us from beyond the grave? How is socialism's great antagonist, liberalism, faring in this new world, and what are the prospects for an accommodation between the two? Granted that no single nation-state can bridle untamed capitalism, could a federal Europe do so? How do the special peculiarities of the British state, the identity it embodies and the political economy over which it presides relate to these wider issues?

I have, I hope, addressed these questions, albeit sometimes obliquely, but I do not pretend to have answered them. The chapters collected here do not represent a final 'position' or even a developing approximation to one. The world was changing fast while I wrote them, and I was changing too: in their case, the academic convention of a static, impersonal, authorial 'we' is even more misleading than usual. They are best seen as milestones on an intellectual journey which began long before the first of them was written, and which still continues. As Andrew Shonfield once said of the European project, it is a journey 'to an unknown destination'.[10] Even the comparatively short part of it covered in these essays has followed a course I did not expect it to take when the earliest of them was published; as I peer into the future, the only thing I am sure of is that there will be more new turnings which I cannot now foresee. Yet my journey has a certain symmetry about it, which may not be apparent at first sight. In the rest of this chapter, I shall retrace my steps and, in the light of that encounter with my past, offer an overview of the territory in which I now find myself.

Intellectually, even if not chronologically, I am a child of the golden age; for nearly forty years I based my political credo on the premise that capitalism had not only been tamed, but would stay tamed. More specifically, I am a child of the Attlee government. I was nearly eleven when Labour won the 1945 election, and I left school in 1952, almost a year after Churchill's return to office. I belong, in fact, to the intermediate generation that came of age too late for the war and too soon for the Beatles – the generation for which the robust collectivism of Labour Britain was part of the texture of growing up. For us, there was nothing problematic or surprising about state intervention or even state direction. We had been used to them since infancy. Our childhoods had reverberated with the wartime state's exhortations to dig for victory, to refrain from careless talk, to eat potatoes, to disdain the squanderbug; we took an active state for granted. We eked out our rationed sweets and went off to do our National Service, not always enthusiastically, but without feeling that anything remarkable or untoward had happened. Tamed capitalism was a fact of life too. The struggles which had preceded its taming belonged to the history books. I doubt if many of us saw it as any kind of New Jerusalem.

For some, it was the least bad compromise available; for others a staging post on the road to something better. But if anyone had told us that, in fifty years' time, it would have given way to a new version of its untamed ancestor, that the heads of privatized utility companies would be making fortunes while beggars thronged London's Underground stations, we would have been incredulous as well as appalled. Part of me is incredulous even now.

My own National Service was remarkably uncoercive. I spent virtually the whole of it in the hothouse of the joint services Russian course, and arrived at Oxford in 1954, emotionally immature but intellectually precocious, at the height of the Butskellite consensus. At fifteen I had read and been intoxicated by *The Communist Manifesto*, but James Burnham's *Managerial Revolution* had quickly ended my Marxist period. Between school and university, I had devoured Orwell's essays, Koestler's autobiography and political novels, Ayer's *Language, Truth and Logic* and most of Popper's *Open Society and Its Enemies*. Early university influences included Talmon's *Origins of Totalitarian Democracy*, Plamenatz's *German Marxism and Russian Communism* and Evan Durbin's *Politics of Democratic Socialism*. I was, I thought, an empiricist, a sceptic, a reformist. I knew that revolutions devoured their children, that utopianism led to totalitarianism, that the dictatorship of the proletariat was doomed to become a dictatorship over the proletariat. My watchword was Reason with a capital 'R'; and Reason told me that faith, any faith, was dangerous.

For some time, the child of the golden age ran in uneasy double harness with the grandchild of a much earlier period. Roman Catholics distinguish between converts and cradle Catholics. I am cradle Labour. My father joined the Labour Party in 1918, used to sell the *Daily Herald* outside the Cardiff docks before going to school, and eventually became a Labour minister. My maternal great-grandfather was a founder-member of the ILP and founder-editor of a socialist paper called *Llais Llafur* ('Labour Voice'), where he preached a fierce, blood-red creed that would make the far left of today's Labour Party look palest pink. I was a socialist when I arrived at Oxford, as well as a sceptic; and I was also a would-be historian. The notion that history had come to an end; that, as Jimmy Porter was famously to cry in *Look Back in Anger*, there were no great causes left; that politics had been for ever reduced to management, seemed to me intolerable, and in any case incredible. I had read some Namier in my sixth form, but although I could see that he was a great historian, I was repelled by his approach – a repulsion soon fortified by my mentor and subsequent tutor, A. J. P. Taylor. There was more to politics than interest and ambition. Ideas mattered; mind could not be taken out of history; even modest changes depended on passion and belief. Utopianism was 'suicidal', I wrote in a pre-university paper, but so was apathy; the task of democratic socialism was 'to find a way of applying scepticism to politics without destroying devotion'. Weaving in and out of ludicrously overambitious reading lists, ebullient re-collections of drunken late-night arguments and mournful descriptions of the pains of rejected love, that theme recurs again and again in my undergraduate notebooks.

I wanted a cause, perhaps a hero. For a while, Aneurin Bevan supplied both needs. I heard him speak in my first term at Oxford and was captivated by his defiant artistry. My father's vote for Gaitskell in the leadership election after Attlee retired seemed to me the blackest villainy. Despite my sixteen-year-old abandonment of Marx, I was close enough to the pre-Hungary Oxford Commu-nists for Raphael Samuel, later the founder of History Workshop and then a passionate, inspiring and dedicated party member, to spend four solid hours trying unsuccessfully to convert me. 'Marxism would be emotionally satisfying', I noted regretfully, 'but I don't think it's true.' Soon afterwards the Suez crisis galvanized the entire Oxford left and, for a brief moment, created a defiant popular-front atmosphere reminiscent of the 1930s. (Did I really think a general strike would bring the Government down? I can't find any contemporary evidence to that effect, but I have a strong suspicion that I did.) Suez protest brought me into contact with Stuart Hall, as eloquent and charismatic then as he is now, and with the dissident socialists of what became the first New Left. I was never in their inner circle, but I shared their view that socialism was about culture as well as about economics, and contributed an article on the political significance of the so-called 'Angry Young Men' to the first issue of *Universities and Left Review*, the precursor of today's *New Left Review*.

But no cause or hero could hold me for long. The bump of scepticism was too big. The source of the problem, I decided, lay in Oxford. (I had no doubt that there *was* a problem.) I loved it, but I was also exasperated by it. It infuriated me, even as it shaped me. Dry-as-dust Oxford empiricism, I complained in a *New Statesman* article, written during a vacation job on the paper, had sapped the energies of the undergraduate left. For the university was permeated by a 'tough-minded, disillusioned attitude', emanating from

> its current intellectual heroes: the Nuffield psephologists, the Namierite historians, the linguistic philosophers . . . Linguistic philosophy encourages a cautious, unemotional approach to problems: from caution it is easy to slide into cowardice. Namierite history leads to suspicion of moral judgements and a tendency to believe that ideas don't matter. If you were taught that the Stuarts were wrong and Hampden right, it was possible to believe that Chamberlain was wrong and Cripps right. Now, nobody is wrong . . .
> . . . The new attitude is implicitly right-wing. Namierite history tends to favour the administrator at the expense of the lone voice; to suggest that nothing much changes anyway. But if nothing changes, why propose change? Linguistic philosophy extols an empirical approach. But empiricism has always been a conservative, not a radical catch word . . . So the dilemma of the intellectual Left is this: the new attitude seems impossible to fault, yet equally impossible to reconcile with anything Socialism used to be about.
> Left-wing discussion has . . . been most frightened by the apparent drift to a tellyocratic Brave New World, with a deep gulf between those who take decisions and those in whose name they are taken, and a thin layer of professional public relations experts uneasily sandwiched between. But the connecting link, running through all this confused discussion, has been the basic dilemma: how to reconcile one's emotional attitudes with the intellectual approach which is almost inevitably absorbed in present-day Oxford – how to marry Keir Hardie with A. J. Ayer.[11]

The focus was parochial and the target far too narrow, but I still think there was something in it. Indeed, there was more in it than I could see when I wrote it. A. J. P. Taylor made the same point more elegantly when he wrote that the alternative to the 'Whig' history his professional colleagues condemned was 'Tory history'.[12] Somewhat later, Ernest Gellner's mordant *Words and Things* put forward a much richer and more powerful critique of the small-'c' conservatism inherent in linguistic philosophy.[13] But the 'Narodniks of North Oxford', as Gellner called them, had a long lineage behind them. The frustrations I attributed to the Oxford left – which were, of course, my own frustrations – could not be laid at the door of a few mid-century Oxford dons. My real quarrel went deeper. The 'new attitude' I attacked was not as new as I (or, for that matter, Taylor or Gellner) thought. The cult of tough-mindedness, the suspicion of general ideas, the worship of 'common sense' and the positivist historiography and political science against which I was unwittingly in revolt were the contemporary manifestations of an enduring strand in the public philosophy. But this is hindsight. I was too young, too lacking in self-confidence and, above all, too impatient to realize it then, let alone to explore the implications. On a deeper level, I was, in any case, a prisoner of that same public philosophy. It took the storms of the 1980s to shake me free.

III

Within a few weeks of my *New Statesman* article I was lying on a Mediterranean beach, reading *The Future of Socialism*. Few converts can have been less willing. Crosland, I noted, 'seems unhappily correct. But in that case the Labour Party has no revolutionary part to play. Why belong to it? Above all, why bother to work for it?' Little by little, Crosland's own answer persuaded me. There was no need for a revolutionary transformation, but there was every need for steady incremental improvement. Capitalism had indeed been tamed – so much so that the term was now misleading, and ownership of the means of production almost irrelevant. But it did not follow that there was no room for left politics. Life chances could be equalized; class distinctions could be eroded; public expenditure could be increased; welfare could be enhanced; society could be made more just and more contented. These made up a worthy left agenda, which only sentimentalists would find inadequate.

In retrospect Croslandite revisionism seems to me hopelessly Panglossian and, on the deepest level, incoherent. It took the institutions and operational codes of the British state for granted, and assumed that if revisionist ministers pulled the right Whitehall levers, the desired results would follow. It presupposed continuing economic growth, on a scale sufficient to produce an adequate fiscal dividend. Above all, as Raymond Plant has shown, it failed to argue the moral case for the egalitarianism it put at the centre of the whole project.[14] But this too is hindsight. What mattered at the time was that Crosland seemed to have resolved the dilemma I had described in my *New Statesman* article. He had constructed a socialism fit for the *Zeitgeist* – if not marrying Keir Hardie to A. J. Ayer, then at least making it possible for them to live in sin. I don't think I ever accepted the full Panglossian rigour of the revisionist position, but for the next twenty-five years or so I certainly accepted the main outlines. In the battles between fundamentalists and revisionists that convulsed the Labour Party after the 1959 defeat, I was a fervent revisionist. As a *Guardian* leader-writer, I applauded Hugh Gaitskell's attempt to revise Clause Four of the party constitution and enlisted in the Gaitskellite Campaign for Democratic Socialism. During a brief return to Oxford as a junior research fellow I was selected as a prospective Labour candidate for a safe Conservative seat. After an even briefer spell teaching politics at the University of Sussex I was elected to Parliament in 1966, three years after Gaitskell's death. I gravitated unhesitatingly to what remained of the Gaitskellite camp.

Despite being singularly ill-suited to the feverish inconsequence of parliamentary life, I sat in the House of Commons for eleven years – the first four of them fuflfilling enough; the remaining ones increasingly, and in the end mind-numbingly, frustrating. Most of the issues that preoccupied me seem irretrievably dated now. Yet three broad themes looked forward to the present and the recent past. The first was the theme of democracy, or what I would now call citizenship. The spectre of the 'tellyocratic Brave New World' which I had conjured up in my *New Statesman* article continued to haunt me. A few years before my election to Parliament, it was given new force by John Mackintosh's *The British Cabinet*. Particularly evocative were its conclusion that, 'Governments are restrained not so much by Parliament or by the opposition as by their own desire to keep in step with public opinion' and its impish final question,

> Is the decline of Parliament to be regretted? Most of the proposals for alleviating the decay of the House of Commons are met with the rejoinder: 'Will it work?' By this what is usually meant is: 'Will it work without in any way altering the present dominance of the Executive?' Reports by Select Committees on Procedure or by academic pamphleteers are pointless until the primary question is decided. How much power should the Executive have and how far is it desirable that either the public or a representative chamber should know about or participate in the processes of Government? . . .
> . . . Our forms of government continue to change, perhaps not for the worse, but it is a pity that the thinkers and ideologues sit silent while some 'intimations' are allowed to decline in favour of others.[15]

Three years after Mackintosh, Andrew Shonfield reinforced the message in his trail-blazing classic of comparative political economy, *Modern Capitalism*.[16] Like Crosland, but if possible even more confidently, Shonfield presupposed tamed capitalism; unlike Crosland, he did not think that Keynesian demand management was enough to keep it tamed. For him the secret of the golden age lay less in Keynesian techniques than in 'intellectual coherence' in economic decision-making, based on 'long-range national planning'. Long-range planning required active government; if active government were not to degenerate into arbitrary government, it would have to be made subject to new forms of democratic control, appropriate to an extended state.

The argument seemed impeccable; and, for some years, the Shonfield problem – how to square active government with democratic control – was a central preoccupation both of my parliamentary life and of my occasional journalism. Like most of the 1966 entry and the livelier House of Commons clerks, I thought the key to a solution lay in Parliament itself. I joined John Mackintosh (who soon became one of my dearest friends) on the Procedure Committee of the House of Commons and hitched my wagon to the star of what was then called parliamentary reform. I was for subject committees with teeth; for a new system of expenditure scrutiny; for pre-legislative committees; for a Parliament that would carry out a 'radical and thoroughgoing revision of its procedures, and even more of its assumptions' in order to become 'the watchdog of the bureaucracy'.[17] It took me more than a decade to see that no such revision would take place until there were Members of Parliament with the will and capacity to conduct it, and that no such Members of Parliament would be elected until the myth of the hegemonic mass party, which had been part of my mental furniture since childhood, had been laid to rest. It took me even longer to see that a culture of negotiation and power-sharing, without which institutional changes would make little difference, could be built only from the bottom up.

The second theme is harder to define and has become fully apparent only in retrospect. By the 1960s the revisionist discourse had taken on a darker tinge. We still took tamed capitalism for granted, but we could see that its British version was falling behind other versions; the starting-point of Shonfield's *Modern Capitalism* – for me, at least, the New Testament to Crosland's Old Testament – was a nagging sense that Britain had failed where others had succeeded. Labour revisionists were not alone in feeling this, of course; the same sense ran through the historiography of the Gramscian New Left[18] and the politics of Tory planners like Edward Boyle and even Harold Macmillan. It also ran through the mood of the time. Indeed, Labour owed its election victories in 1964 and 1966 to its superior command of a cross-party rhetoric of modernization, designed to address it. But revisionism was modernist by definition, and the theme of decline and modernization – or, as I later came to see it, of change, adaptation and failure to adapt – had a special resonance for revisionists. It certainly had one for me. I believed the modernization rhetoric I had used on the election platform. I was for indicative planning, an incomes policy and George Brown's ill-fated Department of Economic Affairs; I thought a combination of efficiency and justice could procure a higher rate of growth and help to realize the Croslandite vision of a classless society. When the Wilson government sacrificed its modernization programme to the exchange rate in July 1966 I watched in despair, with a sense of betrayal that still lingers.

With David Owen and John Mackintosh I argued publicly for devaluation (an act of *lèse-majesté* for which John and I were never forgiven). Later we sent a private memorandum to Harold Wilson making the case at greater length, and published a pamphlet, *Change Gear*, setting out a neo-revisionist programme, in which devaluation was the central plank. But this was whistling in the wind. Our battle had been lost before it began. For all its brave talk in opposition, Labour in government had succumbed to the 'conservative enemy' that Tony Crosland had anatomized in his second important contribution to revisionist thinking.[19] But I could not bring myself to face the implications. I persuaded myself that the government would learn from its mistakes; when Roy Jenkins arrived at the Treasury after the forced devaluation of 1967 my hopes seemed vindicated. It took the grosser defeats of the 1970s – the Labour Party-aided frustration of the Heath government's Industrial Relations Act; the orgy of wage inflation fuelled by the 1974 Labour government's 'social contract'; the failure of successive industrial policies under governments of both parties; and the culminating humiliation of the 1976 sterling crisis – to persuade me that the modernization project of the 1960s and 1970s had been flawed all along, that I had a duty to seek a satisfactory explanation and that I could not do so while I was immured in the gilded cage of parliamentary politics.

Well before that realization began to dawn, the experience of watching the Wilson government's flounderings from a ringside seat gave a new edge to the academic project I had started before getting into Parliament. This was a biography of Ramsay MacDonald – the first scholarly biography based on his private papers – that took me thirteen years to write and ran, in the end, to 400,000 words. The parallels between the MacDonald and

Wilson governments were obvious, but as my research progressed I became increasingly sure that they were only the beginning of the story. The important parallels went deeper. I offered my summary in a passage in the opening chapter written in late 1975 or early 1976.

> The problems of low productivity and declining competitiveness, which absorbed an inordinate amount of ministerial time under the second Labour Government have absorbed, if anything, even more ministerial time in the 1960s and 1970s. The vexed question of European security and disarmament ... presented many of the dilemmas which were to face post-war British Governments when they had to decide their attitude to European integration. The official case for building the Singapore base in 1924 was remarkably similar to the official case for staying east of Suez forty years later; the arguments for sticking to free trade in 1930 and 1931 were to be heard again from opponents of the Common Market's agricultural policy in the early 1970s ... [M]ost of the really intractable problems with which MacDonald had to deal as prime minister can be seen as variations on the interwoven themes of declining economic and political power, dwindling freedom of action and sluggish adaptation to the forces which had made it dwindle. All three have sounded even more loudly in the last twenty-five years.[20]

Unwittingly, I had sketched out the basis for a research programme that still continues.

That leads on to the third theme – the sometimes dominant, occasionally quiescent, but ever-present theme of Britain in Europe and of Europeanism in Britain. Revisionists of the older generation were mostly sceptical about, or even hostile to, British membership of the emerging European Community. They had reached political maturity in the 1940s, when continental models were irrelevant at best and sinister at worst. But for their counterparts in my generation and the generation immediately ahead of mine, 'a dynamic and resurgent Europe', as Anthony Crosland called it,[21] was the external face of modernity. Community membership was a vehicle for, perhaps a precondition of, the modernization of Britain. Opposition to membership went with opposition to modernity; it was at one with class-war fundamentalism on the left, backward-looking imperialism on the right, and resistance to change throughout the society. A victory for the opponents would be a victory for the past, miring Britain still more deeply in a bog of archaism and nostalgia.

I shared the Europeanism of the younger revisionists, but before I was elected to Parliament I did not hold it very strongly. Where the leaders of the Campaign for Democratic Socialism were shocked almost beyond bearing by Gaitskell's notorious 'thousand years of history' speech to the 1963 Labour Party conference, I found it, at most, distasteful. At a CDS drinks party immediately after the speech, I remember, I felt like a man in a Bateman cartoon when I dared limply to defend it. What turned me from a lukewarm to a committed European were the 1966 crisis and the dawning realization that revisionist modernization in one country was a chimera. In an essay written in the summer recess after the 1966 crisis I conceded that, in a fully-fledged economic community, member states would no longer be free to regulate economic forces within their own boundaries. But that loss of freedom, I argued, should hold no terrors for modernizing revisionists. Democratic electorates would never tolerate a return to *laissez-faire*; in any case, Shonfield had shown that continental Europe was more hospitable to planning than Britain was. Though national governments would lose their power to regulate their economies, the powers they lost would be transferred to authorities 'capable of exercising them on a continental, rather than on a merely national, scale'. That was a prospect to make Socialists rejoice.

> The last two years have shown that it is much harder to carry out the kind of planning implied in Labour's 1964 election manifesto within the confines of a single nation-state than many of us had supposed . . . [T]oo few of the variables are even potentially under the control of the planners. If planning were carried out on a European scale . . . the whole exercise would be that much more likely to succeed.[22]

In retrospect, I am surprised by the slightly clinical tone: I was a European of the head, but not yet of the heart. As the battle lines over Community entry hardened, however, reason was reinforced by emotion. Membership of the British delegation to the Council of Europe Assembly and of its multinational socialist group, attendance at the annual Anglo-German conferences at Koenigswinter, meetings with Italian socialists and – most of all, perhaps – revulsion from the sour little-Englandism that swept through the Labour Party in the 1970s taught me to feel, as well as think, European. In the language of the Labour whips I was a 'Euro-fanatic'. Worse yet, I was also a 'Jenkinsite'. I devoted long hours to the caballing of the Labour Europeans before the vote on Community entry in October 1971; when the vote came I was one of the sixty-nine Labour MPs who defied a three-line whip to follow Roy Jenkins into the 'yes' lobby. After he resigned from the deputy leadership, I belonged to the dwindling band of those who still hoped against hope that he might one day succeed to the leadership, and who did their best to keep the flag of Labour Europeanism flying in the teeth of the anti-European gale. We Labour Europeans did not spend much time on the niceties of political economy; the battle now was over identity and history. We were held together partly by faith in the rightness of our cause, and even more by intense group solidarity; the time for ratiocination had passed. But my developing Europeanism of the heart did not displace my earlier Europeanism of the head. Identity and history apart, I saw the rationale for Community membership much as I had seen it in 1966. Economic regulation would no longer work in one country: it had to be supranational or nothing. Though the kind of regulation I was thinking of has since become unworkable on any level of government, the essence of the case seems to me unchanged. Either share sovereignty with the rest of the continent to which we belong, or transfer it to the global marketplace.

IV

Resisting the anti-European gale may have been good for the moral fibre, but it was bad for party loyalty. For me, the European question had come to transcend Europe. It had to do with the nature of the modern world, with Britain's place in that world, with her vision of herself and of the kind of society she wished to be. I followed Roy Jenkins (and am eternally proud to have done so), partly out of a mixture of affection and admiration for that most complex of front-rank politicians, but chiefly because he was the only conceivable Labour leader who saw the question in that way. The twists and turns of his front-bench rivals shocked me, not because I thought politicians should never twist and turn – I knew that most of my heroes, from Gladstone to Roosevelt, had frequently done both – but because they implied a myopic *insouciance* about the wider questions that the European question encapsulated. And if the front bench seemed myopic, the back benches seemed downright blind. Most of my parliamentary colleagues, I reluctantly came to see, found my political priorities and, on a deeper level, my approach to political life incomprehensible, even suspect. (A trivial example sticks in my mind. At some point in the 1970s, I can't remember precisely when, I asked the pairing whip, a normally amiable trade-union *apparatchik*, for permission to attend an Italian Socialist conference to which I had been invited to speak. 'Fuck the Italian socialists', he graciously replied. I went anyway.) I was not yet ready to face the possibility that we no longer belonged in the same party. But when a fellow Labour European, less alienated from the mainstream than I was, accused me of being an 'internal émigré', I could not help seeing that he was right.

After the anti-European gale of the early 1970s came the unexpected zephyrs of the 1974 government's so-called 're-nego-tiation' of the entry terms and the two-to-one referendum vote in favour of continued Community membership. I rejoiced at both, but my emigration continued. This is not the place to describe the government's travails; they have attracted a rich literature, written from a variety of perspectives.[23] What matters is that, within a few months of its arrival in office, it was clear that the post-war golden age was over and that, in the cold climate which had followed, the fissures within the Labour coalition were too deep for effective government. Soaring inflation and a plummeting currency were only two of the symptoms of a paralysing ideological gridlock. Meanwhile the revisionist wing of the coalition – hitherto the political tendency closest to the spirit of the times – seemed unable to come to terms with the new realities. Increasingly, it was losing the moral and intellectual initiative to the monetarist right of the Conservative Party, led by Sir Keith Joseph, and to a resurgent neo-socialism, whose most effective prophet was Stuart Holland, on the left of its own party,[24] while its claim to be the vehicle of modernity looked ever more dubious. Yet, with one or two exceptions, revisionist ministers were too preoccupied to notice. Lacking a lead, revisionist backbenchers were increasingly tempted to make peace with the left.

In an attempt to stem the neo-fundamentalist tide in the parliamentary party, some of us set up the so-called Manifesto Group. We lobbied ministers, ran candidates in subject-group elections and organized interventions in parliamentary party debates. But even at the time, I half-realized that this was what psychiatrists call 'displacement activity'. The rot went too deep for parliamentary manoeuvring to stop it. The revisionist centre was losing the initiative because the revisionist project of the 1950s and 1960s could no longer speak to the needs of the time; it would go on losing until revisionism had been revised.

The question was how, and here I floundered. I could see that Croslandite revisionism – the revisionism for which high public expenditure was the ark of the egalitarian covenant – was now a blind alley. The conventional socialist assumption that public expenditure was bound to redistribute income from the better-off to the worse-off, I pointed out in an IEA symposium in 1976, 'is simply not true. Some forms of public expenditure do: others don't. Some may even redistribute it from the worse off to the better off.'[25] I also sensed that the downfall of the old revisionism owed more to the culture and the polity than to the economy. Both Stuart Holland and Sir Keith Joseph, I argued in a letter to my Manifesto Group colleague and friend, John Horam, attributed Britain's economic ills to worldwide factors which, in other countries, were 'perfectly compatible with roaring success'. A better approach was

> to look, not at the things we have in common with more successful economies, but at the differences between us and them. The more we do this, it seems to me, the clearer it becomes that our problems are not really economic in origin, but social, cultural and political. It's not the fact that we have a powerful meso-economic sector that undoes us, but the feebleness and incompetence of the people who manage our meso-economic sector: not the fact that we have too much state interference, but the fact that our state so often interferes in foolish ways; not that we have powerful labour monopolies, but that so many of our labour monopolists are second-rate ignoramuses, besotted by ideological fantasies dating from half a century ago. In other words, our enemy is not the corporate state as such. It's the uniquely arthritic British version of the corporate state.
> ... Holland's proposals – given the arthritic nature of our political culture and institutions – would lead, in practice, to more protectionism, more subsidisation of inefficiency, more ganging up by vested interests against the consumer, more bureaucratic empire-building – not because there is something *ipso facto* conservative and protectionist about more state intervention, but because of the in-built conservatism and protectionism of the *British* state. But the same is true of Joseph. In effect, he says the answer is less state intervention. That would be fine if we could trust the private sector to work efficiently, but if we could do that we wouldn't be in this mess at all. It's not new economic policies we need ... It's political and institutional changes to break the vicious circle of deadlock, inertia and class conflict.[26]

But these were, at most, pale intimations of the revised revisionism which the times required. Britain *was* exceptional, but not in the way or to the extent that I imagined. By the mid-1970s 'roaring success' hardly described the economic performance of the rest of the OECD world. The conditions which had made tamed capitalism possible – the conditions which modernizers hoped to fortify in Britain – were everywhere under threat. I don't think I could have been expected to realize that at that time, but I should have seen that the connections between British continuities and global changes needed a much more searching analysis than I gave them in my letter to John Horam. The trouble was that searching analysis was out of the question for a beleaguered revisionist MP, caught in the trench warfare of Labour politics. For there was a contradiction between the imperatives of those politics and the imperatives of intellectual renewal. The Labour right was fighting for survival. The trade unions were the only power centre within the Labour movement from which it could hope for support. If it allowed itself to think the thoughts I had sketched out in my letter to John Horam, to explore the connections between trade-union behaviour and economic decline, to challenge traditional Labourism as well as resurgent fundamentalism, no trade-union support would be forthcoming. Yet if it censored itself so as to accommodate trade-union susceptibilities, it would have nothing worthwhile to fight for.

It took me a long time to see the contradiction as clearly as that, but it hung in the Westminster air like an insidious smog. For a while I did my best to ignore it. I concentrated on finishing my MacDonald biography and tried to forget about contemporary politics. But in early 1976 the MacDonald manuscript went to the printers and Harold Wilson retired from the prime ministership. Roy Jenkins's defeat in the ensuing leadership election – above all, the discovery that many of his admirers were too frightened of potential far-left *putschists* in their constituencies to vote for him – was a moment of truth. 'The House of Commons – the PLP – even the Manifesto Group – seemed like a prison', I wrote later. 'One could barely breathe.'[27] I didn't know where my search for a post-Croslandite social democracy would end. By the summer of 1976, I was sure that it would never begin unless I broke out of the straitjacket of parliamentary Labourism.

V

I left Parliament in early 1977. After eighteen months in Brussels, as a rather implausible *haut fonctionnaire* of the European Commission, I returned eagerly to academic life in the autumn of 1978. Seven months after my return, Mrs Thatcher became prime minister. Six months after that, Roy Jenkins delivered the Dimbleby Lecture, calling on the 'radical centre' to end the tyranny of the existing party system and opening the road to the creation of the SDP.

In Brussels I had written little, but brooded much. Two themes had preoccupied me – the mismatch between the purposes and structures of the European project, and the relationship between the crisis of revisionist social democracy and the malaise of the British state. My time as a Commission official fortified my Europeanism, both of the head and of the heart, and deepened my alienation from the narcissistic insularity of the British political class. But it also made me more critical of the existing Community institutions, and more aware of the evasions at the heart of the founding treaties. Community Europe, as I saw it from the inside, was a technocrats' Europe. The commissioners gave themselves airs appropriate to ministers in a national government; their staffs bolstered their illusions. Both were performing a charade. Technocrats, however grand, are only technocrats; a technocracy could not magically evolve into a polity. The Monnet vision of economic integration spilling over into political union was utopianism disguised as pragmatism; only a political route could lead to a political destination.

These meditations inspired my first post-Brussels publication – a 150-page tract for the times called *Parliament for Europe*.[28] It called for a 'parliamentary Europe' in which the Commission would make itself accountable to the soon to be directly elected European Parliament, and in doing so harness the democratic legitimacy of the latter to the cause of integration. In retrospect, it too looks hopelessly utopian. I had assumed that the shock of direct elections would prise the commissioners out of their technocratic habits and inspire them to behave like politicians after all. I had forgotten that my own analysis had shown that that was exactly what they could not do. But although my prescriptions were flawed, the descriptive parts of the book have, I think, stood the test of time. It is true that a political Europe can be built only by political action. Though this did not become clear until much later, it is also true that, in a global political economy which is spinning out of control, a political Europe is even more necessary than it was before.

It was more difficult to get to grips with the crisis of social democracy. In the 1970s, I had chafed against the frozen *immobilisme* of the labour movement. Now the problem was how to keep pace with its apparent meltdown. Labour's defeat in the 1979 election broke the dam which had kept the Labour coalition stable;

Michael Foot's election as Labour leader in November 1980 made a social-democratic breakaway inevitable. But, as events drove on, tactics and organization loomed so large that it was hard to focus on the fundamental questions of purpose and direction. In my case, that difficulty was compounded by two others. Inevitably, I was engaged in a kind of intellectual parricide. Before I could address the present and future, I had to escape from the shadow of my past. The process was necessary, psychologically as well as intellectually, but it sometimes led me into a needless refighting of old battles. Inevitably too, I suffered from intellectual indigestion. After twelve years out of academic life, I had a lot of ground to make up. I read as widely as I could, but I did not find it easy to weave the insights I garnered into a whole. Four literatures influenced me most. One was the 'adversary-politics' literature attributing Britain's economic woes to the policy lurches of successive dogma-intoxicated governments. Another was the public-choice literature originating with the Virginia School, particularly as mediated by Mancur Olson.[29] The third was the burgeoning literature on human rights and constitutional reform to which I was introduced through a seminal article by Anthony Lester.[30] The fourth was the new historiography of the progressive tradition in British politics, to which the most exciting contributor was Peter Clarke.[31] All four were enriching, but they did not all point in the same direction.

The adversary-politics theorists were essentially conservative. They posited a known stock of centrist policies, which would have worked well if only the party system had not got in the way. Thus, Michael Stewart's mordant study of the 1960s and 1970s, *The Jekyll and Hyde Years*,[32] depicted a cycle of decline, with bouts of dogmatic nonsense punctuating periods of pragmatic common sense. The start of each new government – irrespective of its party – saw the rationally social democratic Dr Jekyll elbowed aside by the crazed ideologue, Mr Hyde. Hyde was always eclipsed after a time, but too late to stop him from giving the economy another downward twist. The obvious implication was that centrist social democracy had not failed. The trouble was that it had not been tried consistently or openly. And thus, in a *Spectator* article published a couple of months before Roy Jenkins's Dimbleby Lecture, I conceded that the broadly social-democratic policies followed by the Heath government in 1972–4 and the Wilson and Callaghan governments from 1974 to 1979 had failed. But this was because social democracy had been 'fighting with one hand behind its back'. Party pressures had forced the governments concerned to disguise their new-found centrism and made it impossible for them to campaign for it. The moral was clear.

[I]f the next social-democratic government is to be more successful than the last, it will have to consist of open social democrats, sailing under their own colours, not of covert ones, sailing under other people's.[33]

Yet that interpretation of the social-democratic predicament never satisfied me. I had no doubt that modernization and revisionism were still umbilically connected, and the notion that the fading centrism of the 1960s and 1970s still pointed the way to modernity was inherently implausible. Paradoxically, I learned more from the public-choice theorists whose values I did not share, and whose policy conclusions I disputed. For them, social democracy *had* failed. The basic social-democratic enterprise – the use of public power to redress the balance of the marketplace – was fatally misconceived. The public domain was a site of bureaucratic empire-building and self-stultifying overload. The corporatist techniques to which social-democratic regimes resorted in order to mitigate the consequences of overload were self-stultifying too: corporatism buttressed the status quo and impeded innovation and growth. I was unconvinced. If this were true for Britain, why was it not true for the equally bureaucratic, even more corporatist, yet plainly far more successful political economies of central Europe? *British* corporatism was self-stultifying, not corporatism as such. The cure was to open it up to the public gaze so as to make the 'great barons of the meso-economy' properly accountable, not to wish it out of existence.

But although I was never a convert, the public-choice critique of the overloaded state gave me valuable food for thought. In particular, it helped me to see that one of the reasons why Croslandite social democracy had gone adrift was that it had relied on state-directed social engineering, based on the assumption that 'if the penny of policy decision is fed into the appropriate slot, the chocolate bar of implementation will automatically emerge.' That, I increasingly came to feel, was a fatal flaw. It was nonsense 'to see the great Whitehall bureaucracies as the moving parts in a machine which would-be social engineers can use as they see fit'.[34] They were collections of men and women, with their own agendas. In any case, social science could not furnish the kind of knowledge that would-be social engineers needed. There was an indispensable role for the state, but as facilitator and partner of what I had not yet learned to call civil society, not as engineer.

That was only the beginning of the story. The flaw in Croslandite social democracy reflected a deeper flaw in the public culture. Borrowing from Anthony Lester's exegesis of Dicey's jurisprudence, I gradually came to believe that what Dicey himself called 'the keystone of the Constitution' – the doctrine of the 'absolute legislative sovereignty or despotism of the King in Parliament' – encapsulated a false and damaging conception of public power and the public realm, which had become part of the mental furniture of virtually the entire political class. Central to that conception, I argued in my Inaugural Lecture at Salford University, was the notion 'that power is something you either have or do not have; that while it can sometimes be limited it can never be shared'.[35] From that notion flowed the assumption that politics revolved around a struggle between Ins and Outs for exclusive control of the state, and the corresponding assumption that the victors were entitled to use state power to change society from the top down. If a new social democracy were to arise from the ruins of the old it would have to abandon that notion, together with the Dicey conception of sovereignty in which it was embedded.

In that perspective, marketization, the panacea of the New Right (and later of sections of the SDP), was a pointless and dangerous diversion. Strangely, I had not yet encountered Albert Hirschman's immortal triad, Exit, Voice and Loyalty,[36] but I was instinctively for Voice whenever possible. I knew in my bones that the new public philosophy for which I was groping should put more emphasis on Voice, not less, and that it should be correspondingly suspicious of Exit. But I also sensed that its conception of the role and nature of Voice would have to differ from that of the old. This is where the new historiography of British progressivism came into the argument. In his evocative *Liberals and Social Democrats* Peter Clarke followed the New Liberal, L. T. Hobhouse, in arguing that reformers could be divided into two categories. 'Mechanical' reformers were essentially pessimistic about the human material with which they had to work. The Dicey conception of sovereignty and the absolutist conception of power that went with it fitted their pessimism like a glove. For them, reform had to come from the top down, by way of the central state. 'Moral' reformers were optimists. They thought the impetus for reform came from the bottom up, and that the reformer's chief task was to change the moral climate by argument and persuasion. The New Liberals of the early twentieth century were 'moral' reformers, and the early Fabians 'mechanical' ones. Armed with Clarke's insight, I saw that Croslandite social democracy had been 'mechanical' too. It had gone adrift, I concluded, not just because it had misunderstood the true nature of the state, but because it had forgotten the 'moral' element in the social-democratic heritage.[37] And what was true of social democracy was true of the public culture as a whole. It too was 'mechanical' and, in an important sense, pessimistic. The first step towards a new politics would be to reinvent the tradition of moral reform.

VI

By the early 1980s, then, I had travelled a long way from the revisionist social democracy to which I had been converted a quarter of a century before. I didn't yet know what to put in its place. I did know that the new social democracy for which I was groping would be participative, decentralist and modest, where the old had been directive, centralist and hubristic. I also knew that the flaws I had detected in the old social democracy were connected, in ways I hadn't fully grasped, with the dominant presuppositions of Britain's public culture on the one hand, and with the archaism of her state and economy on the other. Above all, I knew that I owed it to myself to try to put some analytical flesh on these still fragmentary bones.

I was slower to start than I had expected. Ironically, the chief culprit was the SDP, which I saw, for a brief but brilliant moment, as the catalyst of a new political culture. For the best part of three years, SDP politics dominated my life. I had no time for the book I knew I had to write until Mrs Thatcher was well into her second term and my SDP hopes had begun to wither. *The Unprincipled Society*,[38] as it eventually became, was published in early 1988, but it was a child of the mid-1980s, written in the glare of Thatcherism's high noon. By then, some of the preoccupations of the late 1970s and early 1980s had faded. The Jekyll and Hyde syndrome was no more: Hyde, the crazed ideologist, enjoyed unbroken supremacy. The threat to the social-democratic mix of justice and freedom came from Hayekian neo-liberalism: the neo-socialism of the previous decade was dead in the water. Atomization and exclusion loomed larger than corporatist stagnation or state overload. By the same token, I was able to take my reading further than I had done in the first flush of my return to academic life. (I learned most from the writings of Charles Lindblom, John Zysman, Ronald Dore, Andrew Gamble, Philippe Schmitter and Keith Middlemas on comparative political economy, from the social history of Harold Perkin and from the moral philosophy of Alasdair MacIntyre and Mary Midgeley.)[39] But the continuities between my early gropings for a revised revisionism and *The Unprincipled Society* are more important than the contrasts. My journey had taken me into new territory, but I was following the same course.

The Unprincipled Society was two – perhaps three – books in one. It was a critique of neo-liberalism and of the historiography of the New Right. It proposed an alternative account of the rise and fall of the post-war social-democratic consensus and of the secular relative decline of the British economy. Finally, it offered the tentative outlines of an alternative, communitarian public philosophy, centred on what I now realize was a civic republican notion of 'politics as mutual education'. In it, I argued that what I called 'Keynesian social democracy' – the 'governing philosophy' of the post-war period – had broken down. It had done so because economic change had exposed its fundamental weakness: that it was a philosophy of public intervention, without a notion of the public realm or the public good. Because of this, it could not provide the moral basis for the hard choices that had to be made when the economic climate turned cold; as a result, the public sector became a battleground for predatory private interests instead of the instrument of a coherent public purpose.

But the neo-liberal alternative was a blind alley. (So was neo-socialism, but my treatment of that was perfunctory.) In the first place, it was incoherent. Neo-liberals stood for freedom of choice. They were for a market order on the grounds that the market was pre-eminently the realm of freedom. But, on their own showing, the market order of the past could be re-created only by a sustained exercise in social engineering, carried out by a coercive state. Freedom of choice turned out to be the freedom to make choices compatible with a market system and allowed by a neo-liberal regime. Secondly, neo-liberals offered a false diagnosis of Britain's economic decline, based on a false view of the relationship between states and markets. Their governing assumption, that markets were in some sense more 'natural' or 'spontaneous' than

states, was an absurdity. States and markets were always inter-
twined: 'at the door of the auction room stands the policeman'.
Their conclusion that the relative decline of the British economy
could be laid at the door of state-induced 'distortions' of the
market was equally absurd. The truth was almost the opposite.
The British economy had declined in comparison with competing
economies because Britain had always lacked a 'developmental
state' capable of constructing and guiding a social coalition in
favour of economic change and of harnessing market forces to a
long-term national interest. And that lack reflected a public culture
and public philosophy saturated with a reductionist individualism
that rested on a thin, two-dimensional conception of the self, that
saw the very notion of the common good as 'a sentimental fantasy'
and that therefore had no place for a 'public power standing apart
from private interests'.

The inescapable conclusion was that Britain's political economy
was caught in an impasse. There was no going back to the
Keynesian social democracy of the post-war period; the neo-liberal
alternative led nowhere. But there were no short cuts to a better
alternative. The question was not how to replace old policies with
new ones. It was how to make a fragmented society whole, how to
realize a vision of the human self as a developing intellectual and
moral entity, shaped by and growing through constant interaction
with other selves. Politics as mutual education was not so much an
answer to that question as an approach to an answer. It implied a
radical devolution of power, public and private, and open power-
sharing between public authorities and private bodies. But institutional changes were beside the point without a more profound
change in the public culture, based on a notion of human beings as
learning creatures, and involving a break with the 'common sense
which practical men have taken for granted for the best part of two
centuries'. Of that there could be no guarantee.

> Politics as mutual education implies some notion of a common good
> transcending private goods: of membership of a political community as
> partnership in a common enterprise, which endures beyond the
> lifespans of the individuals who make it up: of politics itself as, in Brian
> Crowley's words, 'a civilised and civilising process'[40] through which
> free men and women assume the burdens of social choice, instead of
> handing them over to a charismatic leader or an impersonal social
> process . . .
> . . . It rules out manipulative short cuts to change, imposed 'reforms',
> technocratic fixes. Its style is humdrum, not heroic: collegial, not
> charismatic: consensual, not ideological: conversational, not declaratory.

It depends on the slow processes of argument and negotiation. It requires patience, open-mindedness and, above all, humility before the astonishing and sometimes exasperating diversity of others. At its core lies the belief that men and women may learn if they are stretched; that they can discover how to govern themselves if they win self-government. But the key words in that sentence are 'may' and 'can'. No one who has lived through any of this century would be foolish enough to replace them with 'will'. To substitute the politics of mutual education for the politics of command and exchange would be to gamble – not, it is true, on the altruism or moral excellence of others, but on their sociability and capacity for growth.[41]

In retrospect, it is not difficult to spot loose ends and clumsy stitches. The developmental state does not, at first sight, have much to do with politics as mutual education. I still think they are connected. A developmental state presumably needs developmental citizens; so, in a different way, does politics as mutual education. Both depend on the possibility of a public interest and on the capacity of an active civil society to recognize and pursue it; both blur the boundaries between civil society and the state. As I argue in chapter 6 of this book, moreover, there is a good deal of evidence that the symbiosis between public and private power which is the essence of the developmental state can now be achieved more effectively on the regional or local level than on the national one. Local developmentalism squares quite well, may indeed require, a public philosophy of dialogue, power-sharing and negotiation. But I should have explored these connections more systematically and spelled them out more fully. A more serious weakness is that, against the thrust of the whole argument, my approach to economic and social change was unconsciously influenced by the managerialism of the 1980s, which was itself the product of an unconscious social Darwinism. Too often, my language suggested that an exogenous entity called 'change' operates as an irresistible force, to which mere human beings have to 'adapt'. It was a new version of the modernizing obsessions of the old revisionism. Were I writing the book again, I would emphasize that the very notions of modernity and modernization are problematic; that changes may be good or bad; that bad ones should be resisted; that there is more than one way to adapt to most changes; and that the choice between them is a political act, not a determinate imperative.

By the same token, debate has moved on. The 'thick' communitarian critique of 'thin' procedural liberalism has become more sophisticated and more voluminous, and it is now possible to detect a distinct republican position, offering at least the germ of an alternative to both.[42] The literature on comparative political economy has changed direction. Debate no longer centres on the relationship between states and markets but on the varieties of capitalism and their moral, cultural and institutional dimensions.[43] As I try to show in chapter 11, important new contributions have been made to the historiography of the British state, suggesting a more nuanced interpretation than the one I offered. When all the qualifications have been made, however, I still think the analysis I put forward in *The Unprincipled Society* was broadly right, and I still adhere to the essentials of the public philosophy I tried to sketch out. In some ways, moreover, both are closer to the spirit of the age than they were ten years ago. Triumphalist neo-liberalism is no more. In the world of policy and decision as well as in the world of ideas and reflection, there is a growing realization that the successful working of a market order depends on values that markets themselves cannot generate, and that uninhibited market-ization may erode them. Where the keywords of the 1980s were 'choice', 'markets' and 'freedom', it is beginning to look as if the keywords of the late 1990s and 2000s will be 'cohesion', 'inclusion' and 'responsibility'. My question – how can a fragmented society make itself whole? – may not capture the mood of the times, but it is much closer to doing so than it was.

Yet I cannot suppress a certain pricking in the thumbs – a nagging sense that the path I have followed for the best part of forty years is blocked, and that it is time for a new turning. Except in the broadest of broad terms, I don't yet know where such a new turning would lead, but in the rest of this chapter I want to explain why I think it has to be found and explore some of the implications of that thought.

VII

The Unprincipled Society ended on a note of qualified optimism. So did its successor of 1991, *The Progressive Dilemma*,[44] in which I called for a new, bottom-up 'progressive coalition' based on 'a marriage between the communitarian, decentralist, participatory radicalism to which the Liberal Democrats are heirs and the communitarian, decentralist, participatory strands in the socialist inheritance'. But an undertone of pessimism ran through both. *The Unprincipled Society*'s call for a politics of mutual education sprang from fear as well as from hope – from the fear that *homo sapiens*, the learning creature, may be learning the wrong things: that the processes of social fragmentation may be reaching the point of no return: that pervasive free-riding may be about to destroy the public good of mutual trust. *The Progressive Dilemma*'s call for a bottom-up progressive coalition was balanced by the warning that a conventional party victory would not be enough, even if it could be procured.

There is still room for optimism, but the qualifications loom larger than they did a few years ago. Capitalism's untaming was already under way when *The Unprincipled Society* was written, and it had gone much further by the time *The Progressive Dilemma* appeared. But both books were written within the framework of the tamed capitalism I had taken for granted since my twenties. They could not be written in that framework today. Untamed capitalism is an omnipresent reality, haunting the new mood of the 1990s, like a spectre at the feast. As a result, the hollowing out of community, which politics as mutual education was meant to check, has proceeded apace – and in countries with relatively solidaristic cultures and 'progressive' regimes as well as in Britain and the United States. There is, in fact, a cruel paradox in the intellectual and political changes of the last few years. One of the reasons why social cohesion and mutual trust loom so large in the new discourse of the 1990s is that the creative destruction associated with untamed capitalism has done so much to undermine them. One of the reasons why the Labour Party has become the focal point of a broad-based progressive coalition of the sort I advocated is that the conditions for successful progressivism are under threat.

Can the paradox be resolved, or has the new discourse come too late? Almost by definition, I can't yet answer that question. The most I can do is to offer a perspective from which it may be addressed. It derives from Karl Polanyi's half-forgotten master-piece of fifty years ago, *The Great Transformation*.[45] Polanyi's text speaks even more loudly to the 1990s than it did to the 1940s, when it was published. For him, the self-regulating free market of the early nineteenth century, entailing the commodification of land and labour, was a 'utopia'. It was unrealizable, because land and labour are not in fact commodities like any other. It was also, in a profound sense, unnatural. It was not a spontaneous product of unfettered human instinct, as its apologists claimed. On the contrary, massive state interventions, pushed through by a ruthless and centralized bureaucracy, were needed to impose it on the Old Society and to uproot the old value-system that impeded it. The interventions did not succeed, of course. They could not, because the utopia they were designed to institute was an impossibility. But the attempt to institute it was a social and cultural disaster, provoking, in the end, an instinctive, unplanned reaction against it. According to Polanyi, the real essence of nineteenth-century history lay in this double movement – state-imposed market utopianism at first, followed by a spontaneous countervailing reaction later. As he put it himself,

> The road to the free market was opened and kept open by an enormous increase in continuous, centrally organized and controlled interventionism. To make Adam Smith's 'simple and natural liberty' compatible with the needs of a human society was a most complicated affair. Witness the complexity of the provisions in the innumerable enclosure laws; the amount of bureaucratic control involved in the administration of the New Poor Laws which for the first time since Queen Elizabeth's reign were effectively supervised by central authority; or the increase in governmental administration entailed in the meritorious task of municipal reform . . .
>   This paradox was topped by another. While *laissez-faire* economy was the product of deliberate State action, subsequent restrictions on *laissez-faire* started in a spontaneous way. *Laissez-faire* was planned; planning was not . . . The legislative spearhead of the countermovement against a self-regulating market as it developed in the half century following 1860 turned out to be spontaneous, undirected by opinion and actuated by a purely pragmatic spirit.[46]

On one level, the long-term implications are encouraging. If a pragmatic counter-movement against the excesses of market utopianism could dominate the second half of the nineteenth century, why should a similar counter-movement not develop in our own day? May not the new discourse of the 1990s be a harbinger of precisely such a counter-movement? But a more sombre reading of Polanyi is at least as plausible. The 1980s and early 1990s were indeed a replay of the early nineteenth century, this sombre reading implies, and inflicted comparable damage on the social integument. A counter-movement is indeed inevitable sooner or later: society cannot indefinitely tolerate alienation, anomie, social fragmentation and personal insecurity on the present scale. But there is no guarantee that this counter-movement will take a benign form. Whether it does so or not is a matter of political choice; and at the moment, the omens are far from encouraging.

For the reaction against market utopianism is currently coming, in the main, from a more or less authoritarian, more or less populist, more or less fundamentalist tribalism. The former communist bloc is particularly rich in examples, but it would be self-deception to imagine that Bosnian Serbs, Russian nationalists and Chechen separatists have no western equivalents. Jewish fundamentalists in Brooklyn, Muslim fundamentalists in Beirut and Irish Republican fundamentalists in Belfast belong to the same family. So does Pat Buchanan and so, in a somewhat different vein, does Newt Gingrich. In Britain, Michael Portillo and John Redwood respond to the same imperatives, and appeal to the same emotions. So does Le Pen in France, and so do Berlusconi, the neo-fascists and the Northern League in Italy. A milder version of the same phenomenon is the ominous fascination with the authoritarian capitalism of East Asia displayed by growing numbers of British politicians and commentators.

As some of these examples show, the tribalisms of the 1990s, unlike their predecessors in the 1930s, are not always dirigiste in economics. Sometimes they combine authoritarian xenophobia with market fundamentalism. Plainly, this is intellectually incoherent. A frenzied insistence on national sovereignty in the political sphere and on traditional values in the social sphere cannot logically go hand in hand with an equally frenzied insistence on the sovereignty of the market place in the economic sphere. But that is not the point. We are dealing with the politics of the gut, not with those of the head: with a desperate yearning for stability, identity and security, which will become all the more desperate the longer it is left unsatisfied. Against that background, the intellectual incoherence evident in the combination of authoritarian nationalism and market fundamentalism is neither here nor there. It is psychically coherent, and that is all that matters. In any case, a counter-movement that starts by trying to combine incompatibles may not continue in the same way. Despite the scorn of dogmatic free traders, Pat Buchanan's mixture of xenophobia and protectionism was intellectually coherent; and if our societies continue to fragment, as they will if free-trade dogma continues to prevail, a lurch into Buchananism, on both sides of the Atlantic, is more probable than not.

Can the left and centre – and, for that matter, the non-fundamentalist right – trump the new tribalism with a tolerant, outward-looking alternative? Can it give the inevitable counter-movement against market utopianism a liberal, pluralistic, social-

or Christian-democratic form? Can it teach society how to protect itself from fragmentation without turning to a modern version of the man on a white horse or the damnation-spouting prophet? These will soon be the central questions in the politics of all western countries. Plainly, there are no certain answers. One point, however, is surely clear. As Robert Skidelsky hinted in a *Prospect* essay not long ago, economic and political liberalism no longer go together, if they ever did.[47] Globally and nationally, we shall sooner or later have to choose between the free market and the free society.

1997

• PART ONE •

Capitalism, Socialism and Citizenship

CHAPTER TWO

Reinventing Civic Republicanism

I

The relationship between the market and the forum, between exchange and persuasion, between the public realm of the citizen and the private realm of the consumer, has been a central preoccupation of social thought since the days of Aristotle. For most of the post-war period, however, and in most western countries, the tensions inherent in that relationship appeared to have been resolved. Then came the 'stagflation' of the 1970s, the rise of the New Right, the associated rebirth of economic liberalism and a variety of more or less successful attempts to clip the wings of the post-war welfare state. Classic questions, which the post-war generation imagined it had answered, returned to the agenda – among them the questions of what citizenship means in a market economy, and of how the promise of citizenship is to be realized in complex modern societies. These questions are of significance to all advanced societies, of course; as the most cursory reading of Václav Havel's essays shows, they resonate with particular force in eastern Europe.[1] Perhaps because she has been the chief European testing ground for New Right theory, however, they have also begun to resonate with unusual power in Britain; and it is plausible to imagine that the British case may be more relevant to the rest of the western world than are the various east European cases. Hence, this chapter. It begins by looking at the British debate and the factors which have given rise to it, and then tries to clarify some of the issues it poses.

The first thing to notice is that it is a remarkably confused debate. On the right, Douglas Hurd and other ministers have proclaimed an ideal of 'active and responsible citizenship', building on the centuries-old 'English tradition of voluntary service'.[2] On the centre and centre-left, a disparate band including the Liberal Democrats Paddy Ashdown and Ralf Dahrendorf and Labour supporters like Raymond Plant and Julian le Grand have suggested that the state should be the guarantor of social-citizenship rights rather than the provider of services, as in the familiar Beveridgean model of the welfare state.[3] The cross-party, but overwhelmingly left-of-centre pressure group, Charter 88, sees Britain's political culture as one of 'subjecthood not citizenship' and demands guarantees of fundamental civil and political (but not social) rights. A Commission on Citizenship, presided over by the Speaker of the House of Commons and including representatives of all the United Kingdom political parties, has warned that citizenship is 'a cultural achievement, a gift of history, which can be lost or destroyed' and set out a programme to save it, focused on voluntary service to the community.[4]

Yet the notion of citizenship has, at best, an insecure place in the British political tradition. The British are subjects of a monarch, not citizens of a state. (At least, the English are: the extent to which Scottish constitutional law follows the English model is a matter of debate.) Sovereignty lies with the Crown-in-Parliament, not with the people; and the sovereignty of the Crown-in-Parliament is absolute and inalienable. The executive consists of ministers of the Crown. They are accountable to Parliament for the use they make of the powers at their disposal, but the powers themselves are the Crown's. A recent study suggests that young people have only a vague idea of what the terms 'citizen' and 'citizenship' mean;[5] if a similar study were made of the adult population, it is hard to believe that the results would be very different. Partly because of this, the terminology of citizenship has rarely figured in political discourse. Then why the current salience of the citizenship theme? Why is there a debate over citizenship, and what is the debate about? What light, if any, does it throw on the problems facing contemporary Britain and comparable societies elsewhere? These questions provide the focus for the discussion that follows.

II

It is convenient to begin with the left and centre-left. The collapse of the explicitly Keynesian, and at least implicitly social-democratic, post-war settlement forced them onto the defensive, not only politically, but intellectually as well. They have had to rethink, not their ends, perhaps, but certainly their means. The rethinking exercise has, of course, been confused; such exercises usually are. Despite the confusion, however, three broad themes have emerged.

In the first place, the New Right critique of the 'overloaded' welfare state, encumbered by professional and producer interests, doomed by the logic of collective action to be the prey of bureaucratic empire-building and, as such, unresponsive or indifferent to the public it was supposed to serve, has plainly struck chords among the left and centre-left as well as on the right. But, on left and centre-left assumptions, rationing by price, the New Right alternative to state provision, necessarily leads to injustice. So what should be the left and centre-left alternative? How can social justice be secured without overload? How can the values of the welfare state be realized without relying on the top-heavy, unresponsive structures which have embodied them for so long? An 'enabling state', guaranteeing defined social-citizenship rights, to be delivered by a variety of agencies of which the state itself is only one, has become an increasingly attractive answer. As Raymond Plant puts it,

> Empowerment cannot just come through the market, it has to come also through political mechanisms. However, the New Right are correct in their view that the forms of empowerment which have been tried in the welfare field have very often spawned large bureaucratic forms of service delivery which have sought to provide services to meet professionally ascribed needs ... and have left little scope for individual choice ... The challenge to the Left, therefore, is to devise forms of individual empowerment through rights which will give people more control over their own lives in the welfare field ...
> [A] rights-based approach would move more in the direction of cash payment rather than service delivery, so that instead of the state providing the service, it might rather regulate, to ensure basic national standards, a range of different private service deliverers with cash or a cash surrogate such as a voucher ... Other additional measures could include changing the contracts of service providers such as teachers, doctors or social workers so that it became part of their contractual duty

to provide a service of a specific sort at a specific level which would then yield entitlements under the contract.[6]

The second theme goes deeper. The collapse of the post-war settlement and rise of the New Right, many people on the left and centre-left have come to believe, came about because there was too little sense of community within society, and no public philosophy of mutual obligation and common purpose. The Keynesian social-democratic state of the post-war period was, by definition, an interventionist state. It sought to alter market outcomes and interfere with market forces: in Albert Hirschman's language, to strengthen Voice at the expense of Exit. But, as Hirschman pointed out, Voice goes with and depends upon Loyalty: upon ties of mutuality which endure through time. You will listen to me only if I am, in some sense, loyal to you. I will think it worth while to try to persuade you only if you are, in some sense, loyal to me. Social-democratic governance, to put the point in ordinary language, depends upon communitarian ties. But in post-war Britain, as memories of wartime solidarity faded and the individualistic, utility-maximizing hedonism which had always been central to Britain's economic and political cultures returned to the centre of the stage, these ties grew feeble.

So long as the economic climate remained warm, no harm resulted. But when the climate turned cold, as it did in the 1970s, social-democratic and quasi-social-democratic governments had to appeal for support on non-hedonistic grounds, on grounds of civic duty or social solidarity, to make their policies work. They discovered that the cultural basis for such an appeal was lacking; that, in a profound sense, they had no language in which to frame one; and that, when they spoke in such terms, they had no audience. The New Right rushed in to fill the political vacuum that resulted. Voice faltered and Exit triumphed, in short, because Loyalty was lacking; the public sector became a battleground for predatory private interests because the notion of the public good no longer resonated. The moral seems only too clear. If Voice is ever to be given a bigger role and Exit a lesser one, Loyalty will be necessary as well; if social-democratic governance is to be more successful in the future than it was in the recent past, the fraying bonds of community must somehow be restored.

This is where the third theme enters the argument. In T. H. Marshall's classic 1950 formulation, citizenship had three dimensions – civil, political and social.[7] Over the preceding three centuries the struggle for citizenship rights had shifted from the first to the second, and then from the second to the third. Civil citizenship, manifested in equal civil rights, had been established in the eighteenth century. Political citizenship was largely the work of the nineteenth. In the twentieth century the focus had shifted to the struggle for social rights. The real meaning of the post-war welfare state was that the principle of social citizenship was now enshrined in legislation. A similar view was implicit in the writings of Anthony Crosland, the high priest of the social-democratic revisionism of the 1950s.[8] The primordial social-democratic ends of greater social and economic equality, Crosland argued, could perfectly well be achieved by and through the existing political system, since that system was already egalitarian. Political rights and political citizenship were secure: because they were secure, democratic socialists could concentrate on social reform and leave the polity to take care of itself.

When Marshall and Crosland wrote, these conclusions seemed almost self-evident. In the harsher climate of the 1970s and 1980s, doubts crept in. The interventionist, social-citizenship state found it increasingly difficult to mobilize consent, and there were growing signs of popular disaffection from its institutions.[9] Many on the left and centre-left began to question the Marshall–Crosland picture of a smooth progression from civil to political to social. Perhaps the reason why the social-citizenship state found it more difficult to mobilize consent was that it was losing legitimacy. Perhaps the reason why it was losing legitimacy was that social citizenship was not, after all, securely founded in civil and political citizenship. Perhaps Marshall, Crosland and those who thought like them had tried to build the top floor of citizenship before the first two floors were in place. And if that were true, the obvious conclusion was that the struggle for political citizenship, which the post-war generation had assumed to be over, would have to be waged anew.

III

So far, I have concentrated on the lessons, or perceived lessons, of the 1970s. The experience of the neo-liberal experiment of the 1980s has also provoked awkward questions and second thoughts, and on the right as well as on the left.

The central purpose of the neo-liberal project is, of course, to narrow the frontiers of the state and to widen those of the market. But, as Hayek was quick to recognize, a market order cannot flourish in a society permeated with non-market values.[10] Since most late twentieth-century societies, at least in the developed West, are indeed permeated with such values, it follows that a market order cannot be created (or re-created) without profound changes of attitude and belief. How are these changes to be procured? And who is to procure them? In Britain in the 1980s, at any rate, the answers have been plain. As Andrew Gamble has put it, the hallmark of the Thatcher era has been 'the free economy and the strong state',[11] with the second as the necessary condition of the first. In order to roll back the frontiers of state intervention and foster an 'enterprise culture', the state has had to become more centralized, more aggressive and, in certain respects, more powerful or at least more willing to use the powers it already possessed. Particularly after the second Thatcher victory in 1983, the triumphant New Right launched an ambitious programme of state-led cultural reconstruction, designed to humble or cripple the intermediate institutions which embodied the collectivist values of the old consensus, and to foster the entrepreneurial values which a market order requires. In short: state aggrandizement here and now, so that the state may withdraw at some stage in the future.

Traditionally, however, British conservatives have stood for a vigorous civil society, with strong intermediate institutions capable, in a characteristic British phrase, of protecting the 'liberties of the subject' against state encroachment. The spectacle of a radical New Right government using state power to uproot collectivist values from a society permeated with them has made some conservatives uneasy. In their unease, some have reached for the communitarian strands in their own tradition; a few have also come to the conclusion that the system provides insufficient safeguards against the abuse of power. Unease on the right, moreover, has been matched by much greater unease on the left and in the centre. Whether the Thatcher governments have, in fact, departed from the spirit of Britain's unwritten constitution is a matter for argument. Since the constitution is unwritten, and since there is no authoritative body to decide what its spirit actually is, no one can be certain. What is clear is that many on the left and centre-left believe that the spirit of the constitution has been violated and, more particularly, that freedoms which the British could previously take for granted have been endangered. For many, this has been a painful awakening. Since the First World War, at any rate, the British left (though not the centre) has shown scant interest in constitutional reform. Its purpose has been to win control of the institutions of the state through parliamentary election, and to use the absolute and unfettered sovereignty of the Crown-in-Parliament in accordance with its ideology. It would be wrong to suggest that the experience of the 1980s has led to a universal change of heart, but there is no doubt that it has led some people on the left to question their previous constitutional indifference and to conclude that uncertain, problematic and fluctuating conventions need to be replaced by explicit and justiciable rights, entrenched in a fundamental law.

What is best described, with deliberate imprecision, as the 'social question' has also provoked unease – again, on the right as well as on the left. Not everyone would subscribe to Ralf Dahrendorf's description of an 'underclass'

> split a hundred ways so that most of its members look for their own personal ways out. It does not care much either way about most issues of current concern. It is lethargic.
>
> But it is alienated. The condition is as important as the sentiment. The crucial fact about the underclass and the persistently unemployed is that they have no stake in society. In a very serious sense, society does not need them. Many in the majority class wish that they would simply go away; and if they did their absence would barely be noticed. Those who are in this position know it. Society to them is above all distant. It is symbolised by nothing so much as the police and the courts, and to a lesser extent by the offices and officials of the state . . . Not caring about the norms and values of the official society has become a widespread habit.[12]

Few on left or right, however, would deny that, after a decade of market liberalization, a 'social question' remains to be answered, or that the mixture of alienation and lethargy described by Dahrendorf has something to do with it. The solution of the radical New Right is a quasi-Trotskyite permanent revolution: more liberalization, more attacks on market-distorting intermediate institutions, more fostering of entrepreneurial values, more state aggrandizement. Not surprisingly, that solution is unacceptable to the left and centre-left; increasingly, their alternative is the social-citizenship project described above. But, even on the right, many lack the stomach for further instalments of Hayekian radicalism. One reason is that it carries obvious political risks, but there is another, and almost certainly a more important reason as well.

There is, after all, a communitarianism of the right as well as a communitarianism of the left. Left-of-centre communitarians are not the only ones to be alarmed by Colin Crouch's spectre of a fragmented society, in which

> Social inequalities would continue and become intensified as different regions and economic sectors enjoyed starkly different fates; but these inequalities would not follow identifiable lines of experienced solidarity, and would therefore not generate solidarities among the under-privileged ...
> ... Electrified perimeter fences, private security guards and dogs would keep the housing estates of the more wealthy free from fear and independent of general norms of behaviour in the wider society ...
> Outside the well-equipped home and the regulated but friendly work place would be the streets. Because not much of life would be lived in public spaces, there would be no informal norms of human interaction to govern conduct in the streets and other non-private places, such as the football terraces. Such locations would become the resort of the dispossessed and unemployed ... This would further reduce general use of public space, concomitantly reducing still further its integration into any form of community ...
> The political requirements and the concept of citizenship practised by most people in such a society would be small: various *ad hoc* subsidies to help with awkward corners of welfare provision ... traffic control and road building; and a heavy dose of policing.[13]

The conservative answer is to make the 'active citizen' the substitute for the social citizenship of Marshall, Crosland and the post-war consensus.

This leads on to a more speculative point. In Britain, as elsewhere, the New Right project has a moral dimension as well as an economic one. But there is a tension between the two. New Right economics are centred on utility-maximizing Benthamite hedonism; at the heart of the New Right's morality lies a critique of permissive hedonism in the name of the Protestant ethic. How is that tension to be resolved? What is the moral justification of an essentially hedonistic market order? As Harold Perkin has suggested, the nineteenth-century answer lay in the 'entrepreneurial ideal' of the active, but abstinent, owner-manager of the first industrial revolution, who raised his own capital, took his own risks and saved his own profits.[14] That answer would carry little conviction in an age of corporate conglomerates, faceless account-ants and predatory takeover bids. Here again, the 'active citizen' – now in the guise of a late twentieth-century descendant of the early nineteenth-century active capitalist – fills the breach. In doing so, moreover, he also fills another breach. A New Right market order would depend upon certain public goods – civility, honesty, mutual trust, community even – which the market itself cannot supply. In the nineteenth century these were supplied partly by the Church and partly by the state. Neither is likely to be of much use today. Once more, the 'active citizen' is pressed into service.

IV

Given all this, it is hardly surprising that the citizenship debate is rather confused. As an aid to clarification, it is helpful to consider two models of citizenship – one 'liberal-individualist' and the other 'civic-republican'.[15]

In the liberal-individualist model, citizenship is a status – a status that belongs unconditionally to all its possessors and that confers rights upon them by virtue of that fact. There is no suggestion that rights have to be earned or that they will cease to belong to their owners if they are not used. The only obligation which citizens *qua* citizens owe to each other is the obligation to respect each other's rights. Occasionally, as in Marshall, there is a faint suggestion that rights are accompanied by duties, but the connection is vague. More often, liberal individualists repudiate any suggestion that citizens may have duties, beyond passive ones like paying taxes and obeying the law. Thus, citizens are under no obligation to participate in the public affairs of the community: participation is a right, but it is certainly not a duty. If they do not make use of their right to participate, that is their affair; they do not cease to be citizens thereby. Indeed, many – perhaps most – citizenship rights are rights *against* the community: rights to pursue private affairs without interference from society or from other citizens. In some formulations there is even a slight suspicion of activity, on the grounds that it may encroach on the rights of others or disturb political or social peace.

Yet there is a paradox here, of which many defenders of the liberal-individualist model seem unaware. What are the rights which citizenship as status guarantees? As already mentioned, the seminal modern formulation is Marshall's: first civil, then political, then social. But what are social rights? There is an important difference between civil and political rights on the one hand, and social rights on the other. Social rights are rights to 'positive' freedom, not to 'negative'; they can be made effective only through state action to redistribute resources. They therefore have to be justified on grounds different from, or additional to, the grounds on which civil and political rights are characteristically justified. The typical justification is agency: without social rights, the argument goes, civil and political rights are empty. But at this point, activity and duty re-enter the argument, after all. If social rights are to be justified on grounds of agency, should not the agents act? If resources are redistributed in your favour, are you not under some obligation to make proper use of them?

The civic-republican conception is altogether more austere. In it, citizenship is a practice, not a status; active, not passive; public not private. In the civic-republican tradition, the term 'private citizen', as Adrian Oldfield puts it, is an oxymoron: the practice of citizenship takes place, and can only take place, in the public realm: virtue is civic virtue. There is, of course, a parallel between citizenship as status and citizenship as practice: only those with the status can engage in the practice. Athenian women and slaves could not practise the civic virtues because they were not citizens. But the differences are far greater. Implicit in much liberal individualism is the assumption that the interest of the citizen may conflict with the interest of the community to which he belongs. In civic republicanism, that assumption is almost incomprehensible; the citizen's interest is the city's interest. By the same token, citizenship is about duties, not about rights. Carrying out the practice entails performing duties associated with it – notably, the duties of honouring, defending and sharing in the government of the city. The active performance of these is the essence of citizenship. What liberal individualists see as rights àre the facilitating mechanisms making the performance of duties possible. Civic republicanism is thus

> a hard school of thought. There is no cosy warmth of life in such a community. Citizens are called to stern and important tasks which have to do with the very sustaining of their identity. There may be, indeed there ought to be, a sense of belonging, but that sense of belonging may not be associated with inner peace and, even if it is, it is not the kind of peace that permits a relaxed and private leisure, still less a disdain for civic concerns.[16]

A further implication is that the practice of citizenship is, as Oldfield puts it, 'unnatural'. Like other practices, it has to be learned and can be forgotten. It is, moreover, a demanding practice, requiring commitment and self-discipline. Citizens are made, not born; though others can help them, in the last resort, they make themselves. Citizenship is growing, becoming, *doing*. In an important sense, it is a task: strenuous, stretching, and at first forbidding. To ensure that free-riders do not escape their obligations, putative citizens therefore have to be trained and motivated for the activities from which growth comes; it is not enough simply to give them opportunities. While civic republicanism is optimistic in assuming that human beings can grow in this way, it is pessimistic (or perhaps realistic) in recognizing that it is hard for them to do so and that they can easily regress. For the danger of backsliding is omnipresent. The soil in which citizenship grows often becomes barren. And one of the most insidious threats to its fertility is the possessive hedonism which lies at the heart of the free-market model of man and society and perhaps of the liberal-individualist conception of citizenship as well.

In all this, civic republicanism has much in common with Protestantism. Indeed, Robert Bellah treats the 'biblical' and 'republican' strands in the American tradition as one, contrasting both with what he calls 'utilitarian and expressive individualism'.[17] There is justice in this conflation. Civic republicanism and Protestantism both stress self-discipline, duty and activity in the world. Both are anti-hedonist. But it is important to note that there are differences as well. The Christian virtues – altruism, charity, turning the other cheek – are not civic virtues. The good Samaritan was a good man, not a good citizen: the whole point of the parable is that the beneficiary of his charity came from a different community, and was not bound to him by ties of common loyalty. The good citizen sacrifices himself for the city, not for God or the human race. His reward is the affirmation of his identity in this world, not eternal felicity in the next.

V

The citizenship debate is best appraised against this background. Plainly, different elements from different traditions jostle confusingly together. This may not matter; eclecticism may be useful. But it is wise to be aware of it. Some differences may not be reconcilable; some distinctions may need to be made; some borrowings may be inconsistent with others.

This applies particularly to the 'active citizen' of Douglas Hurd and the Speaker's Commission. The notion of active citizenship comes straight from the civic-republican tradition. But in terms of that tradition (and still more, of course, in terms of the liberal-

individualist tradition) the Hurdian 'active citizen' is an incomplete, even deformed, creature. The activities in which he is
being asked to engage may or may not be desirable in terms of
some other ethic or tradition (for example, of Protestant Christianity) but they have nothing to do with citizenship, whether liberal-
individualist or civic-republican. They have nothing to do with
liberal-individualist citizenship because nothing is said about the
rights that liberal individualism demands. They have nothing to
do with civic-republican citizenship because they do not embrace
the 'stern and important tasks' which are fundamental to that
tradition. In civic republicanism, the supreme civic duty is to take
part in the government of the city. The Hurdian volunteer could
hardly be asked to do that: almost by definition, one important
part of the New Right project of the last decade has been to narrow
the scope of the civic sphere, to privatize public purposes as well
as public institutions. The truth is that the 'active citizen' as
envisaged by Douglas Hurd and the Speaker's Commission is less
a citizen than an exemplar of what Hurd himself has described
as

> The English tradition of voluntary service . . . Justices of the Peace from
> the fifteenth century to the present, the school and vestry boards of the
> Victorian age, councillors in modern local government represent a long
> outstanding tradition of public service. School governors are unpaid, so
> are jurors, so are residents', ratepayers' and tenants' leaders, so are
> neighbourhood watch co-ordinators, so are the thousands of people
> who give their time freely to the huge and thriving number of British
> charities . . . [S]chemes based on this tradition are often more flexible
> and more effective than bureaucratic plans drawn up upon Fabian
> principles.[18]

The tradition of voluntary service has much to commend it.
Without it, British civil society would be much the poorer. But it is
not a civic tradition; service is a monarchical concept, not a civic
one. 'Citizens', Oldfield reminds us tartly, 'govern themselves.'[19]
Does this matter? Is it not a good thing for people to engage
voluntarily in good works, irrespective of any ambiguities or
contradictions in the language in which their activities are described? From a strictly instrumental point of view, the answer is
presumably 'yes'. If good works are done, then good is done. On a
deeper level, it may matter more than appears at first sight. The
object of the 'active citizenship' project is not, after all, purely, or
even primarily, instrumental. Part of the purpose of the exercise is
to strengthen community ties and to foster a sense of mutual

responsibility. If putative volunteers suspect, however vaguely, that they are being manipulated; that the citizenship in the name of which they are urged to volunteer is incomplete or fraudulent; that they are being asked to engage in the practice without having the status that ought to go with it, and that the practice is in some way demeaning because they do not have any control over it; then the whole exercise is likely to fail.

Left and centre-left demands for an enabling state, guaranteeing social-citizenship rights, and for the explicit entrenchment of civil and political rights are not open to these objections. Both sets of demands come from the liberal-individualist tradition. Both have to do with rights, springing unconditionally from status, not with duties, entailed by a practice. There is a faint echo of civic republicanism in Charter 88's critique of the culture of subject-hood, but the Charter says nothing about duty or activity. As for the social-citizenship rights advocated by Ashdown, Dahrendorf and the rest, these are even further removed from citizenship as practice. They are the badges of status, pure and simple. The whole point of treating them as rights is to sever any lingering connection between status and duty, to ensure that their bearers will enjoy them unconditionally.

For liberal-individualists this is as it should be: rights are what matter, and rights are by definition unconditional. Indeed, even civic republicans can march in the same direction, albeit for different reasons. As mentioned above, what liberal individualists see as rights, civic republicans see as necessary conditions for the performance of duties. You cannot practise citizenship if you are trapped in Ralf Dahrendorf's alienated and 'lethargic' underclass. Your ability to govern yourself is problematic if you live in an elective dictatorship, with no guarantees of the traditional liberal-individualist civic rights. For those who advocate them, the civil and political rights demanded by Charter 88 and the social rights demanded by the proponents of an enabling state are concomitants of full citizenship on the liberal-individualist model. They may also be seen as prerequisites of active citizenship on the civic-republican model; as the tools with which the citizen's duties are performed.

The question, however, is whether the liberal-individualist model and the various demands for individual rights which derive from it can address the problems which this and similarly placed societies face. An enabling state, guaranteeing social-citizenship rights, may avoid the dangers of overload more successfully than the post-war welfare state is widely believed to have done. By the same token, it may come closer to solving the problem of the underclass than did old-style, state-bureaucratic Keynesian social democracy. But it can go only part of the way to a solution. The problem is not only one of resources or rights to resources. It is also one of lack of skill, lack of training and, above all, lack of motivation: of what Dahrendorf calls 'lethargy'. Why should the simple guarantee of social-citizenship rights stir the lethargic into activity? Above all, it is hard to see why an enabling state should be able to halt the decay of community, of which the growth of the underclass is one, but only one, manifestation, or to discover a moral language in which the resource redistribution which a programme of social-citizenship rights must entail may be justified to the 'haves', who will lose from it, as well as to the 'have-nots', who will gain. Individual rights belong, by definition, to individuals. The language in which they are argued for and defended is, of necessity, an individualist language. Terms like 'duty', 'loyalty', 'obligation' do not translate into that language; they belong to a different language, springing from a different conception of human nature and human possibilities. But it is only in those terms that community ties can be described and community obligations asserted. What is needed to restore the fraying bonds of community is Oldfield's

> sense of belonging and commitment. The commitment is to others who share interests, or positions or purposes, and it is also to those who, for whatever reason, are unable to look after their own interests or pursue their own purposes. It is to seek the good of others at the same time as, and sometimes in neglect of, one's own good. It is to approach social relationships in an Aristotelian spirit of 'concord'. It is this that creates the sense of community; and it is this that creates citizens.[20]

And 'concord' is quintessentially a civic-republican concept, not a liberal-individualist one.

VI

If the argument set out above is right, one obvious, if at first sight surprising, implication is that the civic-republican tradition has more to say to a complex modern society in the late twentieth century than the liberal-individualist one; that the protagonists of 'active citizenship' are right in laying stress on duty, action and mutual loyalty, even if wrong in picking certain aspects out of the tradition, while ignoring the rest of the corpus from which they come. If so, two questions arise. What, in fact, does civic republicanism say? What, if anything, can be done to make its precepts operational in a world unimaginably different from the one in which it took shape?

These questions provide a focus for further inquiry. Only a few observations can be made here. The first is that the most important things it has to say have to do with its ethics and psychology. Particularly resonant are its stress on growth, activity, learning, and mutuality: its picture of the Self as something that is shaped through constant interaction with other selves in a common and testing endeavour. This has important practical implications for education, training and industrial policies, to name only a few. That said, the ethics and psychology cannot be divorced from politics. After all, the central message of civic republicanism is that the Self can develop its full potential and learn how properly to discharge its obligations to other selves only through action in the public realm of a free city. The key question, perhaps, is whether that insight is valid or not; and whether, if it is, it has any practical implications for today's world. Inevitably, answers will differ. For what it is worth, my own view is that it is valid, though only after translation into a modern idiom. We cannot go back to ancient Greece or Renaissance Italy; our view of what constitutes a forum will have to be both broader and narrower than Aristotle's or Machiavelli's. We can, however, create decentralized structures – at work and in public services, as well as in the formal political sphere – in which the civic republican virtues may be learned and practised. Indeed, if the civic-republican view of social man is right, we not only can, but must. On civic-republican assumptions, the alternative to decentralization is atomization, leading eventually to a kind of barbarism.

The related problems of motivation and the free-rider remain. Preaching is unlikely to work. Attempts to create a new civic religion have usually had farcical or even sinister consequences. So where can the moral impetus for active citizenship come from? To use the haunting phrase of Robert Bellah and his collaborators, how can complex, secular, multicultural societies in the late twentieth century learn the appropriate 'habits of the heart'? Bellah's answer, addressed to his fellow countrymen, in language drawn from the American experience, is to draw on the resources of an enduring, but reinterpreted, tradition.

We will need to remember that we did not create ourselves, that we owe what we are to the communities that formed us, and to what Paul Tillich called 'the structure of grace in history' that made such communities possible . . .

Above all, we will need to remember our poverty. We have been called a people of plenty, and though our per capita GNP has been surpassed by several other nations, we are still enormously affluent. Yet the truth of our condition is our poverty. We are finally defenceless on this earth . . .

Such a vision is neither conservative nor liberal . . . It does not seek to return to the harmony of a 'traditional' society, though it is open to learning from the wisdom of such societies. It does not reject the modern criticism of all traditions, but it insists in turn on the criticism of criticism, that human life is lived in the balance between faith and doubt. Such a vision arises not only from the theories of intellectuals, but from the practices of life that Americans are already engaged in.[21]

It is hard to believe that similar 'practices of life' cannot be found elsewhere.

1991

• CHAPTER THREE •

After Socialism

I

Believers in American-style private enterprise, declared the historian, A. J. P. Taylor in November 1945, were 'a defeated party . . . which seems to have no more future than the Jacobites in England after 1688'.[1] Most of Taylor's fellow socialists shared his triumphalism, if not his delight in titillating historical analogies. In striking contrast to the mood after the First World War, virtually no one dreamed of returning to a pre-war 'normalcy': this time, memories of pre-war were of destructive abnormality. The question was how not to return; how to construct a just and productive economic order in place of the inhumane and wasteful chaos of the recent past. Coerced by the Red Army, eastern Europe was to find the answer in the command economy patented by the Soviet Union. In most of western Europe, wholly or partially left or centre-left governments – some of them with communist participation – sought it in a combination of nationalization, economic planning and improved social welfare. The swing to the right which took place as the cold war intensified in the late 1940s did not produce a significantly different answer. The governments of Adenauer, De Gasperi and Winston Churchill were not remotely socialist, but they were as comfortable with the 'second-best compromises'[2] which created the characteristic west European mix of market allocation, social welfare and state intervention as were their rivals on the left.

For non-socialists had increasingly come to share the primordial socialist assumption that the age of the individual, of the unorganized, of the classical entrepreneur and the classical free market was giving way to the age of the collective, of the bureaucratic, of the regulated and hence of an economy much closer to socialism than to capitalism as traditionally understood. Not long before, Joseph Schumpeter had famously argued that capitalism was making itself superfluous: that the giant firm was ousting the entrepreneur, the linchpin of the system, and 'expropriating' the bourgeoisie, which was losing both its income and its function. In the end, he had concluded, capitalism would give way to centralized socialism.[3] One of the pivotal assumptions underlying the ingenious defence of the British tradition of autonomous executive power which the British Tory imperialist, L. S. Amery, offered in the mid-1940s was that an increasingly collectivist age needed 'more governmental action and more definite leadership'.[4] In modern conditions, argued his younger colleague, Harold Macmillan, the invisible hand of free competition led to 'discordance, disharmony and confusion'. To remedy these, private industry had already started to plan its own activities. But piecemeal, *ad hoc* planning of this sort was not enough; it was time to supplement it with comprehensive planning on the national level.[5] Even Hayek's dithyrambic anti-collectivist *cri de coeur, The Road to Serfdom*, reads more like a lament for a dying order than a celebration of an order waiting to be born.

Plainly, the boot is now on the other foot. The collapse of the communist regimes of eastern Europe and the former Soviet Union in the late 1980s and early 1990s has destroyed the only rival to the capitalist market economy that the industrial world has ever known. Alternative models of economic organization may still exist in the minds of men and women, but it is no longer possible to point to a living alternative in the real world – or not, at any rate, in industrial societies. On a deeper level, the extraordinary series of popular upheavals that caused the communist regimes to collapse discredited the tradition of thought and action which those regimes claimed to embody. The crowds that thronged the squares of eastern Europe in the final months of 1989, like the crowd that tore down Dzherzhinsky's statue in the heart of Moscow two years later, consisted of citizens, or would-be citizens, not proletarians. They were acting in the spirit of 1776 or 1789, not of October 1917. They were protesting *against* the October Revolution, against the proletarian dictatorship, against the vanguard party, against the foundation myths of the Soviet state and all the states modelled upon it. In doing so, they called into question the fundamental postulates, not just of Stalinism – Stalinism was discredited long ago – but of Marxism-Leninism itself. For if Marxism–Leninism had been true, nothing of the sort could have happened.[6]

Of course, it does not follow that the Marxist tradition – or even the Marxist-Leninist tradition – has nothing more to say. The 'endist' notion that liberal democracy and market economics have won a final and irreversible victory over all actual or possible ideological rivals[7] should be taken with a pinch of salt. As the Counter-Reformation showed, traditions of thought and practice can sometimes reconstitute themselves after the most terrible blows. But if the Marxist or Marxist-Leninist traditions do reconstitute themselves – and, on that question, the jury will be out for some time – they are likely to take a very different form from the ones we have been used to for the last seventy years.

That is only the beginning of the story. The collapse of communism in the east has been accompanied, indeed preceded, by an extraordinary renaissance of economic liberalism in the west. In country after country, markets have been deregulated, state planning dismantled or downgraded, full-employment policies abandoned, welfare budgets reined back and nationalized industries privatized. To take only one example, in the world as a whole, state enterprises worth an estimated $185 billion were sold to the private sector in the course of the 1980s.[8] And just as conservative and Christian-Democratic parties accommodated themselves to the collectivism and *dirigisme* of the 1940s, so socialdemocratic and even communist parties have struggled, with varying degrees of success, to accommodate themselves to the reborn economic liberalism of the last twenty years.

Three examples stand out, each emblematic of a particularly striking aspect of the theme. The Italian Communist Party was once the flagship of western Eurocommunism, with an authentic national tradition to draw upon. Now it has dissolved itself, to be reborn as the Democratic Party of the Left, with a programme placing equal emphasis on the values of liberty and equality, and explicitly designed to appeal to all 'progressive' Italian traditions, democratic Catholicism and social liberalism as well as communism.[9] In the 1970s, the reborn French Socialists sloughed off the compromising centrism of the old SFIO and emerged as the 'pur et dur' champions of a total break with the existing system. Two years after Mitterrand's election as president in 1981, they abandoned the mixture of nationalization, state planning and *autogestion* on which he had campaigned. Now the centrepiece of their economic policy is the undeviating defence of the *franc fort* by means of high interest rates and budgetary rigour, supplemented by privatizations expected to yield FF10 billion, while their rhetoric focuses on that traditional standby of French Republicanism, the rights of man.[10] In the early 1980s, the British Labour Party was the most radical of the traditional, mass working-class parties of northern Europe. It fought the 1983 election on a platform of nationalization, import controls and withdrawal from the European Community. In 1992, it proposed only trivial modifications to the privatization programme carried out by the Conservatives, and campaigned on a combination of 'supply-side socialism' – market allocation, tempered by state intervention to promote national competitiveness – monetary orthodoxy and slightly redistributive tax and welfare policies.[11] The reorientation of Labour rhetoric was even more instructive than the reshaping of Labour policy. Appeals to class solidarity, and even to social equality, were conspicuous by their absence. Instead, Labour tried, somewhat implausibly, to whistle the neo-liberal tunes of choice and freedom. 'At the core of our convictions', insisted the party leader in a personal message at the beginning of its election manifesto, 'is belief in individual liberty'[12] – a proposition which would have raised eyebrows among the most embattled revisionists of thirty years before.

II

So far, so Fukuyama. Before swallowing the 'endist' thesis whole, however, it would be wise to pause and take stock. What precisely do these changes amount to, and what do they imply for the future? Do they all spring from the same causes and point unambiguously in the same direction? Whose corpse, exactly, should we hasten to bury? And are we sure that the corpse is dead?

Certain points are clear enough. It is beyond dispute that the communist regimes of eastern Europe and the former Soviet Union have collapsed. Though this is less certain, there is not much doubt that one reason for their collapse is that those who ran them were no longer inwardly convinced of their own right, or perhaps even of their own capacity, to rule: that the ideology on which their claim to power was based had degenerated into a set of ritualistic incantations, which numbed the mind without stirring the spirit or kindling the imagination; and that, because of all this, they lacked the stomach for repression as well as the humility for repentance. Another reason is that, partly as cause and partly as consequence, it was plain to all that the economic race between the Soviet-style command economy and the managed capitalist economies of the West – a race which the Soviet leadership had itself announced it was running in the late 1950s and early 1960s – had ended in a decisive victory for the West. A third is that it gradually became plain that the irrationalities and misallocations which lay behind the defeat of the Soviet system were *systemic*: that they did not spring from the personal deficiencies of particular leaders, or even from remediable corruption in high places or slack discipline in low ones, but from the inner logic of the command economy and the postulates of Marxist economics; and that it was not possible to correct them without dismantling the command economy, disrupting the nexus of vested interests which had grown up around it and repudiating the ideology which sustained it.[13] The velvet revolutions of 1989 and the failure of the attempted Soviet coup in 1991 all told the same story – elites which had lost faith in themselves; internal contradictions which could not be resolved within the terms of the system; alienated masses which regarded their rulers with outwardly compliant, but inwardly cynical, contempt.[14] In short, a classic revolutionary situation, eerily reminiscent of Trotsky's picture of the Russia of Nicholas II.[15]

It is also beyond dispute that, in western Europe no less than in the East, communism and socialism as doctrines, as well as the political parties that wear (or, in some cases, wore) communist or socialist labels, have made remarkably heavy weather of the economic, cultural and social transformation of the last fifteen or twenty years. The dissolution of the Italian Communist Party has already been mentioned. The fate of its French counterpart is equally instructive. In 1945 it won more votes than any of its rivals. Through all the ups and downs of the Fourth Republic, and the first decade of the Fifth, it remained the dominant working-class party, with a significantly larger popular vote than the socialists. Then, in a series of manoeuvres as audacious as they were guileful, Mitterrand allied the much weaker socialists to it, proceeded to overtake it and finally smothered it. Now it is weaker than it has been since the 1920s. But the virtual disappearance of western European communism as a serious political force has brought scant benefits to social democrats or socialists. Of the major, class-based social-democratic parties of northern Europe, the British Labour Party has been out of power since 1979, and the German Social Democrats since 1982. The Swedish Social Democrats have fared better – having lost power for the first time for forty years in 1976, they returned to it six years later – but in the last Swedish general election, their share of the vote was lower than for more than sixty years. For much of the 1980s, it looked as if the traditionally much weaker, but for that very reason less hide-bound, socialist parties of southern Europe might adapt to the social changes of the period more successfully than their slower-moving, less ideologically agile, social-democratic sisters around the North Sea.[16] With the Italian Socialists mired in scandal, and the French Socialists crushingly defeated in the 1993 parliamentary elections, the contrast between the adaptable south and the sclerotic north no longer seems so telling.

More striking than any of this is the absence of a distinctively socialist or social-democratic project. For the best part of a century, the socialist vision of a world remade haunted the imaginations of the idealistic and the dispossessed. It inspired passionate loyalties, mobilized extraordinary energies and survived innumerable be-trayals and disappointments. As recently as fifteen years ago, it still flickered through the common programme of the French Left and the Alternative Strategy of the British Bennites. Revisionist social democracy, of the sort the German SPD embraced at Bad Godesberg in 1959 and the British Labour Party half-embraced under Hugh Gaitskell and Harold Wilson, did not look forward to a world remade, but it offered a different kind of inspiration: a slow, stubborn, inch-by-inch struggle to remedy tangible injustices, which would gradually make the existing world a better place. Both, moreover, could and did inspire collective projects, alter-native paradigms of thought and action, combining analysis of the present with hope for the future and enabling potential con-stituencies to see themselves and their destinies in new ways.

The SPD's *Modell Deutschland* was such a project. At least in intention, so was the Swedish Meidener Plan. However banal it may seem in retrospect, so too was Harold Wilson's 1964 vision of a growth-promoting, welfare-enhancing economic plan, under-pinned by a marriage between socialism and science.[17] But all these projects presupposed a community of interest, or at least of aspiration, extending right across a homogeneous and solidaristic working class, and a state able to deliver the required combination of policies within its own frontiers. The technological and economic changes which have transformed the occupational structures of all advanced societies in the last twenty years have destroyed the first of these preconditions, while the remorseless growth of international economic interdependence has destroyed the second. The socialism and social democracy of the post-war period cannot encompass these transformations; for the time being, at any rate, their adherents are intellectually becalmed, unable to make sense of a world which has suddenly become alien, and still less able to devise plausible projects for changing it. In a sombre conclusion to a comparative study of the 'crisis' of European social democracy, Fritz Scharpf warned recently,

> The vision is bleak. Unlike the situation in the first three postwar decades, there is now no economically plausible Keynesian strategy that would permit the full realization of social democratic goals within a national context without violating the functional imperatives of the capitalist economy. Full employment, rising real wages, larger welfare transfers, and more and better public services can no longer all be had simultaneously ...
>
> But that need not be the end of social democratic strategies. On the contrary: when not all goals can be realized at the same time, the ability to set strategic priorities increases in importance ... [T]he attempt to pursue all goals at once will not lead to 'system-transforming' reforms or to the realization of other postulates of an anticapitalist rhetoric, but to a war of all against all within the Left. The most likely outcome in that case would be a deepening division between the majority of relatively privileged jobholders in the private and public sectors and a growing minority of persons in long-term unemployment, early retirement, or occasional employment, and of young people who never gain access to regular employment at all ...
>
> This, I believe, is the crucial question for the political future of social democracy. If Social Democrats are unwilling to face it, they will cease to shape the future, leaving the field to the Social Darwinism of the market liberals and conservatives.[18]

The warning is as pertinent today as it was when it was written.

III

Yet there are ironies in all this, which triumphant conservatives and liberals are unwilling to confront. The renaissance of economic liberalism in the West coincided with the collapse of the command economy in the east, but it came too late to cause it. The extraordinary growth of living standards and productive power which forced the command economy onto the defensive began long after the capitalism of the nineteenth-century fathers of free-market economics left the stage, and well before the capitalism of today's New Right made its entrance. The credit for it belongs to the reformed, regulated, corporatist or quasi-corporatist, Middle Way capitalism to which Schumpeter and Harold Macmillan had both looked forward before and during the Second World War, and which then emerged, piecemeal, from the improvisations of post-war reconstruction. Like many false prophecies, A. J. P. Taylor's 1945 prediction that belief in private enterprise was about to go the way of Jacobitism was based on the common human assumption that the future would resemble the past. Before the war, belief in private enterprise had been waning. It had waned because – except in Roosevelt's United States – the reformed capitalism of the post-war period had not yet appeared on the scene; and because unreformed capitalism was in manifest and chaotic disarray. It was the capitalism of the long post-war boom, the capitalism of *Mittbestimmung* and the *Commissariat Général du Plan*, the capitalism of the paid holidays, the tight labour markets and the rising welfare expenditures, that won the race with the regimes of eastern Europe, not the capitalism of the Great Depression. If the contest had been between Herbert Hoover and the command economy, the command economy might have won.

In short, capitalism triumphed because – by the criteria which its apologists shared with its opponents for most of its history – it was no longer capitalist. The reasons why it ceased being so are manifold. The symbiosis between public power and private ownership which used to be called the mixed economy, and which it is now fashionable to call the social-market economy, has a varied ancestry. The interests of big business, the teachings of the Church, the imperatives of national survival in a cut-throat world economy and the aspirations of the professional salariat, private and public, all helped to bring it into being.[19] But it is doubtful if these would have done the trick if two other factors had been absent from the equation. One was the moral and political challenge of socialism-as-doctrine: the fact that there was, in existence, a living tradition whose bearers possessed both a moral yardstick against which unreformed capitalism could be measured and found wanting, and a social vision behind which its victims could be mobilized. The other was the insistent, half-loaf pressure of social-democracy-as-practice: the fact that broadly social-democratic labour movements had the strength, discipline and political creativity to help negotiate the second-best compromises which made reformed capitalism possible. In a wry apologia for the socialist tradition, Leszek Kolakowski pointed out some time ago, 'Even if it is true that we cannot ever abolish human misery, it may at the same time be true that the world would be even worse than it is if there were no people who thought it could be better.'[20] Capitalism became better partly because socialists campaigned to replace it, and partly because social democrats could bargain on approximately equal terms with its defenders.

IV

Now that the challengers are disarmed and the bargainers in disarray, what will happen to the challenged? The endist answer is that nothing much will happen. Victorious capitalism will march ever onwards, its progress disturbed only by occasional petty disputes over the details of the route. It would be unwise to take that for granted. Unreformed capitalism was not much good at marching. Reformed, welfare capitalism is a gift of history, as fragile as it is precious. No iron law decreed its birth or its survival. It emerged, by serendipity, from the compromises and contingencies of war and post-war reconstruction. It has been sustained by a subtle moral and political balance, in which the criticisms of socialists and the demands of social democrats were crucial ingredients. As these pressures have lost force, the balance has become unstable. There are at least two reasons for fearing that, if present trends continue, it may topple over, dragging reformed capitalism with it.

The first is Michael Walzer's.

> One can conceive the market as a sphere without boundaries, an unzoned city – for money is insidious, and market relations are expansive. A radically laissez-faire economy would be like a totalitarian state, invading every other sphere, dominating every other distributive process. It would transform every social good into a commodity. This is market imperialism.[21]

Fear of 'market imperialism' – of unreformed capitalism's relentless pressure to commodify all social goods – has, of course, been central to socialism since the beginning. State imperialism, the classical socialist cure applied in eastern Europe, turned out to be worse than the disease. But, in a remarkable display of social creativity and political skill, western Europe found a way to check the imperialism of the market without surrendering to that of the state. The unzoned city of the market place was zoned after all; money, Walzer's 'universal pander',[22] was denied entry to social spheres where non-market principles of distribution were thought more appropriate; at the same time, market principles were allowed free rein in other spheres. That was the real meaning of the second-best compromises of the post-war years. But the boundaries between market and non-market zones were drawn where the pressures of market imperialism met countervailing pressures; and the real meaning of today's rebirth of economic liberalism is that these countervailing pressures are ceasing to operate. The predictable result is that the universal pander has been set free: that a whole range of social goods which were laboriously de-commodified a generation ago are now being re-commodified.

That is only the beginning of the story. Walzer's fear of market imperialism derives from his pluralist and egalitarian values, and these are not universally shared. But his insight has a broader application. The technological and economic transformations which have made it impossible to practise Keynesianism in one country have not invalidated Keynes's central message – that, in a world of uncertainty and insecurity, in which money is a store of value as well as a medium of exchange, savers do not necessarily invest; and that, in an unregulated market economy, in which uncertainty and insecurity are endemic, there is therefore an inherent propensity for supply and demand to balance at less than full employment. Now, as much as in the inter-war years, uncertainty, insecurity and fear of the future erode the confidence of consumers and investors, with the results that Keynes and his contemporaries knew all too well. But uncertainty and insecurity are the hallmarks of unregulated capitalism. By the same token, they are also the hallmarks of Walzer's market imperialism. The classical free market works through sticks as well as carrots; and insecurity is the biggest stick. It is no accident that the central objective of renascent economic liberalism is to dismantle the post-war nexus of social welfare, Keynesian employment policy and corporatist or quasi-corporatist bargaining, which took the edge off the insecurities of the past. On economic-liberal assumptions, these insecurities were functional: without them, the market would not work properly. For economic liberals, only Hirschman's Exit and the threat of Exit keep producers on their toes;[23] and they do so only because, and to the extent that, they are feared. The Keynesian-corporatist welfare state of the post-war period calmed producer fear. Market imperialism is busy reawakening it. The trouble, of course, is that in doing so it is re-creating the Keynesian paradox of unsatisfied wants in the midst of unutilized resources.

The moral is plain. The capitalist free market is a marvellous servant, but a disastrous master. In one of the greatest achievements of the second half of the twentieth century, a few favoured societies learned to convert it from master to servant. The danger now is that a smug and vainglorious capitalism will not remember the lesson.

V

Before consigning socialism to the tender mercies of the historians of political thought, it would therefore be as well to re-examine it. Granted that it can no longer generate persuasive answers, can it still ask worthwhile questions? Granted, above all, that capitalism is now in the ascendant, is there anything in socialism's legacy to help us to secure the achievements of the post-war period and save the victor from itself?

The first thing to notice is that it is a more complicated creature than the endist hypothesis allows. Socialism had at least five dimensions. It was, in the first place, an ethic. It was a difficult ethic to put into words, and socialists disagreed among themselves about how best to do so. Central to almost all their gropings, however, were words like 'co-operation', 'commonwealth' and 'fellowship'. Classical socialism was not primarily about equality, as the Gaitskellite revisionists imagined in the 1950s. As Brian Barry has argued, it is possible for liberals and anarchists to be egalitarians, while the distinctive socialist belief that the distribution of rewards should be socially determined leaves open what the distribution ought to be.[24] Still less was socialism about liberty, as Roy Hattersley and Bryan Gould have insisted more recently.[25] The term in the revolutionary triad that mattered most to socialists, the term that encapsulated the essence of the socialist ideal, was fraternity. That was what William Morris meant when he said that fellowship was heaven and the lack of fellowship, hell.[26] It also lay behind Marx's gnomic (and inegalitarian) prophecy in the *Critique of the Gotha Programme* that, in the higher phase of communism, society would 'inscribe on its banners: From each according to his abilities, to each according to his needs!'[27] In non-sexist language, we might call it 'community'.

Secondly, socialism was an economic theory. Here too there were disputes, sometimes violent, within the socialist camp. Now that the fires have burned low, however, we can see that the differences were much less significant than the similarities. Socialists of all kinds, Fabians as well as Marxists, gradualists as well as revolutionaries, took it for granted that social ownership would be more efficient than private, and a planned economy than the free market. The mighty productive powers of modern industry were held back by the chaos of private competition. Robert Blatchford's famous contrast between the efficient rationality of the state-owned post office and the wasteful irrationality of the competing private milkmen, unnecessarily duplicating their efforts with two or three carts to a street, was paradigmatic.[28] But in the socially owned economy of the future, in which production would be for use, not profit, and the blind fumblings of the capitalist entrepreneur would be replaced by conscious social direction, the contradiction between productive potential and the capitalist mode of production would no longer exist. The result would be a promethean upsurge of wealth creation – Engels's 'unbroken, constantly accelerated development of the productive forces'[29] – freeing mankind at last from the tyranny of want.

Not only was socialism an economic theory, it was also a science of society. Like their liberal adversaries, socialists were children of the Enlightenment and suffused with its imperious rationalism. Society, they assumed, followed a determinate path towards a knowable goal. That goal was socialism. It was coming, not only or even mainly because it was right, but because it was inevitable. Socialism thus had two faces. Socialists were, of course, committed partisans, embattled advocates of human emancipation. But, in their own eyes at least, they were also dispassionate inquirers, teasing out the laws of social development as chemists and biologists teased out the laws of nature. So, for Engels, Marx was at one moment a second Lavoisier; at another, more famously, a second Darwin.[30] And so Sidney Webb saw nothing improper in founding the London School of Economics with the proceeds of a legacy intended to finance socialist propaganda: the facts were socialist, and dispassionate study of the facts would automatically

promote socialism.[31] These two faces reinforced each other. Socialists claimed a special moral authority by virtue of their special
mastery of social dynamics. Of course, they did not all picture
these dynamics in the same way. Marxist historical materialism
and Fabian gradualism sprang from different philosophical roots,
and pointed to different practical conclusions. As on economics,
however, these differences seem less significant in retrospect than
the similarities. Webb was as confident as Marx that he had
charted the course society was destined to follow and that his
prescriptions for the future were uniquely compelling because he
had done so; once in power, Fabians were as apt as Marxists to
treat society as a set of building blocks, to be rearranged in
accordance with a scientific grand design. And although socialists
like Rosa Luxemburg or even Keir Hardie put their faith in the
spontaneous anger of the masses rather than in the laws of history,
they were in a minority – icons rather than exemplars.

Fourthly, socialism was the vehicle of a social interest – the
instrument, inspiration and mentor of the labour movement. To be
sure, the relationship between vehicle and passenger was often
ambivalent and always problematic. Socialist doctrine, again
whether revolutionary or gradualist, allotted a unique, redemptive
role to the proletariat. Unfortunately, real, live proletarians did not
all want to be redeemers. They cheered the vision of a new society
on high days and holidays, but on weekdays their aims were more
prosaic – better wages, better conditions, a better future for their
children. And so the literature of socialism is full of complaints
about the narrow horizons, limited ambitions, short-sighted materialism and dull-headed stodginess of the working class, ranging
in severity from Ernest Bevin's complaints about 'the inferiority
complex amongst our people'[32] to Lenin's contempt for trade
unionism as the 'ideological enslavement of the workers by the
bourgeoisie'.[33] By the same token, the history of organized labour
is full of tensions between the practical needs of working men and
women and the pure flame of the socialist ideal.[34]

Yet it would be wrong to exaggerate these tensions. In spite of
them, millions of working people came to view themselves and
their destiny through the prism of socialist theory. For, in varying
degrees, socialism shaped the political and economic culture of the
working class in almost all industrial countries outside North
America. It threw a glow of principle over the everyday struggles
of the factory floor, and gave dignity and meaning to lives which
market economics treated as commodities. It was a school for

citizenship, a source of self-respect, a stimulus for self-discipline and personal growth: the Hardies and Bebels, Bevins and Neumanns who found, through socialism, a vocation for leadership had humbler equivalents in every working-class community. By a strange irony, the moral legacy of these achievements still helps to underpin the co-operative understandings on which reformed capitalism depends – not the least of the reasons why the Scandinavian and central European economies, where the working-class movement was most influenced by socialist teaching, have been the most successful in the Atlantic world.[35]

Finally, socialism was a secular religion. It had a heaven and a hell; saints and sinners; martyrs and persecutors; heretics and heresy-hunters; saved and damned; clergy and laity. Its language and iconography were particularly revealing. Socialists had 'faith'; they were engaged on a 'crusade'; their projects were 'New Jerusalems'; they marched to the 'Promised Land' across 'deserts' of tribulation; their leaders were 'prophets';[36] their songs were 'hymns'; their funeral processions were ceremonies of collective dedication.[37] Above all, they had an eschatology – a science of last things. One day, the expropriators would be expropriated, the humble would be exalted and a new society, free of exploitation and injustice, would arise from the ruins of the old. No one knew when that day would come, but there was no doubt that it was coming. By the same token, the details of the new society were a little vague: like Christians, socialists were better at anathematizing vice than at describing virtue. But its vagueness was an asset. It shimmered in the distance, all the more glorious because no one knew what it would be like. And, as with Christianity, the force of that vision justified the most appalling crimes, as well as calling forth the most astounding displays of heroism and self-sacrifice.

VI

Now it is all – or nearly all – over. No one, not even the Chinese, still accepts the economic theory of socialism. A promethean upsurge of wealth creation has indeed taken place, but in the mixed or social-market economies of central Europe and the Pacific Rim. The ancient socialist assumption that public ownership and production for use were bound to be more efficient than private ownership and production for profit has turned out to be the reverse of the truth. The wave of privatizations which has swept across the globe in the last ten years has not been driven wholly, or even mainly, by ideology. At least as important has been the discovery by governments of all colours that publicly owned industries are extraordinarily difficult to discipline, to motivate and to manage; that the state can be as myopic and greedy as any private shareholder; that, in any case, it lacks the knowledge and capacity to control the undertakings it owns; and that efficiency can best be promoted by devolving responsibility to private owners, while retaining regulatory powers to ensure strategic oversight.[38] To be sure, the doctrinaire apologists for the free market are as mistaken as the doctrinaire socialists whom they mimic unintentionally. The economies which have succeeded most spectacularly have been those fostered by developmental states, where public power, acting in concert with private interest, has induced market forces to flow in the desired direction.[39] But the developmental state is as remote from the socialist state as from the Nightwatchman State of classical economics. Its purpose is to constrain the market and to allocate the costs and benefits of economic change in such a way as to enhance the capacity of a capitalist national economy to compete with other capitalist national economies, not to supersede market forces or to socialize the means of production.

The social science of socialism has fared no better. Imperious Enlightenment rationalism and scientific social engineering are now discredited, on the left even more than on the right. We have learned that the social sciences are quite different in character and logical status from the natural sciences; that contingency and unpredictability are fundamental to social life; that the social sciences therefore cannot generate falsifiable laws with strong predictive power; that, as Alasdair MacIntyre puts it, their generalizations have the same logical status as 'the proverbs of folk societies, the generalizations of jurists, the maxims of Machiavelli';[40] and that the socialist theoreticians who thought they could uncover the dynamics of social progress were searching for fools' gold. We have also learned – perhaps even more disturbingly – that the search for this particular fools' gold was dangerous as well as pointless; that the steps from believing that it is possible to predict the future to believing that it is possible to shape it, and from believing that it is possible to shape it to believing that those with the appropriate knowledge have the right to shape it and to force their shape on others, are terrifyingly short. The first lesson implies that civil society cannot be remade to fit a grand design – not just because it is apt to resist, but because the very notion of a grand design is an absurdity. The second implies that it is wrong to try.

To the extent that socialism is still the vehicle of the working class, that is now a handicap rather than an asset. The classical working class, the proletariat which Marx described and helped to form, has almost disappeared. Some of it – in most developed societies, the majority – has been absorbed, for all practical purposes, into a vast, almost boundaryless, middle class. The rest – the unskilled, the handicapped, the victims of racial prejudice – have become an underclass, effectively excluded from full citizenship. However, this underclass has little in common with the disciplined class warriors who were supposed to carry the future in their knapsacks. If anything, it is more reminiscent of the *lumpenproletariat* which the early socialists saw as recruiting material for militarists and strike breakers.

Partly because of all this, the secular religion seems to be losing its power as well. Vestiges of the old language and iconography remain, of course; but the emotional resonance is draining out of them. The agile, and until recently successful, socialist politicians of southern Europe – the Mitterrands, the Craxis, the Papandreous – have had about the same relationship with the socialism of the pioneers as Renaissance popes with the Christianity of the apostles. The heavier-footed, slower-moving social-democratic parties of the north still try to represent the victims of economic change, but they long ago ceased to promise salvation to the elect or damnation to the unregenerate. They stand for reform, progress, amelioration, not for transformation. In the east, meanwhile, the very words 'socialism' and 'social democracy' have been discredited by their association with the old regimes.

Yet in this catalogue of decay, one item is conspicuous by its absence. Nothing has happened to invalidate the socialist ethic. The values of community and fellowship speak as loudly (or, of course, as faintly) to the late twentieth century as to earlier periods. Indeed, in some respects they are more pertinent, if not necessarily more resonant, than they used to be. For with the ethic went an insight – the insight that all societies, even capitalist ones, depend on ties of mutual obligation; and that such ties are public goods, which have to be provided to everyone if they are to be provided to anyone, and which the competitive free market therefore cannot supply, although it may conceivably destroy them. Different socialists expressed that insight in different ways, but almost all of them believed that a society based on the acquisitive individualism of the market place would be a contradiction in terms and feared that, if acquisitive individualism had free rein, if all social relationships were mediated through the cash nexus, the ties of mutual trust which hold society together would snap. A hundred years ago, when the socialist critique of capitalism first developed political momentum, that danger was remote. Marx, Morris, even the young Tawney lived in societies saturated with the communal ethic of the pre-industrial past, and shot through with institutions that embodied it. Churches, universities, municipalities, crafts, professions, armies all, in different ways and to differing degrees, expressed a collective morality of some kind. Indeed, the capitalist free market drew on the moral legacy of earlier centuries, even while depleting it. Now the danger has come close. The old communalism is fading, and no one has yet found a new communalism to replace it.

Perhaps the central question for our time is whether insight and ethic can be brought together in a new project with some purchase on social reality. The only honest answer is that there is, as yet, no way of telling. The obstacles are formidable – the transformation of the world market which has made it impossible to practise even Keynesianism, let alone socialism or social democracy, in one country; the changing patterns of production and employment which are eroding the old solidarities of class and occupation; the simultaneous globalization and fragmentation of culture and identity which make it increasingly difficult to speak resonantly of public, as opposed to private, interests. It is possible to detect the germs of a possible new paradigm – the communitarian critique of liberalism which has become a major theme of moral and political thought; the feminist critique of traditional conceptions of politics and the public sphere; the green emphasis on sustainability and stewardship; the growing realization that human capital and economic co-operation hold the key to high-quality production – but no one has yet succeeded in putting them together into a persuasive whole.

That said, it is hard to believe that Hirschman's cycle of 'involvement', from the private to the public sphere and back again,[41] has, for some mysterious reason, come to a halt at the end of the twentieth century. To be sure, it is equally hard to guess what form a new era of public involvement would take. Outwardly, at least, it is unlikely to bear much resemblance to the socialism or even to the social democracy discussed in this chapter.

Yet some of the pioneers would have been prepared for that. It was, after all, William Morris who dreamed of 'How men fight and lose the battle, and the thing they fought for comes about in spite of their defeat, and when it comes turns out not to be what they meant, and other men have to fight for what they meant under another name.'[42]

1993

CHAPTER FOUR

Liberalism's Revenge? Resolving the Progressive Dilemma

I

Among them are those who see, and cannot help seeing, many sides of a case, as well as those who perceive that a humane cause promoted by means that are too ruthless is in danger of turning into its opposite, liberty into oppression in the name of liberty, equality into a new, self-perpetuating oligarchy to defend equality, justice into crushing of all forms of nonconformity, love of men into hatred of those who oppose brutal means of achieving it. The middle ground is a notoriously exposed, dangerous and ungrateful position. The complex position of those who, in the thick of the fight, wish to continue to speak to both sides is often interpreted as softness, trimming, opportunism, cowardice . . .

. . . The ambivalence of such moderates . . . stems, in part, from the historic position of nineteenth-century liberals for whom the enemy had hitherto always been on the right – monarchists, clericals, aristocratic supporters of political or economic oligarchies, men whose rule promoted, or was indifferent to, poverty, ignorance, injustice and the exploitation and degradation of men. The natural inclination of liberals has been, and still is, towards the left, the party of generosity and humanity, towards anything that destroys barriers between men. Even after the inevitable split they tend to be deeply reluctant to believe that there can be real enemies on the left. (Isaiah Berlin on the dilemmas faced by liberals confronting a challenge from the extreme left)[1]

The dilemmas of the middle ground are part of the stuff of politics. They were peculiarly harsh and painful for the nineteenth-century Russian liberals of Turgenev's generation – torn between their loathing of Tsarist oppression and their fear that the hard young radicals on their left would trample on the essentials of a

liberal culture – whose agonies of conscience Isaiah Berlin anatomized in the passage from which my quotation comes. Nothing in
the recent experience of mainland Britain approaches those agonies in scale or intensity. (Recent Irish experience is a different
matter.) Yet even in Britain, the middle ground has often been a
stressful place. For most of the twentieth century, British liberals
have faced a dilemma, milder than, but reminiscent of, the
dilemma faced by their nineteenth-century Russian counterparts.
They too have had to decide whether to throw in their lot with a
harder, more impatient, culturally and emotionally threatening
movement on their left. They too have hesitated – torn between
their sympathy for the underdog and their fear that the underdog's
new champions might endanger the values that liberals have
cherished most. Their hesitations hold the key to a long saga of
division within, and consequent failure on the part of, the entire
British left. In doing so, they also provide a thought-provoking
perspective from which to approach the question that forms the
central theme of this chapter: the question of whether that saga is
now coming to an end.

The twentieth-century British version of the recurrent dilemma
of the middle ground – the 'progressive dilemma' of my title[2] –
first became acute during the political upheavals that accompanied
and followed the First World War. By the early 1920s it was clear
that the rising Labour Party might replace the Liberals as the main
anti-Conservative party in the state. By the end of the decade it
was clear that it had done so. Liberals – both with a big and a small
'l' – were confronted with a choice not unlike the choice faced by
Turgenev and his contemporaries sixty years before. If they stood
aloof from Labour they might lose all hope of influencing events;
they might even help to keep the Conservatives in power. Yet if
they joined it they would have to surrender their values, in a
profound sense their very identities, to a Labourism that seemed to
them narrow and illiberal. Some joined; some stood aloof. And,
because not all joined, Labour failed to construct a new, Labour-
centred version of the Liberal-centred social and ideological
coalition which had dominated British politics for the best part of
a decade before the First World War. This was not the only cause of
the seventy-year-long period of Conservative predominance that
began in the early 1920s, but there can be no doubt that it was an
important cause.

That is a narrowly British perspective. A wider perspective also
deserves attention. In most of continental Europe liberals faced

essentially the same dilemma, often in a much harsher form, and responded in essentially the same way, often with much more destructive consequences. Of the major western countries, only the United States breaks the pattern. The Roosevelt coalition that dominated American politics from the 1930s to the 1960s was, in essence, a transatlantic version of the coalition that kept the Liberals in office before 1914, and that fell apart during and after the First World War. But the much-discussed resilience of American liberalism did not last for ever. The Roosevelt coalition eventually unravelled. One of the reasons why it did so is that American liberals, in their turn, found themselves facing a challenge from contemptuous radicals on their left, to which they responded with an agonized ambivalence that might have come from the pages of Turgenev or a debate at a Liberal Summer School. The British story examined here is, in short, part of a much wider story, and if we are to find our way through the confusions and ambiguities of the former, the latter must be kept firmly in mind.

II

The dilemma facing twentieth-century British liberals, uncertain of their attitude to a strong but alien Labour Party on their left, has had three dimensions. The first and most obvious has been ideological. To be sure, the immediate programmes of the Labour and Liberal parties have often coincided. Sometimes the Liberal programme has been more radical than Labour's. That was conspicuously true in 1929, when Lloyd George campaigned on a proto-Keynesian platform of loan-financed public works, and it can at least be argued that it was equally true in 1997. In government, moreover, Labour's economic and social policies have carried a strong liberal imprint. As Alec Cairncross has shown, the 1945 government soon abandoned its 'nebulous, but exalted' yearnings for a socially controlled economy, in which resources would be allocated through administrative processes rather than by the price mechanism, and settled for a mixture of Keynesian economic management and a Beveridgean welfare state.[3] The Wilson governments of the 1960s tried, not very successfully, to couple macro-economic Keynesian management with a form of micro-economic indicative planning designed to raise the level of investment and speed up the rate of growth. A commitment to planning, however defined, was part of the Labour tradition, of course. But the Wilson government's planning experiment is best seen as the logical continuation of the experiment launched by the Macmillan government a few years before, and it would be as plausible to trace its descent from the famous Liberal Yellow Book of 1927 as from any Labour source.

Yet ideology is not a matter of election platforms and government policies alone. As Michael Freeden argues, ideologies are 'thought practices', compounds of 'genuinely conscious beliefs, of unconscious assumptions and of dissimulatively rhetorical statements'.[4] They are encoded in and transmitted by ritual and myth; they shape perceptions and influence behaviour, not only or even mainly on the level of the head, but also on the level of the heart. On that second level – the level on which the party has recognized itself and defined its vocation – Labour has differed radically from its Liberal *frère semblable*. In however confused and fluctuating a fashion, it has been a socialist party, one of the family of parties that trace their ancestry back to the Second International. More significantly in some ways, it has also been a proletarianist party. Whatever might be true of individual members, the party as such has never accepted the Marxist doctrine of the class war; even a class analysis of politics has been alien to the Fabian and, in some respects, to the ILP strands in the party's tradition. But, for all that, the old Clause Four of the party constitution, indeed the party's very name, have both implied a primordial, inescapable conflict of interest between workers and owners, and a special vocation for the former.

All this has been profoundly problematic for liberals, again with a small as well as with a big 'l'. The logic of the 'New' or social liberalism which has suffused the assumptions of most big-'L' Liberals for most of this century, and which has given the modern Liberal Party its justification and rationale, points in a quite different direction. The New Liberals of the turn of the century sought to reconcile capital and labour, to moralize market relations, to achieve a just distribution of resources within a capitalist framework. Their project was based on the premise that this attempt was feasible as well as right; that capitalism was sufficiently flexible and productive for it to be reformed in such a way. In spite of their frequent programmatic propinquity, the early socialists and the New Liberals were therefore divided by a chasm of understanding and assumption. If socialism was right, New

Liberalism was wrong; if New Liberalism was right, socialism was unnecessary.

This dimension of the progressive dilemma was particularly acute for big-'L' Liberals who had belonged to the New Liberal camp before the First World War, and who then had to decide what to do when the Liberal Party ceased to be a plausible contender for power in the 1920s. But it continued to haunt their intellectual descendants in the 1930s and after the Second World War. The Attlee government was, from one perspective, the lineal descendant of the Asquith government. But that was not how the members of the government saw themselves or their achievement. In their own eyes they were socialists. The fact that they had not created a socialist commonwealth merely proved that the path to socialism was long and arduous. They had at least laid the foundations for one. There was nothing in this to allay liberal hesitations or to resolve the dilemma they faced. In the mid-1950s, it is true, Anthony Crosland's *The Future of Socialism* proposed a resolution. In effect (though, of course, without acknowledgement) socialism was redefined to mean updated Hobhousian New Liberalism. By the same token, however, Hugh Gaitskell's failure to rewrite Clause Four in a Croslandian spirit gave the dilemma a new twist. It showed that, although the Labour Party contained distinguished radical intellectuals in its ranks, one of whom was its leader, it was not prepared explicitly to jettison its socialist and proletarianist ideology when they urged it to do so. Had Gaitskell won, it is hard to believe that the Liberal revival that began under Jo Grimond would have taken place; his defeat reinforced liberal suspicions of the Labour Party and gave liberals of all stripes a new reason for standing aloof from it.

The second dimension of the dilemma is less obvious, but in some ways even more important. It has had to do with political organization and the parliamentary process. Notoriously, the late nineteenth and early twentieth centuries saw two profound changes in the structure of political life: the coming of a mass electorate and the emergence of the disciplined mass party, seeking total control of the machinery of the state as a means towards hegemony over civil society. These were, of course, symbiotically connected: the mass party was there to organize the mass electorate. Both antedated the rise of the Labour Party (though not of the German SPD). Indeed, the Liberal Party had acquired some of the characteristics of a mass party long before the Labour Representation Committee was thought of. But liberal assumptions and mass politics were uneasy bedfellows. For nineteenth-century liberals, a free market in ideas was as important as a free market in commodities: if competition among ideas were free, the best ones would prevail. From that premise sprang John Stuart Mill's vision of representative government as a kind of discovery process, through which 'not only the general opinion of the nation, but that of every section of it, and as far as possible of every eminent individual whom it contains, can produce itself in full light and challenge discussion'.[5] Parliament, in this vision, was quintessentially a forum for free debate, while the point of parliamentary debate was not only to state opinions, but to change them. And if opinions were to be changed, the Member of Parliament had to be an unfettered representative, making up his mind on the merits of the case after testing his own opinions against those of his peers, not a mandated delegate.

As times changed, and the conditions of parliamentary life were transformed, big-L' Liberals had to water down the pure milk of the Millian vision. But the values it implied retained a hold even on big-'L' Liberals, and remained central to the small-'l' liberal view of how politics should be conducted. It is, of course, incompatible with the mass-party model, according to which the primary task of the Member of Parliament is to carry into law a programme decided upon by a disciplined party and approved by a mass electorate. It is not an accident that, despite the pressures on it to conform to that model, the Liberal Party never managed to do so. But Labour was, almost by definition, a hegemony-seeking mass party: indeed, it was a quintessential mass party long before it even dreamed of hegemony. It came into being to define, mobilize and prosecute the Labour interest. Later, it acquired the grander purpose of social transformation. It did not need hegemony for the first, but it did for the second, and it needed discipline for both.

Above all, it needed a conception of representative government utterly at odds with Mill's. It saw itself as a kind of battering ram, with which working people would break into the citadels of power. It also saw itself as the property of its members, rather than of a parliamentary elite. In theory, at least, its policy was decided outside Parliament, by its own 'parliament', the annual conference. In practice, of course, it did not follow the mass-party model as consistently as this vision suggested. To prosper in the Westminster village, Labour MPs had to adopt the mores of the existing villagers, and even in the twentieth century those mores have been in tension with the presuppositions of the mass-party model. But for all that, Labour's conventions and understandings were profoundly un- or even illiberal. It did not believe in a free market in ideas. It believed in duopoly – socialist transformation against the status quo; workers by hand and brain against capital. For it, Parliament was less a forum than a factory, where legislative workers transformed programmatic commitments into laws. In such a setting, there could be no place for Millian representatives, testing their opinions against the opinions of their colleagues in untrammelled debate, and changing their minds when they had been persuaded to do so. And for liberals – including the many instinctive liberals who joined the Labour Party and, in some cases, became Labour Members of Parliament – the Labour conception of the role of Parliament and the nature of the political party was oppressive and even demeaning.

That leads on to the third and most elusive dimension – the existential dimension of culture and self-identity. Labour's culture has been solidaristic, collectivist, group-centred. Its values have been those of the (male) working class, hammered out in and necessitated by a long struggle for dignity, sometimes for survival, in the harsh conditions of early industrialism. Loyalty to majority decisions has been its paradigmatic virtue; disloyalty, its most heinous crime. These values have, of course, been functional for an organized, hegemony-seeking mass party. Ironically, their existential consequences have had much in common with those of the 'regimental', hierarchical values of the Conservative Party, even though they have sprung from an utterly different moral and cultural source. They have also had great emotional and moral resonance: they are the sediment of a long, proud history, the expression of a tough, resilient tradition of collective endurance and shared sacrifice. As such, they have been an important source of political strength. The hold of the Labour tradition on the party's core constituency helps to explain its rapid growth after the First World War, its recovery from the catastrophe of 1931 and the ease with which it saw off the SDP–Liberal Alliance in the 1980s.

Unfortunately, these values have also been a source of weakness. They, more than anything else, account for Labour's uneasy relationship with the liberal-minded radical intelligentsia, on which it has always depended for ideas. To good Labour men and women, the radical intelligentsia has often seemed finicky, unreliable, even frivolous; for their part, radical intellectuals have chafed at the constraints imposed by the Labour ethos of loyalty and solidarity, and found the disciplines of party life intolerable and stifling. For liberal-minded people outside as well as inside the party, the bouts of heresy-hunting and accusations of disloyalty which have punctuated its history since its earliest days – the dark side of its collectivist culture – have been one of its ugliest features. As such, they have been a potent cause of its persistent failure to cross the social and cultural boundary between its core constituency and potential supporters beyond it.

III

At this point in the argument, re-enter the question with which I began. Is this saga of division and failure coming to an end? Has the progressive dilemma been resolved – or is it, at any rate, on the point of resolution?

On the level of electoral politics, there is a strong case for saying 'yes'. The 'Blair project' in the United Kingdom is particularly instructive. In the 1987 general election – only ten years ago, be it remembered – the SDP–Liberal Alliance polled a respectable 23 per cent, only 2.9 per cent down on its 1983 figure and the second-best centre-party achievement since 1929. Though Neil Kinnock had begun the long march from Old to New Labour, he had travelled only a tiny distance. The neo-socialist baggage of the early 1980s had been jettisoned, but Labour was still, in all essentials, the familiar old party it had always been. As a result, it was still confined to its familiar old fortresses. In the 1987 election, its share of the vote was only 31 per cent – its worst performance, apart from 1983, since 1931. The obvious question for the centre-left was how to construct an electoral coalition capable of stemming an apparently unstoppable Conservative tide. The obvious answer was that Labour and the Alliance should make common cause, presumably on the basis of a new political agenda, combining elements from both Labour and Liberal traditions.

Alas for obvious answers. The long-awaited realignment of centre-left politics has taken place, but without a party realignment. Blair's great achievement has been to reposition the Labour Party, while remaining within the two-party 'mould' that the SDP once hoped to break. Instead of making common cause with the Liberal Democrats, Labour has taken over the ideological territory once occupied by the SDP–Liberal Alliance. Indeed, in an electoral equivalent of Guderian's *Blitzkrieg*, it has swept through that territory into territory once occupied by moderate Conservatives. As a result, the rift in the anti-Conservative lute that began when Labour overtook the Liberals in the 1920s has now been healed. At least for the moment and for most practical purposes, Tony Blair's 'New Labour' Party has become a new version of the broad-based progressive coalition that disappeared in the 1920s, or at least the pole around which such a coalition can take shape. It has done this by deliberately reinventing and repositioning itself so as to remove those of its pre-Blair characteristics that alienated non-Labour 'progressives' – notably by revising the old Clause Four out of all recognition, by weakening the link with the trade unions, by slimming down the trade-union block vote and, above all, by constructing a rhetoric pitched at non-Labour 'middle England'. This is, by any reckoning, a historic achievement. Other Labour leaders – Ramsay MacDonald in the 1920s, Attlee in the 1940s, Harold Wilson in the 1960s – have appealed successfully to a non-Labour constituency, at least for a while. None has remade the Labour Party itself.

That is only the beginning of the story. Blair's achievement would not have been possible a decade ago. It took place against the background of a much more fundamental change in the ideological climate, the real meaning of which is that the doctrinal quarrel between liberalism and socialism has been settled in liberalism's favour. Capitalism has won its historic contest with socialism, and pluralist democracy *its* historic contest with the vanguard party. *Pace* Francis Fukuyama, this does not mean that history has ended. What it does mean is that it has taken an extraordinary new twist. The old debate between capitalism and socialism is over, but as I tried to show in chapter 1, lively debates are now in progress over the forms of capitalism and their ethical and moral underpinnings, and over the cultural and ethical prerequisites of a sustainable market order and a successful capitalist enterprise. From these debates, the faint outlines of a new approach to political economy are beginning to emerge. Among those who share this approach, there is growing agreement that a sustainable market order depends on non-market values, capable of generating an ethos of mutual loyalty and reciprocal obligation; that economic success depends, in part, on the social capital of mutual trust, generated by a way of life involving reciprocity and mutuality; that it is simplistic to imagine that 'individualistic'

Anglo-American capitalism is the only capitalism on offer; and that, by virtue of the social dislocation and the erosion of social capital it brings with it, unbridled Anglo-American capitalism may be self-stultifying.

But although this approach to political economy is new in the perspective of the recent past, some of its features, at any rate, are not so new in the perspective of the last 100 years of centre-left history. And the intriguing thing about them is that, *mutatis mutandis*, today's critics of unbridled capitalism have much more in common with early twentieth-century social *liberals* than with socialists of any period. The same applies on the level of party competition. Socialist parties, where they survive as serious political forces, are essentially social-liberal not socialist: their projects are far closer, in all but name, to Hobhousian New Liberalism than to Marxist or even Webbian socialism. Many of them have abandoned the symbols that tied them to their socialist pasts. All of them accept market allocation and capitalist property relations, just as the New Liberals did. Also like the New Liberals, however, they seek to reconcile market allocation and capitalist property relations with social solidarity and just distribution. Donald Sassoon's description of what he calls 'neo-revisionism' contains the gist:

> It implies that markets should be regulated by legislation and not through state ownership. It means accepting that the object of socialism is not the abolition of capitalism, but its co-existence with social justice; that regulation of the market will increasingly be a goal achieved by supranational means . . . It means that the historic link with the working class, however defined, is no longer of primary importance, and that the trade unions are to be regarded as representing workers' interests with no *a priori* claim to have a greater say in politics than other interest groups. It means giving a far greater priority than in the past to the concerns of consumers.[6]

But that project presupposes that capitalism and the market can be moralized in this way – precisely the claim that the New Liberals made a century ago and that socialists denied.

The French and Italian socialists' emphasis on 'republican' values and British Labour's more tentative talk of human rights and constitutional reform point in the same direction. In an important sense, liberalism is about process; socialism (and, for that matter, social democracy) have been about outcomes. Typically, socialists dismissed the liberal concern with process as artificial, frivolous, even deliberately deceitful. For classical Marxists, 'bourgeois' freedom, 'bourgeois' citizenship and 'bourgeois' parliamentarianism were shams. For Webbian, and later Croslandian, Fabians and social democrats the Liberal constitutional and political agenda, and the Liberal anxiety about the British state that underpinned it, were diversions. The system was sufficiently democratic to ensure majority rule; 'individualistic' constitutional tinkering might make it more difficult for a majority to have its way. The task of the left was to deliver redistributive and efficiency-enhancing welfare and economic outcomes without bothering about process.

In this domain as well, two linked experiences have provoked a change of heart, giving liberalism a sort of revenge. The failure of the communist regimes to reform themselves from the top, and the growth of dissident movements using the language of civil society to define their aims, encouraged western socialists who used to pooh-pooh the traditional liberal fear of concentrated power and the associated liberal demand for civic rights and constitutional checks and balances, to engage in second thoughts. 'Bourgeois' freedom and 'bourgeois' constitutionalism might not be enough, but they were better than nothing; in any case, the east European experience showed that civil society might well need protection against the depredations of the state.[7]

The so-called Thatcher Revolution in Britain, and quasi-Thatcherite imitations elsewhere, have pointed a similar moral. In Britain, the socialist and social-democratic left discovered to its horror that Westminster parliamentarianism did not, after all, provide effective protection against the abuse of power by a determined government. They began to suspect that 'bourgeois' checks and balances and entrenched 'bourgeois' civil rights might have made it more difficult for the radicals of the neo-liberal right to unpick the social-democratic post-war settlement and to embark on a programme of cultural reconstruction from the top down. The current discourse of citizenship and constitutional reform was a product of this change of heart. Its central premise is that there was, after all, an unfinished radical agenda; that the 'universal abolitionism' that Bernard Shaw once mocked and that the rising Labour movement (whether social-democratic or socialist) dismissed as being of no account should now be retrieved. The rise of Charter 88, the Scottish Constitutional Convention and New Labour's commitment to a substantial, if somewhat incoherent, programme of constitutional reform all show that that agenda now has a new appeal, not only to liberals but to formerly sceptical socialists and social democrats as well.[8]

On a different level, technological and social change have helped to erode the economic, and perhaps even the cultural, bases of the Labour tradition, and with them the barriers between Labour's core constituency and the wider society. Notoriously, there was a symbiotic relationship between 'Fordist' mass production and classical socialism, classical social-democracy and the classical Labour movement. But in 'disorganized', 'post-Fordist' capitalism, the mass, male working class of the old kind barely exists. Heroic proletarianism on the Marxist model has, in any case, been discredited by the ugliness and corruption of the regimes that prayed it in aid in eastern Europe. Because the historical conditions that gave rise to it no longer exist, the humdrum version that once suffused the culture and understandings of the British labour movement is now in its death throes too, even if it is not quite dead.

All this has broken the moral mainspring of the disciplined and hegemony-seeking mass party. For its logic was, almost by definition, transformative. At least in the long term, its purpose was to transform society in accordance with its ideology. It aspired to total control of the power of the state because state power was the vehicle for social transformation; it saw its parliamentary group as the battering ram of an extra-parliamentary 'movement' because its ideology was the property of the movement and embodied in it. The goal of social transformation made hegemony necessary and the pursuit of hegemony legitimate. If hegemony were to be pursued successfully, coalition with other parties had to be ruled out, except as a short-lived tactical device in emergencies. By the same token, individual party members had to subordinate themselves to the disciplines of the group. Take away the goal of social transformation, and the whole hegemonial edifice falls apart. New Labour, to take the example closest to home, is no longer in the business of transformation. Why should it need hegemony or the disciplines associated with its pursuit? And, if it no longer needs them, what is to stop it from embracing a politics of negotiation and coalition-building, not as a temporary expedient, but as a permanent feature of the landscape?

That is only part of the case for a post-hegemonial politics. Today's variegated and turbulent societies, criss-crossed with social fissures that the old mass-party model ignored and rich in social movements that it cannot encompass, are, in any case, barren soil for hegemonial ambitions, at any rate on the left. In such societies, opposition to the status quo comes from a variety of sources, and its political expression is almost bound to be complex and heterogeneous. As a result, parties of the left can exercise power successfully only if they are willing to share it with partners – sometimes with awkward partners – in broad-based, fluid coalitions. That is the logic of the Prodi coalition in Italy. It has come into existence, among other reasons, because the Communist Party has abandoned the hegemonial ambitions which were once of its very essence.[9] If former Italian Communists can accept the logic of post-hegemonial politics, why should the same logic not apply to Britain? If it does, New Labour should be happy to share power with other 'progressive' forces and to jettison the first-past-the-post electoral system that made Old Labour's hegemonial ambitions appear feasible.

IV

Yet paradoxes abound. Labour's transformation into a social liberal party, no longer aiming at social transformation, and no longer entitled to seek the kind of hegemony that the promise of transformation legitimized and necessitated, has been achieved by making the internal structure of the party more hegemonic, in some ways, than it was before. New Labour may be 'progressive', but it is not pluralistic, or not, at any rate, in its conduct of its own affairs. Its constitutional agenda points to a new approach, not just to the machinery of the state, but to the conduct of politics. Yet the changes which have been made in the party's internal governance, together with the iron discipline which the leadership has imposed on the parliamentary party, point towards a personalized, public-relations-driven presidentialism on the American model, as remote from the liberal ideal of a reflective and deliberative politics of free discussion and debate as was the solidaristic, 'collectivist' Labour-ism of the past.

That leads on to a deeper paradox. A reinvented progressive coalition has become possible at the very moment when the idea of progress has lost its appeal to the intellectual descendants of its inventors: when, for the first time since the French Revolution, the right is more comfortable with the rhetoric of progress than is the left. As Albert Hirschman has pointed out, the claim that ineluct-able trends are carrying society willy-nilly in a desirable direction, that, in John Reed's famous phrase, 'I have seen the future and it works', has always been a central trope of 'progressive' rhetoric.[10] But that claim now comes chiefly from Hayekian neo-liberals who insist that the inexorable pressures of globalization and techno-logical change rule out any attempt to tame the capitalist free market. That does not mean that their claim is valid, of course: the rhetoric of globalization should be taken with a pinch of salt. As Paul Hirst and Grahame Thompson have argued, globalization is not an irresistible force, carrying all before it. In some domains, at least, today's world market conforms less closely to the model of the globalization theorists than did that of the late nineteenth century.[11] But that is not the point. The point is simply that the right has the self-confidence and *élan*, the all-important sense that history is on its side, to use the rhetoric of progress, and that the left's attempts to recapture it (as when Tony Blair talked of Britain as a 'young country') are unconvinced and unconvincing. Colin Crouch's analysis of the implications of the 1996 Italian elections is particularly pertinent:

> Seen in general terms, the Prodi Government is a social Christian coalition after the manner of Jacques Delors' European Commission . . . that forged something of a European social agenda during the 1980s . . .
> It is an alliance that addresses the most fundamental issue of our age – how to construct a capacity for collective action in societies where individual advance and wealth accumulation seem so much easier to achieve if only collective responsibilities do not improve – by bringing together two assertions of the priority of the collective. In the past, they have presented bitterly rival visions and their mutually inflicted wounds will not heal easily. They have also both become defensive visions, since they feed on past sources and experiences while the forces of unbridled market capitalism are very contemporary.[12]

There are comparable paradoxes in liberalism's revenge. It has coincided with growing tensions within the liberal ideological family, indeed growing incoherence in liberalism itself, as liberals try to make sense of, and cope with, the dynamics of renascent capitalism and cultural transformation. One manifestation of these tensions is the death of the clerisy and the absence of an heir. Nineteenth-century liberalism was, *par excellence*, the creed of the clerisy: of what Stefan Collini has called the 'public moralists'.[13] It presupposed a vigorous, self-confident intellectual and political elite, whose members had the capacity and will to act as schoolmasters to the demos. For the liberal vision of a reflective (and reflexive) polity of free discussion and debate did not imply that all values were equally legitimate or all arguments equally valid. On the contrary, there was a truth to be discovered, and some people – the elite – were better at discovering it than others. It was their duty to communicate it to their fellows and, by inference at least, it was the duty of their fellows to listen to them. In all this, of course, liberalism embodied the assumptions and legitimized the claims of the professional mandarinate, whose rise Harold Perkin has charted.[14] But the authority of – indeed, the preconditions for – such a clerisy have been undermined by the 'demotic and antinomian' cultural revolution of our time.[15] That revolution is both parent and child of unbridled capitalism and the global marketplace, of what Benjamin Barber calls 'McWorld':

> Education is unlikely ever to win an 'open market' competition with entertainment because 'easy' and 'hard' can never compete on equal ground, and for those not yet disciplined in the rites of learning, 'freedom' will always mean easy. Perhaps that is why Tocqueville thought that liberty was the most 'arduous of all apprenticeships'. To grow into our mature better selves, we need the help of our nascent better selves, which is what common standards, authoritative education and a sense of the public good can offer. Consumption takes us as it finds us, the more impulsive and greedy the better.[16]

The Murdoch empire and its foreign counterparts have done more to subvert old cultural authorities and prevent the emergence of new ones than have any number of roads protesters, cannabis smokers or single mothers – not the least of the reasons why the familiar conservative mix of traditional values and market freedom has also come under increasing strain. But the demotic anti-nomianism they have helped to foster has less obvious sources as well. One of them is the 'thin', rights-centred liberalism, a bastard form of which has become one of the dominant ideologies of our time. For this bastard liberalism, the very suggestion that some rights are more worthy of respect than others, that we can have 'better selves' to which we should be encouraged to aspire, and that some people may aspire to them more successfully than others, is a cloak for privilege or elitism. The result is a paradox of cultural regression. The vision of a free market in ideas, which Mill and his contemporaries saw as a mechanism for weeding out error and spreading enlightenment, has become a cover for the global market's race for the bottom.

The growing communitarian (or perhaps republican) critique of 'thin', rights-centred liberalism suggests a more wide-ranging and, at the same time, more disturbing thought. Communitarianism can, of course, be conservative, even authoritarian. But not all communitarians are. There is a left communitarianism, too, exemplified *par excellence* by Michael Sandel and Michael Walzer.[17] Three intuitions emerge from the debates provoked by this left communitarianism or republicanism. One is that a flourishing political community depends on mutual obligations, shared loyalties and civic virtues which the language of individual rights cannot capture. The second is that a culture of rights without obligations is self-stultifying, much as the unbridled, trust-eroding capitalist free market is self-stultifying, because it inhibits the cultivation of civic virtue and undermines the institutions that promote it.

The third intuition is more complex. The civic virtues on which a free society depends themselves depend on mutual trust. Trust goes with stability, and stability with institutions. As John Kay has argued, long-term 'relational' contracts depend on trust and actually breed trust; short-term 'spot' contracts don't.[18] A society with a dense network of stable and authoritative intermediate institutions, which give their members meaning, dignity and security, will have a higher level of mutual trust than a society of disaggregated isolates, in which the intermediate institutions are fluctuating, unstable and lacking in authority. Stable and authoritative institutions have to be, in some sense, hierarchical; someone has to be in charge, and people have to know who that someone is. And the hierarchy has, of course, to be legitimate: people have to believe that the someone in charge has a right to be in charge.

Looked at in that light (strongly influenced by the 'cultural theory' of Mary Douglas),[19] the demotic antinomianism of our time takes on a sinister meaning. It denies the very possibility of legitimate authority and corrodes all hierarchies, except perhaps the hierarchies of spectator sport and pop music. The result is a lurch from stability to instability; from legitimate hierarchy to authority-undermining self-assertion; from trust to distrust. David Manet's *Olleana* was generally taken to be an attack on militant feminism and nothing more. In a different, and I think more productive reading, it is a kind of parable of this cultural mutation. The hypocritical, middle-aged, authority-mocking professor – a classic example of the soft-faced men who have done well out of the 1960s – is confronted, and in the end destroyed, by his own creation: the ruthless self-assertion of political correctness. In the micro-world of the university, a particular version of liberalism has undermined the conditions for its own existence.

One obvious implication is that there is now a tension, perhaps even a contradiction, between social liberalism and procedural liberalism, and therefore between the socio-economic and political aspects of the 'revenge' discussed above. Historically, social liberalism was communitarian by definition. Its exponents pre-supposed shared values, embedded in realized ways of life, and appealed successfully to them. That was why they could practise the 'moral' reformism I discussed in chapter 1. This in turn implies that a viable social-liberal project in the economic domain – a project aimed at 'moralizing the market' of the sort I discussed a moment ago – would have to be underpinned by an essentially republican public philosophy. But the public philosophy implied by the dominant strand in the constitutional reform movement is not republican. In the terminology proposed by Adrian Oldfield and discussed in chapter 3, it is 'liberal individualist'. It is a philosophy of individual rights, not of civic activism. Yet it is the growing appeal of that philosophy that accounts for the political aspect of liberalism's revenge.

V

The prospects for a feasible 'progressive' project (and *a fortiori* for a sustainable progressive coalition) depend on whether these paradoxes can be resolved in practice. Obviously, there can be no way of telling. Yet certain features of the current British scene may be suggestive. The first is that what I have called the radical intelligentsia does not seem particularly enthusiastic about the new progressivism of Blair's New Labour Party, assuming that that is what it is. Part of the explanation, it may be, lies in his 'moral reformism'. Like the hero of *Olleana*, a large swathe of today's radical intelligentsia belongs to the class of 1968. Many of those concerned have drunk so deep of the procedural liberalism of rights that they have become viscerally suspicious of any talk of duties. But I doubt if that is the whole story. They may also sense potentially damaging ambiguities and confusions in the 'Blair project'. Even if they don't, ambiguities and confusions un-doubtedly exist.

In the crucial domain of the political economy, the project is negative, not positive. Old-style proletarianism and Clause Four socialism have gone, but it is not at all clear what has replaced them. On the central question in contemporary political economy – the question of how to protect social cohesion and rebuild the public domain in the face of renascent untamed capitalism; of how to moralize the market in today's conditions, as the New Liberals tried to moralize it in their generation – New Labour has so far had little to say. One reason, of course, is that in detail and in practice, it is an extraordinarily difficult question to answer. Yet it does not follow that it is inherently impossible to define the broad outlines of a public philosophy from which detailed, practical answers might be drawn. The central themes of such a philosophy are clear enough. The public domain should be safeguarded from invasion by the market domain. Enterprises should take account of stakeholders as well as owners. Wealth should be redefined to include well-being. The sovereignty of a supranational Europe should countervail the sovereignty of the global market place. There is nothing particularly arcane about any of these. New Labour has failed to hammer out a public philosophy embodying them because it has been unwilling to do so, not because it does not understand what is at stake.

By the same token, there is no sign that it has constructed an intellectually coherent rationale for the bundle of constitutional reforms to which it is, in principle, committed. As Oldfield points out, in the concrete situation of 1990s Britain, the practical implications of republican and liberal conceptions of citizenship are not necessarily in contention with each other. What the latter sees as rights inhering in a status, the former sees as the necessary conditions for a practice or set of practices. But since the proposed reforms are extremely radical, perhaps even revolutionary, in the context of this particular political community of Great Britain, the absence of an overarching philosophy to legitimize them and to arm their proponents for a hard dialectical battle, may have damaging consequences. The 'mechanical', Fabian 'democratic collectivism' that old Keynesian social democracy, old socialism and old Labourism all shared, is patently bankrupt. That is why liberalism has enjoyed its revenge and why New Labour has accepted the case for reform. But there is something curiously makeshift about its conversion. To carry conviction, it must be able to articulate a coherent vision of the purposes reform is supposed to serve: to point to a spine of theory holding its proposed reforms together and linking them with the rest of its programme. Above all, it must be able to spell out its implications for the fundamentals of British statehood and theirs for it. So far, at least, it has done none of this.

In the main, it has advocated constitutional reform on liberal-individualist grounds, not on communitarian or republican ones. The emphasis has been on rights against the state, not on activity within it; on the danger that public power may be abused, not on the need to facilitate and legitimize collective action. As a result, its constitutional agenda has looked, all too often, more like a rag-bag of concessions to radical-individualist *chic* than a set of building blocks for a politics of social cohesion and public purpose. Yet there is a republican, social-democratic case for reform which has little to do with liberal individualism. At the heart of that case lies the proposition that the British state is not, and cannot be, a proper vehicle for the values of solidarity and common citizenship. It wears the trappings of democracy, but its institutions, its iconography, the symbols and rituals that tell its managers who they are and the operational codes that tell them what to do are all saturated with pre-democratic values. It can deliver (has historically delivered) high-quality public goods from the top down, but the very notion of a politics of civic activism runs against its grain. Twice in this century, Labour has had the opportunity to reconstruct it. On each occasion, Labour ministers persuaded themselves that they could use the existing machinery for their own purposes; that social-democratic outcomes could emerge from pre-democratic processes. Their reward was frustration in office, a Conservative recovery and still more frustration in opposition. Now reconstruction is more urgent than ever. Indeed, as I argue in chapter 10, reconstruction of a kind has been in progress for a decade. As a result, the status quo is no longer an option. The question is how it will be changed, and in accordance with what principles. The second question is more important than the first. If New Labour does not answer it, others will – almost certainly in an 'un-progressive' way.

It would be wrong to end on a pessimistic note. Notwithstanding global pressures, economic constraints, intellectual confusions and policy ambiguities, the prospects for a reborn progressive coalition are better than they have been since the lights went out in August 1914. We cannot know if the promise will be fulfilled. What is certain is that fulfilment will depend on a rare mixture of openness, generosity and intellectual honesty, in civil society as well as in government. By a nice irony, politicians and public alike have more to learn from Turgenev and Mill than from any of the paladins of twentieth-century mass politics. No one could pretend that they will find it easy to do so. The real question is whether they have the humility to try.

1997

• PART TWO •

Europe

• CHAPTER FIVE •

The Politics of Monetary Union

I

Monetary union has twice been a live issue in the politics of the European Community – first, in the late sixties and early seventies, when the Werner Group proposed a phased plan for the achievement of monetary union by stages, and when member governments rashly committed themselves to full-scale monetary union by 1980; and, second, in the late seventies, when Roy Jenkins's Florence speech 'relaunching' the concept in October 1977 was followed not more than a year later by the decision to set up the European Monetary System. Both in the first, 'Werner', phase and in the second, 'Jenkins', phase, the most enthusiastic advocates of monetary union clearly appreciated that it had immense political and institutional implications. The final report of the Werner Group explicitly said that in the final stage there would have to be a 'centre of decision for economic policy' and a 'Community system for the central banks'.[1] Jenkins did not go quite as far as this, but in his Florence speech he said that monetary union 'would imply a major new authority to manage the exchange rate, external reserves and the main lines of internal monetary policy';[2] and in a

* This chapter was originally published in 1982, and refers to the debates over monetary union that followed Roy Jenkins's 'relaunching' of the Community's monetary project in the late 1970s, and the creation of the European Monetary Union System in 1979. I republish it here in its original form because the basic arguments over monetary union and its political implications seem to me to have changed very little in the intervening decade and a half.

speech to the European Parliament a few weeks later, he declared
that in a monetary union 'two of what are generally regarded as
the more important functions of a modern government – control
over the exchange rate and control over the money supply – would
be exercised by a central Community institution instead of by
governments'.[3]

Unofficial bodies were equally aware of the political implications. The 1975 Marjolin Report declared that, in a monetary union,
'national governments put at the disposal of the common institutions the use of all the instruments of monetary policy and of
economic policy whose action should be exercised for the Community as a whole'; this implied a 'European political authority, an
important Community budget and an integrated system of central
banks'.[4] The MacDougall Group of economists, which reported on
the role of public finance in European integration in April 1977, did
not itself say much about the political implications. In a working
paper on the budgetary powers of the European Parliament,
however, one member argued that, if the Community budget were
increased in the way that the Group thought necessary, a political
authority of some kind would have to be created to determine how
the money should be spent.[5]

Yet, by a revealing paradox, both in the comings and goings
which followed the publication of the Werner Report, and in the
more recent transactions which culminated in the establishment of
the EMS, the authorities involved kept the political and institutional implications firmly in the background. The Commission's
Communication to the Council following the Werner Report made
no reference to political union, and said nothing about the need for
a 'centre of decision'; by the same token, the Council's decision of
March 1971, expressing the Community's political will to establish
monetary union by the end of the decade, did not provide for any
institutional expression of that will. Much the same was true of the
second 'Jenkins' phase of the monetary-union debate. The EMS fell
far short of monetary union; in striking contrast to what had
happened during the 'Werner' phase, the governments which set it
up did not even commit themselves to full-scale monetary union at
any stage in the future. In these circumstances, it is not surprising
that they said nothing about the institutional and political implications of a move towards full-scale monetary union, should the
EMS eventually develop in that direction. The Commission's
attitude was more surprising. The central premise of Jenkins's
Florence speech was that monetary union had to be taken neat or

not at all; that there was no point in trying to construct a half-way house; on Jenkins's logic, therefore, such value as it had lay in its capacity to develop into full-scale monetary union at a later stage. Yet in the discussions between the Florence speech in October 1977 and the decision to set up the EMS in December 1978, the Commission carefully refrained from drawing attention to institutional aspects of the question. Moreover, though Werner and Jenkins both explicitly recognized that monetary union would involve a major political step, and as such represent, in Jenkins's words, 'a formidable challenge to our institutional inventiveness', neither devoted much time or energy to exploring the nature of that political step, or to discussing what sort of institutional arrangements would be necessary either during the transition stage towards monetary union or in the final stage of full-scale union when it finally came to pass. The Werner Group suggested that its 'centre' of economic decision-making should be made responsible to a directly elected European Parliament. In his speech to the European Parliament in January 1978, Jenkins saw 'a wide range of possibilities: at one end, a body under the continuing and permanent surveillance of finance ministries; at the other something like a Federal Reserve Board which, I add in passing, is responsible to Congress rather than to the Executive of the United States'. The Werner Group's suggestions, however, amounted to little more than hints and Mr Jenkins's to little more than an aside. On the official level, in other words, even among those who were prepared explicitly to recognize that monetary union had a significant political and institutional dimension, discussion of these political and institutional aspects did not go beyond generalities.

II

Almost certainly, the reason was twofold. In the early seventies, France was in favour of monetary union itself but was unwilling to accept the supranational implications of the Werner Report. The Commission and the other member states feared that if they insisted on an explicit commitment to the institutional changes advocated in the Report, the French would take fright and the whole project would have to be abandoned. By the late seventies, supranationalists were, if anything, thinner on the ground than at the beginning of the decade, and opponents of supranationalism thicker. Not only the French, but the British and perhaps even the Danes could be expected to oppose institutional changes on Werner lines; and it was far from clear that even the Germans would support them. It must have seemed to the Commission that it was better to settle for the EMS, which was at least a modest step in the right direction, than to insist on the qualitative leap which Jenkins had advocated at Florence, and risk getting nowhere; in these circumstances, it could plausibly be argued that discussion of the political and institutional implications of full-scale monetary union would be, at best, premature and, at worst, damaging.

But that is only part of the explanation. Where the federalists of the late forties had thought in terms of mobilizing political forces and creating political structures, the 'neo-functionalist' conception of integration, on which the Community's founding fathers operated for most of the time, was, in an important sense, anti-, or at any rate, apolitical. The architects of the Coal and Steel Community of the early fifties and the Economic Community of the late fifties were trying to set in motion an irreversible process, with an irresistible dynamic, through which national governments and national parliaments would be more and more tightly constrained. Once integration had been achieved in one field, they imagined, it would 'spill over' into neighbouring fields. As it spilled, national governments would find themselves unable to take decisions, or at any rate to make their decisions stick, in an ever-expanding cluster of policy areas. In respect of policy area after policy area, they would sooner or later be forced to conclude that effective decisions could be taken only on the European level. Integration was rather like tobogganing. Once the toboggan had been given an initial push, the governments, parliaments and peoples perched on it would be carried along willy-nilly by the momentum of the integration process itself. Arguments about the political and institutional implications of the process were to be avoided, since they could only slow the toboggan down. The important thing was to get it moving, and that could best be done by patiently removing the technical obstacles to its descent, not by engaging in time-wasting theoretical disputes about its goal or direction.

Hence the Community's institutional structure, in which the role of 'motor of integration' was assigned to an appointed Commission, whose authority was derived partly from the text of the treaty establishing it and partly from the technical skills of its members and staff rather than from popular election. Hence, too, the

Commission's increasingly bureaucratic and diminishingly political conception of its own task. For although it attempted to play a political role in the early years of the Community, when Dr Hallstein was president, it was soon brought to heel by President de Gaulle. Since the mid-sixties it has shrunk from political conflicts with member governments, and has made few attempts to mobilize political forces in support of its policies. Its essentially technocratic and apolitical approach to the issues raised by the Werner Report and later by Jenkins's Florence speech was thus all of a piece with its approach to almost all the policy areas with which it deals, and for that matter all of a piece with the logic underlying its own creation.

The central contention of this chapter is that that logic and that approach – however appropriate they may have been to the problems of 'negative' integration, which were uppermost in the early years of the Community – are profoundly inappropriate to the enormously more difficult measures of 'positive' integration implied by a commitment to monetary union. The Werner Group may have drawn exaggerated conclusions from its analysis, but it is hard to quarrel with its judgement that monetary union must, at any rate, entail 'the total and irreversible convertibility of currencies, the elimination of margins of fluctuations in exchange rates, the irrevocable fixing of parity rates and the complete liberation of movements of capital'. The key words in that sentence are, of course, 'irreversible' and 'irrevocable'. Both imply big reductions in the freedom of action of member governments, rules to ensure that they do not recover their freedom at a later date and – most important of all – an authority or authorities to ensure that the rules are obeyed. Though this is more controversial, it seems fairly clear that both also imply an authority or authorities to discharge at least some of the functions which will no longer be discharged at the national level. The net effect must be a big transfer of power – and therefore of political activity – from the national to the supranational level. That, in turn, implies far-reaching changes in the Community's present institutional structure.

Monetary union, it is worth remembering, is not as novel an idea as is sometimes imagined. The nineteenth century saw three attempts at monetary union in Europe – a short-lived monetary union between Austria and the German *Zollverein*; a rather more durable 'Latin' union between France, Belgium, Switzerland and Italy; and a Scandinavian union which lasted for a generation. The Austro-German union was destroyed by the war between its

members. The other two fell apart because the members retained
the freedom to follow independent policies, and in the end used it
in a way that made continuation of the union impossible. It is true,
of course, that conditions have changed since the nineteenth
century. But it is hard to see why the changes should have made it
any less likely that the parties to a monetary union will sooner or
later behave in ways which are incompatible with its survival if
they have retained the freedom to do so. For there is an ominous,
but instructive, parallel between monetary union and disarmament. If governments did not want arms, disarmament would be
easy, but it would also be unnecessary: it is necessary because it is
difficult. If the parties to a monetary union knew that there would
never be any question of their changing their exchange rates
against each other, they would not need to establish a union. It is
because they know that they are likely to be under pressure either
to change their exchange rates or to allow the rates to change that
it is worth their while to agree to make such changes impossible.
The trouble is that the pressures which lead to exchange-rate
changes in the absence of such an agreement will still be in
existence after the agreement has been made. Indeed, the value of
the agreement is proportionate to the strength of the pressures:
monetary union, it is worth remembering, became an issue in
Community politics only when the Bretton Woods system was
beginning to break down and when the consequential monetary
disturbances began to call the existing *acquis communautaire* into
question. By the same token, one of the main arguments for the
EMS was that some dramatic step was needed to create a zone of
stability in a continent where stability would otherwise be lacking.
If the pressures are not to prevail in the future as they have
prevailed in the past, the governments concerned will have to
behave differently. To assume that they will behave differently
merely because they have promised to do so is to assume that their
unwillingness to break their word will be a strong enough
constraint on their behaviour to outweigh the pressures. To put it
at its lowest, that assumption does not square well with the
experience of the last fifteen years.

It is sometimes said that the freedom of action which the parties
to a monetary union would have to surrender is nowadays
illusory: that, in western Europe at any rate, governments no
longer enjoy real, as opposed to formal, sovereignty over their
exchange rates, or even over their monetary policies, in any case.
Clearly, there is something to be said for that view. As the last

British Labour government discovered, control over the exchange rate is very far from conferring complete freedom of action on its possessor, and it is not possible to follow a loose money-supply policy for very long if the rest of the world is following a tight one. But it would be a mistake to push that argument very far. A country with a floating exchange rate can at least choose its own rate of inflation. This is not the place for a long discussion of the social and political forces which lead different societies to opt for different inflation rates, and a non-economist would in any case be unwise to venture into such contentious territory. To put it at its lowest, however, it seems clear that the forces at work are both complex and powerful; and that if entry into a monetary union entails giving up the right to determine one's own rate of inflation, it follows that these forces will sooner or later impinge on the authority or authorities to which that right has been transferred. If the UK joined a monetary union, the authorities of which had a 'German' view of what the rate of inflation ought to be, the forces which have hitherto produced a 'British' rate of inflation in the UK would not suddenly disappear. They would make themselves felt in the union, just as they used to make themselves felt outside it. They would either prevail, or not prevail. If they prevailed, the Germans would find themselves moving in a 'British' direction against their will. If they did not, a good many people in the UK would presumably find themselves subject to disciplines which they did not wish to accept.

Governments, moreover, do not at present behave as though they had no effective sovereignty over these matters: if they did, stability would have arrived already, and there would be no need for special measures to establish it. It can, of course, be argued that governments behave in the way that they do merely because they are too stupid or too short-sighted to recognize how limited their real freedom of action is. But even if that is true, there is no reason to believe that they will suddenly cease being stupid and short-sighted merely because they have promised to behave more wisely in the future. In fact, the statement is only half-true. Thanks to the monetary instability of the seventies, to the growing interdependence of the economies of the EC and perhaps also to the growing ability of wage bargainers to see through the 'money illusion', member governments of the Community have less freedom to do what they want in the exchange-rate and monetary fields than they once had. But it does not follow that they have no freedom at all. Both on the money supply and on the exchange rate, after all, the

Thatcher government's policy differs markedly from its predecessor's; even in government, the latter's policy was by no means identical with that being followed at present. Their policies differ because they have different constituencies and different ideologies, and because, as a result, they have made different trade-offs between various objectives of economic policy. The government may find it convenient to suggest that it has no alternative to such trade-offs and the last government said much the same about its (different) policies. The suggestion is nevertheless misleading. It is Sir Geoffrey Howe, not God, or even the market, that is keeping interest rates and the exchange rate up. He could lower interest rates if he wanted to, and if he did, the exchange rate would probably fall as well. If the Opposition came to power it might discover that the changes it is currently advocating yielded fewer benefits than expected, and imposed more costs. But it would still be free to make them. In a monetary union, such questions would not be decided on the national level at all.

III

This example shows, moreover, not just that the powers which the parties to a monetary union would have to surrender are real, though limited, but that their exercise (or non-exercise) is inherently controversial. In Federal Germany there seems to be a fair degree of political consensus, not perhaps on the details of exchange-rate and monetary policy but at any rate on the assumptions underlying them. The consensus may perhaps be fortified by the constitutional position of the German Bundesbank, as an independent authority free of government control, but it is unlikely to have been caused by it. There is no such consensus in France, Italy or the UK, and no reason to believe that the ideological divisions which prevent consensus at present would suddenly disappear if the governments of those countries joined a monetary union. There, decisions on the exchange rate and the money supply will be vulnerable to controversy, and the decision-makers subject to attack, no matter where the decisions are taken. The notion that monetary policy can somehow be 'taken out of politics' has obvious attractions for the authorities charged with its management, and may well have wider advantages as well. But it is hard to see how that notion can be anything more than an academic fancy in a society with a Communist Party as powerful as those of Italy and France, or a trade-union movement with the political and economic attitudes of the British. At present, the controversies are settled on the national level. In a monetary union, they would be settled on a supranational level. It would be as unreasonable for a British citizen to blame the London government for the rate of interest in the UK as it is for a Mancunian to blame the Greater Manchester Council for the rate of interest in Manchester. But one of the reasons why the Greater Manchester Council is not blamed is that aggrieved Mancunians have someone else to blame instead; that there is an identifiable government in London which is known to be responsible for decisions of this kind, whose right to take them is accepted even by those who disagree with them and which can be thrown out at the next election. If there were no identifiable government in London, but only an anonymous committee of borough treasurers, the Greater Manchester Council almost certainly would be blamed; and if members of the Greater Manchester Council found that they were being blamed for the borough treasurers' decisions they would be forced, in self-defence, to claw back the power which they had transferred to the borough treasurers. If controversies over the exchange rate and the money supply are to be settled on the supranational level, there must be a supranational institution or institutions capable of settling them – capable, that is to say, of making its decisions stick in the face of opposition from those who are disadvantaged by or disagree with them.

Budgetary considerations point in the same direction. As the MacDougall Group pointed out, in most modern nation states – and, for that matter, in developed federal states – the weaker regions or states are shielded from the adverse balance-of-payments effects of monetary union with the stronger ones by substantial flows of public finance. No European Monetary Union would survive for long unless it created a similar shield. The MacDougall Group estimated that resources could be redistributed on a sufficient scale from the stronger economies to the weaker ones if the Community budget were made deliberately redistributive and if it were expanded so as to account for between 5–7 per cent of total Community GDP. That figure is, of course, very much smaller than the equivalent in any existing national or federal state. Nevertheless, the 'MacDougall' budget would still be more than five times as big as the existing Community budget, and would require a substantial development of new Community policies. That, too, implies institutions to decide what the policies should be and how the money should be spent. These institutions, too, would have to make controversial decisions, benefiting some regions and groups at the expense of others; their decisions would not stick unless the decision-makers could defend themselves against attack, and unless their right to make them were accepted by those affected.

The Community's existing structure must be examined against this background. The founding fathers seem to have imagined that the integrationist toboggan which they hoped to set in motion would lead, sooner or later, if not to outright federation then at least to something not far short of it. After a transition stage, most Council decisions were to be taken by a complicated system of weighted majority voting. Since Commission proposals could be amended by the Council only if the Council were unanimous, this would enhance the Commission's influence and authority, and, *a fortiori*, the influence and authority of the Assembly, to which it was accountable. At some unspecified, but presumably fairly early, stage in the process, the Assembly was to be directly elected. Majority voting would change the whole character of the Council of Ministers. It would cease to be a kind of standing inter-governmental conference, and become something much more akin to a legislative body – to an embryo upper house or Chamber of States, in President Hallstein's words, on the model of the early US Senate or perhaps of the German Bundesrat.[6] Direct elections, meanwhile, would turn the Assembly into an embryo lower house or House of Representatives. The Commission would presumably be the embryo government, accountable to its directly elected Parliament as real governments are accountable to theirs. Thanks to the 1966 'Luxemburg compromise', however, the treaty provisions on majority voting were never properly implemented. The Council of Ministers did not change in character, and the Commission did not gain the extra influence and authority which majority voting in the Council would have given it. It still retained its treaty-conferred monopoly of the right of initiative. Increasingly, however, it eschewed the role of embryo government. More and more, the Council of Ministers became the real centre of power in the Community; more and more, the Council became a forum for intergovernmental negotiations of the traditional kind rather than a Community institution, with a coherent view of the Community interest. Increasingly, too, real decision-making took place on the margins of the Community structure, or even outside it altogether. Increasingly, it is by the European Council, rather than by the

Commission or even by the Council of Ministers, that really important initiatives have been taken – not least, the decision to set up the EMS. Yet the European Council is unknown to the treaty, and does not answer to any Community institution.

Clearly, then, the Community is not a federal state, or even a quasi-federation. There is no government, even in embryo. The Council of Ministers consists of a floating population of national ministers, with different ministers attending different specialist councils, most of whom are concerned with Community affairs only spasmodically. In practice, the Council often takes decisions by a majority, but even when it does so, its proceedings are almost always conducted in the shadow of a possible veto. The Commission exercises some governmental functions, but only some. In any case, it is not elected, and therefore lacks the authority which is one of the essential attributes of a government. Although the Commission is accountable to and removable by the European Parliament, commissioners are more anxious to keep on good terms with the governments which appointed them, and which have the power to reappoint them (or to appoint them to other positions), than to win or hold the confidence of a parliament with only a negligible influence on their personal careers. Still less is there a clear dividing line between the Community sphere and the national sphere, as there would be in a federal state. The treaty no longer provides much guidance. It committed its signatories to sweeping measures of 'negative' integration and to a few measures of 'positive' integration. Most, though not all, of its 'negative' commitments have been carried out, but so far the only important measure of 'positive' integration is the Common Agricultural Policy. In spite of the treaty, the Community still lacks a common transport policy and has hardly begun to co-ordinate national economic policies.

Nor, however, is the Community a coalition of states. Community laws take precedence over national laws and the Community Court over national courts. The *acquis* of the last twenty-two years is now, in effect, entrenched law in the member states, and cannot be altered by national legislation.[7] Since 1975, the Community has been financially independent of the member states, its revenues being derived, not (as the present British government has sometimes appeared to imagine) from national contributions, but from its own resources. None of this has a parallel in any other international organization. The same is true of the 'supranational' element in the Community's institutional structure and decision-making. With all its weaknesses, the Commission exists, and plays a central part in the Community's legislative process. It also plays crucial parts in other aspects of Community life – for example, in trade negotiations with extra-Community countries or in deciding whether or not to bring infraction proceedings against a member state in breach of its obligations under Community law. On a different and more intangible level, moreover, the old functionalist dynamic still has considerable constraining force. The fact that the Community is a community – that virtually all Community officials and a great many national officials share the same 'communautaire' ideology; that the Permanent Representatives and their delegations live and work cheek by jowl with the Commission, in the same, small Eurovillage; that some interests in all members states are now articulated at the Community as well as the national level; that Community business flows on, covering a wide range of subjects, and that member governments therefore know that if they are to have their way tomorrow they have to make concessions today, and that if they have had their way today they will probably have debts to pay tomorrow – exerts a constant, hidden pressure on member governments, countervailing the centrifugal pressures which make themselves felt in national capitals.

IV

Community decision-making, then, is neither national nor supranational, but a baffling amalgam of, or perhaps half-way house between, the two. Three consequences follow. The first is that it is only dubiously and fitfully accountable either to the public, in whose names decisions are taken, or to their parliamentary representatives. The second is that it is not likely to become accountable unless the whole institutional structure is changed. The third is that, in the absence of such changes, it is equally unlikely to be able to cope with the political strains which monetary union would generate.

The Community's parliamentary institutions operate either on the national or on the supranational level, and are ill-equipped to venture into the intervening no-man's-land, where most Community business is transacted. The European Parliament can call the Commission to account through questions, debates and the threat of a vote of censure. Through its committees, and still more through informal contacts between its staff and the Commission staff, it probably has more influence on the 'pre-legislative' phase of Community policy-making than Westminster MPs have on the UK equivalent.[8] Yet even in its relations with the Commission, the European Parliament operates within fairly narrow limits, some formal and others informal. In the first place, the Commission is collectively accountable, not individually. Parliament can censure only the whole Commission, not individual commissioners. There is no equivalent to the Westminster motion to reduce an individual minister's salary. Thus, lazy or incompetent commissioners – and, what is much more important, lazy or incompetent Directorates-General – can shelter behind their hard-working and competent colleagues. In any case, censure motions require a two-thirds majority of the total membership to pass – a larger majority than any post-war British Government has had at Westminster. More significant than these formal limits, however, is the fact that, from the earliest days of the Coal and Steel Community, the High Authority and later the Commission, on the one hand, and the Assembly, on the other, have seen each other as allies, not as adversaries or antagonists. Most MEPs have wanted to support the Commission, not embarrass it; to prod it into taking further action, not to criticize the actions it has already taken. The result is that Parliament's attempts to hold the Commission to account contain a large element of shadow-boxing.

In any case, the European Parliament's ability to hold the Commission to account is nothing like as valuable as it would have been had the founding fathers' toboggan proceeded as planned. What matters now is influence over the Council and, even more perhaps, influence over the strange, bureaucratic limbo between the Council and the Commission. The European Parliament faces formidable obstacles in its search for this. To be sure, it does have some power over the Community budget. As became clear in December 1979, this enables it to throw the Community process into considerable confusion, and so to force member governments to negotiate with it, even if not to do what it wants. Given skill and determination, moreover, its budgetary powers might be used to extract changes of policy – not necessarily in big, set-piece battles, but in small guerrilla skirmishes unreported by the press. By the same token, Parliament could use its power to censure the Commission as a lever to acquire a say in the appointment of the Commission president, or perhaps even all commissioners. A really determined Parliament might use the same weapon to force the Commission to give it a share in the right to the initiative. Treaty amendment would be needed to give Parliament a formal right of initiative of its own, but there is nothing in the treaties to stop the Commission from adopting Parliament's initiatives as its own, or from putting them to the Council thereafter. Thus the simplistic notion that the European Parliament has no worthwhile powers at all, and that its role in Community decision-making cannot be enhanced without a fundamental change in the treaties, is wide of the mark.

But all this is in the future conditional, not in the present. It would be absurd to pretend that Community decision-makers are accountable to the European Parliament at this moment. Indeed, it is difficult to see how the Council of Ministers ever could be, for the obvious reason that it consists of national ministers, who are separately accountable to their own national parliaments. Even if the Council evolved into a Community 'upper house', on the lines hinted at by President Hallstein, it would not be accountable to the European Parliament, any more than the US Senate is accountable to the House of Representatives. The future conditional can be turned into the present, moreover, only if a majority (or, more probably, a series of majorities) in the Parliament wish it to do so. Such majorities may emerge; it was because such a majority emerged during the arguments over the 1980 Community budget that Parliament voted as it did in December 1979. But, as that example itself suggests, such majorities are likely to be evanescent. The MEPs who then voted overwhelmingly for rejection later accepted a budget differing only marginally from the one they rejected seven months before. Almost certainly, the reason is that the December majority reflected only the institutional ambitions of the MEPs who composed it, rather than pressures from their parties or constituents. It would be wrong to suggest that rebellious parliamentary majorities will always crumble in that way. But if they do not, it will be because the pressures which have brought them into existence have also made themselves felt at the national level. If the pressures are felt at the national level, the Council will itself be affected by them sooner or later, and will presumably modify its policy without any great battle with Parliament.

There is, in short, no automatic toboggan slide to accountability on the Community level. What of the national level? National parliaments have responded to Community membership in a wide variety of ways. In France and Luxemburg, Parliament has, for all practical purposes, no special machinery to deal with Community affairs. In Denmark, a special committee of the Folketing has been set up, which has to approve the negotiating briefs which Danish ministers take to the Council, and to give its approval if a change in the Commission proposal makes it necessary to change the brief. The British House of Commons has set up a kind of parliamentary sieve, designed to ensure that all important Commission proposals are debated on the floor of the House before the Council takes a decision on them. In the German Bundestag, the Dutch Second Chamber and the Italian Chamber of Deputies, Community business is scrutinized by ordinary committees. The House of Lords, the Belgian House of Representatives, the Italian Senate and the German Bundesrat have set up special committees on Community affairs, with varying terms of reference. In Ireland, a joint committee of both Houses operates in much the same way as the special committee in the British House of Lords.[9]

On closer inspection, however, it emerges that a national parliament faced with the problems posed by Community membership has four options (not, of course, mutually exclusive) from which to choose. It can fail to differentiate between Community issues and 'normal' issues, and rely on its customary procedures. It can try to tie its ministers down in advance of Council meetings, as the Folketing does. It can try, as the House of Lords does, to influence its government at an early stage in the Community's legislative process, before firm proposals have gone to the Council, and leave it to the government to decide what to do when the Council meets. Or it can try to bring influence to bear on the government at a later stage, when a decision is more or less imminent. It also emerges, however, that none of these options is particularly satisfactory. The first is unsatisfactory because Community issues are not 'normal'. The second is unsatisfactory because, in practice, it merely substitutes one unaccountable body for another. The Market Relations Committee of the Folketing undoubtedly exerts tight control over Danish ministers. But in order to do this, it has to meet in secret; otherwise ministers could not divulge their negotiating tactics to it. The system works because its members are leading figures in their respective parties, and can therefore 'deliver' the Folketing at large.[10] It is less a mechanism for ensuring parliamentary accountability than a kind of mini-coalition government concerned with only one aspect of politics.

The last two options are less unsatisfactory than the first two, but neither goes to the heart of the matter, and both suffer from the same built-in contradiction. The purpose of both is to bring influence to bear on government, either early or late, while leaving it to government to decide what to do once the influence has been brought. But influencing people does not make them accountable. In any case, if the government can be trusted to pursue the national interest as it thinks best during Council meetings, why not trust it to decide for itself what the national interest is before the meeting has begun? And if it cannot be trusted to decide what the national interest is before the Council assembles, why should it be trusted to defend that interest thereafter? This contradiction springs, of course, from the very nature of the Community; and that, in turn, suggests not only that it is impossible to make a Community process accountable to a national parliament, but that it will remain impossible so long as the Community retains its present form. Accountability depends on clarity. If decision-makers are to be accountable, someone must always be in a position to use Harry Truman's motto, 'The buck stops here.' In the Community, such clarity is lacking. No one is unambiguously answerable for anything. The buck is never seen to stop: it is hidden from view in an endless scrimmage of consultation and bargaining. National parliaments are no more able to penetrate the confusion than is the European Parliament, and no more likely to acquire the ability to do so.

As the Common Agricultural Policy shows, opaque and un-accountable decision-making is singularly ill-adapted to the problems of resource allocation. Agricultural prices are fixed in a secret, and effectively unaccountable, cabal of agricultural ministers, all of them subject to intense pressure from their respective farm lobbies. Each knows that if prices are kept down, he will be blamed by his farmers. Each also knows that if prices are increased someone else will have to find the money to pay for the consequent surpluses; and that, whereas the farmers' indignation with low prices will be particular and precisely focused, the consumers' indignation with high prices will be generalized and diffuse. From the point of view of the Community as a whole, it would be rational to lower farm prices so as to reduce the surpluses. From the point of view of each single agriculture minister it is rational to vote for higher prices so as to avoid rows with farmers. The results are well known; and it is hard to resist the conclusion that in the absence of changes in the decision-making process, an enlargement of the Community budget on MacDougall lines would produce similar results in other fields. Yet, as we have seen, an enlargement of the Community budget on MacDougall lines is a prerequisite of monetary union. Somewhat different considerations apply to decisions on the money supply and the exchange rate, but – as I tried to suggest in my imaginary example of the likely relationship between the Greater Manchester Council and a committee of borough treasurers – they point to the same conclusion. At present, member governments are rightly blamed (or praised) for what happens to the money supply and the exchange rate. They would still be blamed or praised in a monetary union, unless it had an identifiable political authority which could be blamed or praised instead. But in a monetary union they would no longer be free to take decisions on these matters and would therefore have to take the blame for things which they had not done, or for failing to do things which they could not do. Since no one willingly puts himself in such a position for very long, the union would be unlikely to last.

The implication is clear. The founding fathers of the Community assumed that politics would follow economics. In fact, the reverse is the case. Economic union requires monetary union, but monetary union requires political union. And political union requires a different institutional structure, not merely when it has been achieved but as a condition of achieving it.

1982

CHAPTER SIX

The New Medievalism

I

Ever since the nation-state first appeared on the stage of European history, its nature, worth and destiny have been the subjects of fierce controversy. The controversy has, of course, taken different forms at different times; many schools of thought have contributed to it. In Britain, however, three have been particularly influential. Even today, preconceptions derived from their accounts of the matter provide the intellectual framework for the burgeoning debate on the territorial dimensions of the British state and of the evolving European Union of which Britain is part. Yet, as so often in similar circumstances, the protagonists in the debate are apt to forget the provenance and logic of their own assumptions. If we are to make sense of their arguments, and come to terms with the complex and contested place of nationhood, nation-states and sub-national territorial entities in present-day Europe and, *a fortiori*, in present-day Britain, we should look at the accounts which these schools of thought have offered.

The simplest and most dramatic of them is the Marxist. Its central premise is that the proletariat – by definition, the carrier of the future – is also by definition internationalist. The workers have, and can have, no fatherland. If they think they have one, they are either the victims of false consciousness or the prisoners of a pre-proletarian past or both. For nationalism, however defined, is the reactionary, petit-bourgeois, above all *irrational* refuge of doomed social forces, whose only possible future lies in the dustbin of history. The future is international, not national – first internationally capitalist, then internationally socialist. Indeed, it is internationally socialist in the long run only because it is internationally capitalist in the short or medium run. For capitalism is, in a crucial sense, 'progressive': the 'unconscious tool of history' as the British were in India.[1] It sweeps away the divisions between the petty, introverted communities of the past and drags them, willy-nilly, into a world market governed by worldwide imperatives. In the exhilarating phrases of *The Communist Manifesto*,

> In place of the old wants, satisfied by the production of the country, we find new wants, requiring for their satisfaction the products of distant lands and climes. In place of the old local and national seclusion and self-sufficiency, we have intercourse in every direction, universal interdependence of nations. And as in material, so also in intellectual production. The intellectual creations of individual nations become common property. National one-sidedness and narrow-mindedness becomes more and more impossible, and from the numerous national and local literatures there arises a world-literature.
>
> The bourgeoisie, by the rapid improvement of all instruments of production, by the immensely facilitated means of communication, draws all, even the most barbarian, nations into civilisation. The cheap prices of its commodities are the heavy artillery with which it batters down all Chinese walls ... It compels all nations, on pain of extinction, to adopt the bourgeois mode of production; it compels them to introduce what it calls civilisation into their midst, i.e. to become bourgeois themselves. In one word, it creates a world after its own image.[2]

Nationalism was thus an attempt to spit into the wind of history, a refuge for sociological detritus. And this was, above all, true of the 'barbarian', pre-modern, provincial nationalisms of small and backward peasant communities, trying to resist assimilation by the advanced, modern, cosmopolitan nationalities whose languages and cultures have become the vehicles of the highest forms of bourgeois civilization. The advanced, 'historic' nationalisms of the Germans, the English, the French and, in the New World, the Americans may serve, however unwittingly, as the agents of modernity. The nationalisms of the small, historyless Slavic peoples of central and eastern Europe belong to essentially the same historical category as African or Red Indian tribalism. The motive force behind them is a blatant wish to cling to a pre-capitalist, pre-scientific past, from which capitalism offers a kind of liberation. Insofar as they represent anything more than straightforward sentimentality, they are camouflage for social interest and formations which are becoming steadily more obsolete.

Not only is nationalism reactionary and irrational, it is a diversion from the battle that really matters. The only social conflict in which the proletariat has real interests at stake, the only social conflict that holds out the promise of ultimate human emancipation, is the conflict between classes. If national conflict cuts across the primordial conflict between classes, distracting the proletariat from its historic mission to prepare itself for the destruction of capitalism, only the bourgeoisie will benefit. Sometimes, it is true, a national cause may serve the proletariat's cause; the Irish struggle for national liberation, Marx thought, deserved the support of the English working class, since it was directed against the common enemy of both. More often, nationalism is a tool of the bourgeoisie, which uses it to further its own ends.

The Leninist derivative of the Marxist account adds a further twist. Before the Revolution, the Bolsheviks were for national self-determination, but only when it served the interests of the proletariat. As Lenin put it, they were concerned with 'the self-determination of the *proletariat* in each nationality rather than the self-determination of peoples or nations'.[3] After the Revolution, Communists did not see the Soviet Union as a nation-state or even, in essence, as a multinational state. Its very name asserted an internationalist ideology rather than a national identity or even a set of national identities; as that name implied, it was the multinational embodiment of the principle of proletariat internationalism, claiming the allegiance of the working class throughout the world. Though Stalin used Russian national sentiment to buttress his position, particularly during the Second World War, when he needed all the support he could get, it is a mistake to see him as a Russian or, for that matter, as any other kind of nationalist. His regime trampled on Russian traditions at least as savagely as on other national traditions; the Russian people suffered at least as much from the terror it unleashed in the name of proletarian internationalism as did any other Soviet nationality.

II

The second account is that offered by what are best termed liberal internationalists. Its parentage is not as obvious as that of the Marxist account, but possible authors include Adam Smith, Richard Cobden and John Stuart Mill. There are some intriguing similarities between liberal internationalism and Marxism. For it, too, nationalism of any sort is suspect, and the nationalism of small and 'backward' peoples, not merely suspect but reactionary, irrational and harmful to the peoples concerned as well as the progress of civilization. To John Stuart Mill, the champion of tolerance and minority rights, it seemed beyond dispute that it would be better for a Breton or a Basque to be a Frenchman, with all the privileges of French citizenship, than 'to sulk on his own rocks, the half-savage relic of past times, revolving in his own little mental orbit, without participation or interest in the general movement of the world'.[4] As that implies, another similarity between liberal internationalism and Marxism is that both are, in an important sense, teleological doctrines. For both, history is moving inexorably and inevitably towards a knowable goal – in one case, towards the goal of worldwide socialism and in the other towards the goal of worldwide capitalism.

But there is a difference as well. Marxism is a doctrine of conflict, though not of national conflict. Liberal internationalism is a doctrine of *harmony*. Individual and social interests are naturally harmonious. Provided the free, competitive market is not distorted by private monopolists or by a foolish and power-hungry state, and provided all recognize that the free competitive market allocates resources more efficiently than any other mechanism, the laws of political economy will work to the benefit of all. And what is true of societies is also true of the world. The pursuit of prosperity is not a zero-sum game. 'As a rich man is likely to be a better customer to the industrious people in his neighbourhood than a poor', Adam Smith pointed out, 'so likewise a rich nation'.[5] Given the chance, worldwide free trade, also operating according to the laws of political economy, will spread wealth from rich nations to poor ones. And, as all nations realize that they all benefit from the free working of the world market and from the international division of labour which the world market makes possible, national conflicts will become things of the past. As the Anti-Corn Law League put it, the greatest result of free trade would be 'to draw men together, to thrust aside the antagonism of race, creed and language, and unite us in the bonds of eternal peace'.[6]

The third account – that of what might be called liberal nationalists – is the most difficult to describe. Its adherents often overlap with the liberal internationalists; often liberal internationalists slip into liberal nationalism without realizing it.

However, it is best understood as a third account, not as a sub-theme of the second. Its champions include Mazzini, Thomas Jefferson, Gladstone, in some of his multifarious manifestations Lloyd George, and above all Woodrow Wilson. According to it, nationalism is neither reactionary nor irrational. On the contrary, it reflects an important – in some versions, a supremely important – part of the human psyche. Liberal nationalism agrees with liberal internationalism in holding that national interests are naturally harmonious. It adds, however, that this natural harmony will become manifest in practice only if all nations enjoy their natural right to self-determination. National conflicts result from the oppression of one nation by another: from denying to some nations their right to self-determination and from thwarting thereby the natural, proper, laudable wish of national groups to live in freedom according to their own laws and customs. Statehood, in short, is essential to full nationhood. But once all nations enjoy statehood, the reign of worldwide harmony will dawn as in the account given by the liberal internationalists.

This leads on to the most obvious and, in some respects, the most important practical differences between liberal nationalism and liberal internationalism. Where liberal internationalists disdain small and 'backward' peoples, and applaud their assimilation by 'advanced' and metropolitan cultures as a form of progress, liberal nationalists display a special sensitivity to their claims. Gladstone championing the Bulgarians and Montenegrins; Lloyd George leading the 'pro-Boers'; Woodrow Wilson insisting that the small Slavic nations of central and eastern Europe must enjoy the right to self-determination – these are characteristic expressions of one of the central themes of liberal nationalism. It is quite alien to the instinctive, if often only half-conscious, metropolitanism of the liberal internationalists. It follows that there is a certain tension within liberal nationalism which is missing from liberal internationalism. Suppose a small people, having rightly struggled to be free, and having thereby achieved self-determination, does not wish to join the harmonious world order which liberal nationalists join with liberal internationalists in seeing as the ultimate expression of their ideal? Suppose, indeed, that a small people is struggling for the freedom to stick to an illiberal culture, with illiberal values? What should the conscientious liberal nationalist do then? In the golden age of liberal nationalism, in the late nineteenth and early twentieth centuries, these questions were rarely addressed. As the rest of the twentieth century has amply demonstrated, they were always implicit in the liberal nationalist project.

III

The complex and paradoxical history of the twentieth-century European nation-state must be seen against this background. Few would deny that it has made nonsense of the first account. Except on rare occasions, working-class parties have succeeded in conditions of pluralist party competition only when they have abandoned proletarian internationalism, and to the extent that they have abandoned it. The reason is only too obvious. The workers *have* had fatherlands; they have been much more willing to die for their fatherlands than for the dream of proletarian internationalism; even in time of peace, nationalism has been a far more potent agent of mobilization than internationalism. Even more obviously, the system built on the Leninist version of the Marxist account has collapsed, in large part because nationalism has inspired the masses, whom that system was supposed to represent, to revolt against the political elites which derived their legitimacy from the memory of the October Revolution. Now even the Soviet Union is unravelling, in large measure because the nationalities of which it is composed, including the supposedly dominant Russians, are reasserting national loyalties, national identities and national interests against the increasingly bewildered custodians of Bolshevik internationalism.

The fate of the liberal-internationalist account is more mixed. Two terrible European wars, which eventually became world wars, not to speak of a multiplicity of national conflicts in the Third World, hardly conform to the prognosis it implied. Its champions could, however, explain some of these unfortunate experiences away. After all, the founding fathers of liberal internationalism did not say that the world was bound to become conflict-free; they only said that it would be conflict-free if governments had the sense to follow liberal-internationalist teachings. The two world wars and, for that matter, the disheartening national conflicts of the Third World, can be accounted for, within the liberal-internationalist paradigm, as the predictable results of irrational attempts to achieve national economic self-sufficiency by deliberately avoiding the disciplines and eschewing the benefits of the international division of labour. Governments were too stupid or too wicked to see that the reign of international harmony would dawn if only the principles of *The Wealth of Nations* were universally applied. They put their faith in national autarky instead of in international free trade; the resulting trade wars led inexorably to real wars.

At first sight, moreover, the history of post-war western Europe gives great comfort to the liberal-internationalist camp. The European Community, which has been one of the great success stories of post-war history, can be depicted, without much violence to the facts, as a triumph for the liberal-internationalist ideal. The creation of a vast European market in place of narrow national markets; an attempt to maximize prosperity all round by removing barriers to trade and facilitating cross-border competition; the pursuit of these goals through the pooling of national sovereignties and the transfer of competence from national states to supranational institutions – if Cobden were alive today, he could be forgiven for seeing all this as a logical extension of the principles underlying his famous free-trade treaty with Napoleon III's France.

Beneath the surface, however, the picture is more complex and problematical. Upward transfers of competence from national capitals to Brussels, Luxemburg and Strasburg have been accompanied by growing turbulence below the level of the state. The story of Community Europe has been one of supranational integration, but of sub-national differentiation. The pressures behind the latter have varied a good deal from place to place; no single explanation will do justice to them all. That said, they all have one crucial feature in common. In the German Federal Republic, in which sub-national territorial identities have been constitutionally embodied from the start, such pressures have been virtually absent. In the other large member states of the European Community (and in at least one of their smaller member states) territorial groupings which do not feel that their identities, aspirations and interests are fully satisfied by the nation-states concerned have demanded recognition for these identities, aspirations and interests. An incomplete, but impressive roll-call of the groupings concerned includes the Scots, the Welsh, the Bretons, the Basques, the Alsatians, the Occitans, the Corsicans, the Frieslanders, the Flemings, the Catalans and the Sardinians. In all the large Community member states apart from Britain, moreover, governments have embarked on policies of regionalization, downward devolution or even federalism or quasi-federalism to accommodate the identities and aspirations in question.[7] The liberal-internationalist model, in short, has applied only to the relationships *between* Community members; *within* them, forces for which that model has no place, and with which it cannot easily come to terms, have become increasingly significant.

Then does the third account provide a satisfactory guide to Europe's post-war experience? At first sight, the answer appears to be 'yes'. The challenge to the collapsing citadel of Bolshevik internationalism – particularly in the Baltic states and the Caucasus and even, to some extent, in the Russian Republic itself – has been phrased in language which might have come straight from Woodrow Wilson. As Scotland, Flanders and the Basque country all show, the same is true of some (though by no means all) the territorial challenges which the established nation-states of western Europe have faced from within their own borders. On a closer inspection, however, the experience of post-war Europe has dealt a severe blow to the liberal-nationalist account as well as to the other two. It is simply not true that national conflicts are everywhere the fruit of the oppression of nations, rightly struggling to be free, by unjust alien intruders. As such names as Belfast, Brussels, Estonia, Transylvania, Kosovo and Nagorno-Karabakh bear anguished and sometimes bloody witness, the suppressed major premise of the liberal-nationalist account – the assumption that all nations occupy clearly demarcated territories to which no other nation can have a legitimate claim – has turned out to be dangerous nonsense. The fact is that ethnic groups do not come in neat territorial parcels, easily separated from each other. They overlap – obviously in space; less obviously in time and in the myths and counter-myths which encapsulate memories of past time. That, of course, is why attempts to settle complex territorial disputes in accordance with liberal-nationalist doctrine, as by the Allies in 1919 and by innumerable Third World regimes since 1945, have so often come to grief.

IV

For different reasons, then, none of the classical accounts I have tried to describe can encompass the experience of post-war Europe. The proletariat has not proved more internationalist than the bourgeoisie; if anything it has been less so. Though the member states of the European Community have, in some respects, conformed to the precepts of liberal internationalism, smaller territorial groupings have pulled in the opposite direction. Though territorial aspirations have often been articulated in the language of liberal nationalism, the central premise from which that language derives its persuasive force has turned out to be false. So where do we turn instead? How *should* Europe's post-war experience be interpreted?

I cannot hope to offer a complete answer to these questions. The most I can do is to sketch out a possible approach. It begins with another look at the strange and, at first sight, paradoxical coincidence between supranational integration and sub-national differentiation. The first is fairly easy to understand. As I suggested a moment ago, it can be assimilated without much difficulty to the models of liberal internationalism. The nation-states of western Europe, devastated by the second of the two terrible wars, decided to knit their economies together and to integrate some of the most important economic functions of their respective governments in order to do so. The result was that their economies become more and more interdependent, with the further result that their governments became less and less able to exercise sovereignty in the economic sphere. Little by little, they were impelled to the conclusion that their polities would have to follow where their economies had led: that sovereignty which could no longer be exercised on the national level would have to be exercised on the supranational level instead.

The second process – the process of sub-national differentiation – has been far more complicated. It is clear that the historic nation-states of western Europe have faced pressures from below as well as from above: pressures to devolve as well as pressures to integrate. It is clear too that, if these two sets of pressures continue to operate in the future as they have in the recent past, the end product will be a Europe at once enormously more united and enormously more variegated than the Europe of the last 200 or 300 years – a Europe in some ways more reminiscent of medieval Christendom than of the nation-state-dominated Europe of the late nineteenth and early twentieth centuries. Pre-modern Europe was, after all, a patchwork of city-states, all of them subject to the authority of a pan-European Church. The first task of the emergent nation-state – or rather of its rulers – was to obliterate the ancient boundaries which were the legacy of that patchwork, to impose the language and culture of the capital upon the whole of the territory over which they had jurisdiction and, in the process, to build a 'nation' out of disparate, localized communities to which the notion of nationality meant nothing. But the 'national' identities thus procured were the products of contestable (and contested) political programmes, not of objective cultural or even economic realities, while the geographical boundaries of those identities owed more to the accidents of battle and the vagaries of dynastic marriage than to some inexorable fate. No iron law of history decreed that the peasants of Franche-Comté would one day be turned into Frenchmen rather than into Burgundians or even Germans,[8] that Madrid was to be the capital of a Spanish nation-state and Lisbon of a Portuguese one but that Barcelona was not to be the capital of an independent Catalonia, or that the low German dialect which the English call 'Dutch' was to become the official language of a nation-state known as The Netherlands.

Pace the rival teleologies of Marxism, liberal internationalism and liberal nationalism, history is now turning back on its tracks. Ancient boundaries, ancient identities, even, in some cases, ancient languages are coming in from the cold. So far from accepting cultural euthanasia, the submerged, historyless peoples whom Marx and Mill consigned to oblivion, and many whom even Gladstone and Woodrow Wilson forgot, have been on the march. In doing so they have called into question the single most important of the ideological premises of the European state-system – the double proposition that people and nation are one, and that the nation is, or should be, embodied in the state. The result is that the nation-state, for so long the supreme focus for European political loyalties, is now caught in a nutcracker embrace between Brussels, Strasburg and Luxemburg on the one hand and a host of local, regional and provincial centres on the other. For if people and nation are not necessarily one; if territorial identities cannot always be subsumed in an overarching national identity; if there are stateless peoples and multi-peopled states; then the claim of the sovereign nation-state to be the supreme political embodiment of the sovereign people is hard to sustain. And if the nation-state is no longer seen as its embodiment, why should it not be embodied, at least in part, in a European union? Scots may not be English or Basques Frenchmen, but they are all Europeans.

At this point in the argument, it is only fair to add, the teleologists are likely to object that many – perhaps most – of the non-state territorial pressures I have mentioned are not really 'national' in character, but only 'regional'; and that, since 'regional' identities and 'regional' claims are obviously less deserving of respect than 'national' ones, they cannot have the effects I have attributed to them. This may appear to be a narrow semantic point, but an important political question is concealed within it. What is to count as a nation? Plainly, there is no objective test. For what it is worth, my own view is that there is and can be no generally acceptable definition, according to which some territorial entities can be classified as regions and others as nations. Nations are regions which made it, which succeeded in establishing a claim to nationhood, sometimes conquering other regions in the process. National cultures are regional cultures which were successfully imposed on other regional cultures. One man's nation rightly struggling to be free is another man's potential alien oppressor: one man's trivial and rightly subordinate region is another's nation rightly struggling to be free. When territorial aspirations are described as 'regional', particularly when they are then contrasted with other aspirations described as 'national', it is usually with bad faith, the intention being to suggest that the first set of aspirations are somehow less serious, and therefore deserve less consideration, than the second.

A few examples will help to pin down the point. One possible criterion of nationhood as opposed to regionhood – a criterion much favoured by the Scots – is that the territory in question should once have been a state. But Bavaria, Hanover, Tuscany and Piedmont, which are not normally classified as nations, were states of sorts much more recently than Scotland; Wales, which is normally so classified, at any rate when Welshmen are present, was never a state in the modern sense. Another possible criterion is the existence of a separate language. Unfortunately, that criterion gives the Flemings and perhaps the Basques and the Catalans a better claim to nationhood than the Irish, who now possess an indubitably separate, sovereign nation-state of their own. A third possible criterion is the possession of a historic identity, giving rise to common loyalties and shared memories which endure through time. But virtually all the territorial groupings whose aspirations I have mentioned can and do point to a historic identity of some kind. That is one of the reasons why they have the aspirations. The truth is that these groupings are no less 'organic', or 'natural', or 'historic' than the nation-states within whose boundaries they lie, and that the identities they embody are no less real. Sometimes, those identities are proclaimed under a national banner and sometimes under a regional one, but the distinction between the two is artificial. What matters is that the proclamations are becoming louder and more resonant.

V

The question is, why? Two answers, or sets of answers, stand out. The first has to do with the technological and structural changes which have transformed the economies of the industrial world in the last twenty years. Notoriously, the information revolution, the growth of small-scale 'flexible specialization' in industry, the shift of mass-production manufacturing from Europe to the so-called Pacific Rim and the possible emergence of a new kind of 'disorganized capitalism' in place of the organized capitalism of the post-war period[9] have made it increasingly difficult for nation-states to promote economic development from the centre – either through indirect macro-economic manipulation or through direct intervention. But there is no warrant for the recently fashionable conclusion that public power *as such* no longer has a worthwhile economic role, and that the market should therefore be left to its own devices. On the contrary, there is plenty of evidence that, in this new world of disorganized capitalism as much as in its organized predecessor, economic development depends upon a complex symbiosis between public and private power. The central state is not, however, the only agency capable of bringing public power to bear on economic activity; and in the new era of disorganized capitalism, sub-national institutions are in a better position than national ones to cope with the problems and to seize the opportunities which technological change is bringing in its train.

One reason is that the technological and economic upheavals of the 1970s and 1980s exacerbated the familiar problem of territorially uneven economic development. Inevitably, the old industrial regions, where traditional mass-development manufacturing was concentrated, bore the brunt of the Schumpeterian 'gale of destruction' which accompanied the technological and economic transformation of the period. As so often in history, the shift of resources from old activities to new was also a shift from certain regions to others – from the English north-east to the Thames Valley, from north Germany to south, from Wallonia to Flanders, and so on. At the same time, the central state found it more difficult to shield weaker regions from the consequences of uneven economic development – or, at any rate, to do so by and through the instruments on which they had relied in the boom years of the 1950s and 1960s. In that period, regional policy focused on the provision of incentives to attract footloose mass-production, multi-branch industry into depressed regions. But one of the chief consequences of the current economic transformation is that footloose industry of this sort is no longer available to be attracted on the necessary scale. Meanwhile it became increasingly clear that the factors which cause depressed regions to fall behind are more complex than was realized twenty years ago, and that locating the branch plants of multi-branch firms in such areas is unlikely, by itself, to enrich their indigenous resources – particularly the human resources on which economic development increasingly depends.

Yet the issues of territorial justice, which traditional regional policy was designed to address, have not been – cannot be – banished from the political agenda. The social and economic arguments against allowing economic development to be disproportionately concentrated in favoured regions, while the less favoured sink into a vicious spiral of depression, emigration and deteriorating social capital, are as powerful and as resonant today as they were in the 1960s or, for that matter, in the 1920s. The obvious implication is that these issues will have to be addressed with different policies, implemented with different instruments. In the knowledge- and skill-intensive economies of the late twentieth century the crucial resources for regional economic development are, by definition, knowledge and skill. Sub-national agencies, closer than central government can possibly be to the entrepreneurs and information flows of the region for which they are responsible, are much better placed to strengthen local networks of skill and knowledge than is central government, and therefore much more likely to develop the indigenous capacities of the region. The *Land* government of Baden-Württemberg is one classic case in point; the Scottish Development Agency another. As both these examples suggest, moreover, one way to disperse knowledge and skill is to disperse political power. Centralized polities, with dominant capital cities, which act as magnets for the head offices of firms and the associated research and development activities, inevitably foster centralized economies. Political decentralization, as in Federal Germany or the United States, encourages economic decentralization.[10]

Powerful though they may be, however, 'hard' economic arguments of this sort would not have cut much political ice if attitude and sentiment had been adverse to them. The reason they have carried conviction is that they have increasingly chimed with the mood of the times. In this respect, at any rate, cultural change and economic change have run together. The age of flexible specialization and disorganized capitalism is also the age of Samuel Beer's 'romantic revolt'[11] and of Ronald Inglehart's 'post-materialism'[12] – an age which, in almost all western countries, has seen a new stress on the values of authenticity, autonomy and personal fulfilment and a new revulsion against externally imposed identities of any kind. Associated with these values are a growing belief in the need for popular participation in decision-making, a growing suspicion of bureaucracy and particularly of remote, large-scale bureaucracy, a growing unwillingness to take traditional authority on trust and a growing yearning for the familiar, the small-scale and the face-to-face in a world which seems ever more rootless, more homogenized and more impersonal. The result is a challenge to established authority in the name of a new populism, a challenge to class and group loyalties in the name of a new individualism, and a challenge to the central state in the name of a new provincialism. Most Europeans want supranational institutions to make public policy in certain limited areas where the nation-state can no longer make its will effective, but few want an American-style melting pot. And, for an increasing number, 'national' identities, constructed in and imposed from the capital cities of the Community's member states, do as much violence to this yearning for authenticity as would a pan-European melting pot constructed in Brussels, Luxemburg and Strasburg.

VI

The logic points to a Europe of the regions in place of the present Europe of the states – to a Europe in which the macro-economic functions of government are mostly discharged by Community authorities, while micro-economic intervention is mostly left to regional or provincial ones; in which sovereignty is shared out between different supranational, national and sub-national tiers of government, according to the principle of subsidiarity; and in which political identities are multiple rather than singular, with both a European and a regional or provincial dimension as well as a national one. Whether such a Europe will in fact come into existence it is impossible to tell. As the pace of supranational integration speeds up, and the Community's 1992 project makes it still more difficult for the national tier of government to exercise its imagined sovereignty in the economic sphere, the economic role of the sub-national tier is likely to become even more important. As regions and provinces become more powerful, they are likely to loom larger in the consciousness of their peoples. They are also likely to form more cross-national alliances on issues of common concern, and to develop more direct links with the Community's supranational institutions. But there is a big gap between evolutionary, *de facto* regionalization on these lines and a *de jure* regional structure, with clearly demarcated functions and lines of accountability, and that gap will not be crossed without a decisive act of political will. Because of this, there is not much point in speculating about the precise form which the constitution of a Europe of the regions might take. The only certainty is that it would run with the grain of the times and that the elements out of which it might be constructed lie around us.

1991

CHAPTER SEVEN

Reinventing Federalism

I

Europeans have lived for so long in the warm cocoon of the Community system that we have almost forgotten what our history was like before the astonishing burst of institutional inventiveness that culminated in the Rome Treaty a generation ago. If present trends are allowed to continue we may be brutally reminded, with consequences we cannot now imagine. The demons of European history – chauvinism, xenophobia, irredentism, racism and scapegoat-hunting – are on the march all over the former Soviet bloc. In Community Europe they are still relatively quiescent. But no one who has watched the rise of the French National Front or the German Republicans – no one, for that matter, who watched the 1993 Conservative Party conference in this country – can pretend that they strike no chords on this side of what used to be the Iron Curtain. There is an ample supply of combustible material lying about in western Europe as well as in the east. If anyone puts a match to it the entire Community system may be destroyed.

To be sure, its institutional structure is not at risk. Institutions, particularly international institutions, often limp on, pale shadows of their former selves, long after events have squeezed the life out of them. The real danger is that they will bombinate in a vacuum; that the mountains of paper, the hours of talk, the agitated comings and goings of self-important personages will be so much spitting in the wind; that, while preserving the forms of a supranational

Community, the reality of European life will be one of beggar-my-neighbour attempts to sneak competitive advantages in an ever more cut-throat world economy, accompanied by increasingly raucous chauvinistic drum-beating and deepening national rivalries in politics as well as in economics.

For the current trend in the brave new European Union inaugurated by the Maastricht Treaty is emphatically towards a two- (or even a multi-)speed Europe. Like the currency upheavals which destroyed the snake in the 1970s, the currency upheavals which have inflicted so much damage on the European Monetary System in the recent past have shown that the mere exercise of political will cannot force through the economic convergence which is the necessary condition of a monetary union between the 'strong' currency core of the European Community and the 'weak' currency periphery. If present trends continue there is not much doubt that the deutschmark-dominated core – with or without France – will continue along the path to further economic and monetary integration. In the periphery, meanwhile, a vigorous 'race for the bottom', led by the United Kingdom, is likely to accelerate.

Britain's social-chapter opt-out is a classic example of free-rider politics. In effect, Britain has been allowed to escape her share of the social costs of the single market. She is riding free on the backs of the other member states, in an attempt to make herself that much more attractive to inward investment, and that much more competitive in the cheap and shoddy end of the global market place. And she is justifying herself by banging on a peculiarly crass and nasty xenophobic drum. The Community can survive one free-rider. It could not survive several. Yet, if John Major's free-riding succeeds, it is hard to believe that all the other member states will refrain indefinitely from following suit. If he is followed, the process of competitive social dumping which the social chapter was designed to stop is likely to start after all. If it does, member states with high standards of social protection will be under enormous – and understandable – pressure to defend themselves against unfair competition from those who have followed the British road. And the lesson of history is that that sort of self-defence quickly spreads, and quickly becomes self-stultifying.

It is equally clear that, on present trends, the institutional framework of the Union will, for the foreseeable future, remain essentially intergovernmental rather than supranational; that an unholy alliance between France and the United Kingdom will continue to block all attempts to correct the democratic deficit in decision-making, as it did before the Maastricht summit; and that, because of this, the institutions will remain weak, opaque and lacking in democratic legitimacy. If this prediction is borne out, the people of what is now supposed to be the European Union will remain apathetic and, at least to a certain extent, alienated from the whole process. All this will create fertile soil for 'fundamentalist' nationalism and populist demagogy, of the sort that surfaced in the French and Danish referendum campaigns on the Maastricht Treaty and that the miscalled 'Euro-sceptics' in both major British political parties have employed ever since membership first became a serious political issue.

A further and, in some ways, even more alarming implication follows as well. This is that a social-democratic European project will continue to be, in practice, utopian. It will be utopian because the nation-states of the Union have already surrendered too much power to supranational institutions to implement it on the national level, while the institutions of the Union will continue to be too weak to implement it on the supranational level. And if this is at all true, the clear implication is that Europe will continue to be dominated, in practice, by the political right and centre-right; that capital will continue to sit in the driving seat, with little to fear from the political left or from organized labour – even if nominally left or centre-left governments hold office in certain capitals, as is the case at present in Spain. Though the Spanish socialists are still in office, it is worth remembering, their programme is not very different from that of the neo-Thatcherites under John Major in this country. And if this is all true, the likelihood is that European governments will continue to respond to international competition by hollowing out the welfare state, arguably the greatest achievement of European civilization in this century.

Last, but not least, eastern Europe will, on present trends, remain outside the new Union, an impoverished hinterland, cut off from the rich and complacent west by a new kind of Berlin Wall – a wall of patronizing indifference, tinged with suppressed fear, rather than of concrete. There is, of course, an argument for keeping the countries of eastern Europe out of the Union. It is a spurious one, but that does not make it any less persuasive to those who want, for other reasons, to accept it. It is that the economies of the eastern countries are too weak to sustain the competition implied by full membership; that if they were to become full members on terms that made it possible for them to escape the rigours of competition, the famous 'acquis communautaire' would be fatally jeopardized in the existing member states; and that this would compromise the whole European project. The premise is true, although the conclusion does not follow; and because the premise is true, the argument has great resonance in the capitals of western Europe and still more, perhaps, in the strange Euro-half-capital that clusters around the Berlaymont building in Brussels.

The trouble is that it carries great dangers – dangers symbolized most poignantly and most powerfully by the word 'Sarajevo'. The problems of transition in eastern Europe have turned out to be enormously more difficult, and the solutions enormously more painful, than anyone expected in the euphoria of 1989. The former Czechoslovakia apart, the societies which will be suffering the pains have few or no democratic traditions to draw upon and, in almost all of them, ethnic hatreds and irredentist ambitions are rife. Fragile new regimes, long on hope but short on experience, necessarily dependent on the bureaucracies they have inherited from their Stalinist predecessors and encumbered by expectations they cannot satisfy, may well see in these ambitions their only reservoir of popular support. That is the inner meaning of the Bosnian tragedy; and there are plenty of other potential Bosnias in eastern Europe. These potential Bosnias are far more likely to suffer the fate of the real Bosnia if eastern Europe is excluded from the Union taking shape in the west than if it has a reasonable prospect of joining it in a timescale which is not impossibly remote. If they do suffer that fate, it is hard to believe that smug and prosperous western Europe could insulate itself from the ensuing conflicts, any more than the western Europe of 1914 could insulate itself from the consequences of what happened at Sarajevo then.

If there are plenty of potential Bosnias in eastern Europe, there are far more in the former Soviet Union, where the Stalinist terror was even more savage and did even more to destroy the mutual trust which provides the basis of a civic culture. Partly because of this, and partly because of the very nature of the Soviet regime, economic dislocation has already gone much further in its successor-states than in the lands between the new united Germany and the former Soviet border, while ethnic conflicts and resentments are even fiercer. For the collapse of the Soviet Union has spelt more than the collapse of another economically irrational and politically illegitimate communist regime. It has also spelt the end of the last great European empire; and the end of empire is almost always a bloody business. So far bloodshed has been much rarer than it was in the Indian subcontinent after the end of the British Raj, or in North Africa during the war against the French, but upheavals on that scale cannot be ruled out.

II

Why should these trends, so gloomy compared to those that seemed to be in operation in the late 1980s and early 1990s, in the aftermath of the Single European Act and the dismantling of the Berlin wall, appear to be in the ascendant now? I shall argue that the answer to that question lies in a series of confusions, of paradoxes, perhaps even of contradictions at the heart of the European project, at least in its contemporary form. In trying to explore these paradoxes and contradictions, I hasten to add, I imply no criticism of the founding fathers of the European Community. On the contrary, I believe that Monnet, De Gasperi, Schuman and the rest were giants in their generation. They were statesmen of extraordinary inventiveness and extraordinary cour-age. If there is a criticism to be made, and I think there is, it should be directed not to them but to their latter-day followers who trod mechanically in their footsteps without realizing that times had changed.

What are these paradoxes? The first is a paradox of identity. We speak of the European Union, or the European Community, but what is meant by 'Europe'? Where are its boundaries? What are the essential features of a European identity? The founding fathers never asked these questions. They never defined what they meant by 'Europe'. They did not define it because they had no need to define it. Their Europe was, in practice, the Europe of Charle-magne, with the addition of southern Italy. It was the Europe of the Po Valley in northern Italy and of the lands clustered around the River Rhine: the Europe of Adenauer's Germany allied to the Europe of Charlemagne's France. And this Europe – the little Europe of Charlemagne – huddled in the shadow of American power, which it saw as its only feasible protector against the perceived threat from the east. Community Europe was in reality Carolingian Europe until Britain, Ireland and Denmark acceded to it twenty-one years later. Then, in the early 1970s, Community Europe expanded to include a northern addition; and in the early

1980s, it expanded again to include the Iberian peninsula and Greece. Apart from the last-named, it is worth noting, this was, to a very considerable extent, Catholic Christendom (including, under that heading, formerly Catholic countries which became Protestant in the sixteenth and seventeenth centuries). To be sure, it did not include the whole of Catholic Christendom. Austria, Poland, what until recently we knew as Czechoslovakia, and the northern parts of what we used to know as Yugoslavia, were also part of Catholic Christendom in the Middle Ages, but did not belong to the Community either of the nine or of the twelve.

Now if 'Europe' does mean Catholic Christendom – and implicit in the arguments of many of the participants in the debate about further enlargement is the assumption that this is the most that Europe can ever mean – then clearly Poland, the Czech Republic, Hungary, Croatia and Slovenia, as well as Austria and Scandinavia should, at least in principle, and at least in due time, become part of it politically. But why should Europe be defined as Catholic Christendom? What about Orthodox Christendom? Greece, after all, is already in the Community and Greece is part of Orthodox Christendom, not of Catholic Christendom. And if 'Europe' includes Orthodox Christendom then there is no legitimate reason for excluding Romania, Bulgaria, Serbia (if Serbia should eventually become a democracy of some sort), the Ukraine and perhaps Russia. Is Russia 'European' or not? If Greece is 'European', why is Russia not 'European'? Following the collapse of the communist regimes of eastern Europe and the subsequent collapse of the Soviet Union these questions are now, at least by implication, on the table.

Secondly, there has been a paradox of territory. At the heart of this paradox lies a coincidence between economic convergence in the dynamic core of the Community and divergence in the periphery. Increasingly, the economic geography of late twentieth-century Europe is coming to resemble the economic geography of the late Middle Ages. At the heart of the Union is a grid of prosperity, where the line of Lombardy to the Rhine to the North Sea crosses the line of Munich to Marseilles and perhaps to Barcelona. That grid has become enormously, inconceivably more prosperous than ever before. But while economic integration has speeded up the development of this grid of prosperity, of the core of the Community, its impact on the periphery has been less benign. In absolute terms, of course, the periphery has also become more prosperous. In the boom years of the 1950s and 1960s, moreover, the gap between the periphery and the core narrowed significantly. But in the last twenty years or so, the gap between the periphery and the core has remained static at best, and widened at worst.[1]

This pattern is, of course, a familiar feature of all capitalist economies. Capitalism is centripetal. The free market rewards those who are well endowed for the market place, and punishes those who are badly endowed; and endowment includes geographical location. Nineteenth-century Britain was the classic case. The creation of a single market and monetary union between backward Ireland and advanced mainland Britain plunged the former into destitution and famine. In modern welfare democracies, however, there are strong countervailing tendencies. The tax and welfare system redistributes resources from richer to poorer territories as well as from richer to poorer persons – in large measure, of course, because there is a higher proportion of poor persons in poor territories than in rich ones. One reason why the tax and welfare system does this is that electoral competition gives the poorer territories political clout with which, at least to some extent, to redress the balance of market competition.

In the virtual one-party state which is the present-day United Kingdom, it should be noted, these countervailing tendencies have been blunted because the political party that represents the poorer territories has been out of power for so long that these territories have lost much of their political clout. But that merely underlines the point. In a normally functioning welfare democracy, the ballot box gives the poorer territories an instrument with which to mitigate the pressures towards ever greater concentration that emanate from the capitalist free market; the reason that these pressures are not effectively mitigated in present-day Britain is that present-day Britain has ceased to be a normally functioning welfare democracy. And that leads on to the really critical point. The mechanisms of territorial redistribution – electoral competition combined with a modern tax and welfare system – do not exist in the European Community. Plainly, the tax and welfare system remains under national control. In a strange way, the same is true of the electoral system. The European Parliament exists; political forces compete for representation in it; but it is not a European equivalent of a national Parliament. The political forces which are represented in it organize and compete on a national, not on a European, level. In any case, it is so weak that electoral competition for representation in it has little more than a symbolic significance. Such political clout as poor territories possess – and it is not very impressive in quantity or quality – derives from the representation of poor *states* in the Council of Ministers, not from the representation of poor *people* in the European Parliament.

The problem is political, not technical. As I showed in chapter 5, the MacDougall Report suggested that a Community budget, accounting for 5–7 per cent of total community GDP, could be as effective an agent of territorial redistribution as are the budgets of federal states.[2] This, of course, was in a Community of nine. In a Union of twelve the proportion would need to be larger. The real significance of the MacDougall Report, however, is that it quickly became a dead letter – not because of any technical imperfections in the case it set out, but because the political will which would have been needed to implement the kind of project it advocated simply did not exist. And herein lies the essence of the paradox of territory. The real obstacles to monetary union – the forces that actually generated the waves of speculation which have inflicted so much damage on the European Monetary System – are territorial. Monetary union between the core and the periphery would speed up the process of concentration. It would be good for the core. It does not follow that it would be good for the periphery, any more than monetary union between nineteenth-century Ireland and mainland Britain was good for Ireland or than post-unification monetary union between northern Italy and the Mezzogiorno was good for the Mezzogiorno. Until these economic realities have been addressed, there will be no monetary union, however fervently political leaders may proclaim their commitment to it, and half-way houses on the lines of the European Monetary System will always be vulnerable to speculative pressure. But the realities cannot be addressed through technical fixes. Here, as in so many areas of social life, only politics can countervail markets.

That brings me to the third paradox: the paradox of supranationalism. Supporters of the European project customarily proclaim that its object is to transcend the nation-state or national sovereignty. I suggest that the truth has always been more complicated. The founding fathers did wish to transcend the nation-state in certain crucial areas of policy, but they wished to transcend it because they also wished to reconstruct it. Above all, they – or at least the most important of them – wished to reconstruct the two key nation-states of Carolingian western Europe, Germany and France. Adenauer in one way, and the governments of Fourth

Republic France in a slightly different way, both saw in the formation of the European Community a means to give their weak and insecure regimes greater legitimacy and greater efficacy. With extraordinary genius they saw that the best way to do this was to surrender control over certain key areas to supranational institutions. And, as Alan Milward has brilliantly argued in his latest book, they succeeded.[3] On any reasonable definition, the nation-states of France and Germany are far stronger than they were when the Community was set up forty years ago. They are more respected. They are more firmly based in popular support. They are more efficacious; and they have greater legitimacy than they did at the beginning of the post-war period.

To be sure, the United Kingdom is an exception. The trajectory of the British state has been downwards, not upwards. But it is a piece of Anglocentric insularity to imagine that, because the British state has lost strength, efficacy and legitimacy since the early 1950s, the same must necessarily be true of all nation-states. In most of western Europe, the reverse is the case. This, however, is where the paradox comes into the story. The nation-states of Carolingian little Europe, of the Europe of the six which is still and will, for the foreseeable future, remain the heartland of the Union, have become stronger because they have created a chain of interdependencies which has made it impossible, or at the very least extremely expensive, for them to act unilaterally in certain key areas – notably in the key area of macro-economic management, and latterly even in the key area of industrial policy. The nation-states have not transcended sovereignty exactly. They remain sovereign: indeed, they cling to their sovereignty. They also remain overwhelmingly the most important focus for political loyalty and political activity. Yet the very processes through which they have regained the legitimacy and efficacy which they lost during the Second World War have made it increasingly difficult for them to act in the ways in which the social-democratic state of the post-war period used to act.

III

That leads on to a fourth paradox. I shall call it the paradox of functionalism. By that I mean that the process of integration, as it has been conceived up to now in Europe, has gradually become self-stultifying – not because it has failed, but because it has succeeded. A brief historical reminder may be appropriate at this point. As everyone knows, the late 1940s saw a vigorous debate among supporters of European union between those who favoured a functional approach and those who wished to see the early creation of a federal system. As everyone also knows, function-alism prevailed. Functionalism prevailed because the interests of the nation-states and the aspiration for European unity could, so to speak, join forces in seeking gradual integration of key sectors of the economy. Now, in the early 1950s, integrationists assumed that this process would set in motion an irresistible, ineluctable pressure for ever more integration, until in the end political union would come about almost of its own accord. It was a kind of bastard Marxism. Economics was the base, politics was the superstructure; to change the metaphor, economics was the horse dragging the cart of politics behind it.

From that key assumption flow some of the preconceptions which now bedevil debate on the future of the Union. The debate over 'widening' versus 'deepening' in relation to eastern Europe is the most obvious case in point. Wideners and deepeners have different aims, but they share a critically important assumption. Both those who want to see the Union enlarge first and engage in further integration later, and those who want more integration first and further enlargement later, if at all, take it for granted that politics follows economics. Wideners, for the most part, wish to slow down the process of integration in the existing Union. They are for widening because they are against deepening; for incorpo-rating the eastern European countries because they want to weaken the forces making for further integration in the west. The deepeners object to widening for exactly the same reason. They fear that, as things are at present, widening would indeed inhibit deepening; and they are against it for that reason.

A parallel set of assumptions has shaped the debate about the single market and monetary union in western Europe. Central to the case for monetary union is that it is the logical, inevitable concomitant of a single market and the logical, preordained precursor of political union. On one level, that is true. A single market combined with stable exchange rates and with the free movement of capital across national boundaries is inconceivable, in the long run, without a single currency; and a single currency is inconceivable in the long run without an authority of some kind to run it. Ultimately, then, a single currency entails a qualitative jump towards political union: to that extent, Lady Thatcher and the British Euro-sceptics are right.

IV

Unfortunately, this logic does not apply to the first step in the process. Though it is true that a single currency entails a qualitative jump towards political union, it does not follow that a single market *entails* a qualitative jump towards a single currency. The débâcle which has overcome the European monetary system and the stalling which has taken place in the various countries of western Europe since the Maastricht Treaty was signed point in a less comforting direction. So long as there is no political authority to ensure territorial justice, to overcome the centripetal tendencies inherent in a capitalist free-market economy, the periphery will not be able to sustain monetary union; and so long as the periphery cannot sustain monetary union, monetary union will be incomplete. There is, in short, a contradiction between the monetary ambitions of the Union and its territorial divergences. Unless and until that contradiction is resolved, the Union is as likely to move backward as forward. And the contradiction can be resolved only by and through political institutions.

The implications are plain. The Maastricht Treaty, it is now clear, did not go nearly far enough. Indeed, in certain crucial respects it went in the wrong direction. For Maastricht was rooted in the technocratic economism of the Community's salad days. It was based on the assumption that a single market would lead ineluctably to monetary union, and a monetary union to political union. There was no need to mobilize consent for the eventual political union; it would emerge, of its own accord, from the bosom of history. By the same token, there was no need to examine the political obstacles to monetary union or to try patiently to overcome them. Monetary union was a technical matter, to be achieved by technical means.

As so often in history, developments since Maastricht have shown that economism of this sort is usually false, and often dangerous. The notion that politics can be a sort of cart, dragged along by the horse of economics, has no place outside the fairy-tale worlds of classical Marxism and classical economic liberalism. In the real world, politics is always the horse and economics the cart. Now that this ancient truth has been painfully rediscovered, the

European left, above all, should draw the obvious conclusion. Recognizing that its aims cannot be achieved in the half-way house created by the Maastricht Treaty, and that there is no future in reverting to the beggar-my-neighbour myopia of an 'Europe des patries', it should embrace a new version of the federalism of the forties, based on the good Christian-democratic principle of subsidiarity.

The kind of subsidiarity now needed, however, is not the kind implied in the Maastricht Treaty. Maastricht-style subsidiarity is offered as a principle of universal validity, to be realized in the same way in all parts of the emerging Union. In the Europe in which we live and will continue to live, that approach is likely to prove a blind alley. For a long time to come, the level of government on which decision-making will be effective will vary, not just from subject to subject, but from country to country. In the Community's hard-currency core, whose members can already meet the Maastricht conditions for monetary union without much difficulty, decision-making in the monetary sphere would be conducted more effectively on a supranational level. In the weak-currency periphery, that is not yet true.

The real question is how much diversity an emerging political union can stand without dissolving into its constituent parts. Plainly, that question cannot be answered *a priori*. But it is worth noting that in the United States, arguably the world's most successful continental-size federation, the role of the federal government was, by the standards of contemporary European nation-states, extremely limited until well into the twentieth century, and that the states differed hugely both in economic performance and in the scope of public power. If the Community were to develop along the lines suggested here, there would have to be a significant redistribution of functions between the regional, national and supranational tiers. Responsibility for foreign and security policy would pass quite quickly to the Community. In the core countries, the same would be true of monetary policy. But since the pursuit of Community-wide free competition would have taken a back seat, at any rate as far as the new eastern and central European members were concerned, the deregulation and re-regulation needed to achieve a Community-wide 'level playing field' would not have to be extended to them; and the competences which Community institutions have had to assume in order to carry it out in the little Europe of the west could be left at the national level. In the west European periphery, the same would be true of monetary policy for a long time to come. To put the point in another way, the model of Community federalism would be closer to that of the early nineteenth-century United States than to that of late twentieth-century Germany.

The result would be untidy. Politically the Community would be a federation, but of a loose and limited kind. A wide range of functions would be devolved to the regional, rather than to the national level. Economically, things would be much less clear. In the little-European heartland there would be a single (and social) market, on 1992 lines. To the east, to the south, and across the Channel, there would be a variety of economic regimes, all moving slowly towards full incorporation, but at different speeds. At first sight it would look rather like the Europe of 'variable geometry' which has sometimes been seen as a way of solving the British problem. But economic variation would be combined with political union, instead of being seen as an excuse for delaying it.

1994

• PART THREE •

Britain

CHAPTER EIGHT

History Derailed?

I start with a quotation. It comes from H. G. Wells's marvellous political novel – in my view one of the greatest novels of political ideas ever written – *The New Machiavelli*, published in 1911. The novel traces the hero's intellectual and emotional journey from the Liberal back-benches in the House of Commons and a fairly conventional social-liberal creed to membership of the Conservative Party and an idiosyncratic mixture of Milnerite social imperialism, feminism and marital infidelity. At a fairly early stage in his peregrination, when he is still a Liberal MP and only half-aware of the gulf of attitude and belief that divides him from colleagues, he muses as follows on the nature of his party:

> Liberalism never has been nor ever can be anything but a diversified crowd ... It is a gathering together of all the smaller interests which find themselves at a disadvantage against the big established classes, the leasehold tenant as against the landowner, the retail tradesman as against the merchant and moneylender, the Nonconformist as against the Churchman, the small employer as against the demoralising hospitable publican, the man without introductions and broad connections against the man who has these things ... It has no more essential reason for loving the Collectivist state than the Conservatives; the small dealer is doomed to absorption in that just as much as the large owner; but it resorts to the state against its antagonists as in the middle ages common men pitted themselves against the barons by siding with the king. The Liberal Party is the party against class privilege because it represents no class advantages, but it is also the party that is on the whole most set against Collective control because it represents no established responsibility. It is constructive only so far as its antagonism to the great owner is more powerful than its jealousy of the state. It is

organised only because organisation is forced upon it by the organisation of its adversaries. It lapses in and out of alliance with Labour as
it sways between hostility to wealth and hostility to public
expenditure.[1]

Time is too short to tease out all the assumptions which
underpin that vivid caricature. Three, however, seem reasonably
plain. The first and most obvious is the quintessentially Fabian
assumption that the intellectually and organizationally tidy should
and would prevail over the variegated, the spontaneous and the
unruly. The weight of numbers, Wells was saying, might, for a
time, enable a Liberal-style 'diversified crowd' to overwhelm its
rivals, as the Liberals had overwhelmed theirs in 1906. But such
success could only be temporary. In government, as in war,
heterogeneity, diversity and variety were handicaps. Lasting success went to the expert, the disciplined, the well-drilled. The
second assumption was that the omnicompetent 'Collectivist state',
managed by tidy-minded experts, was bound to be the wave of the
future. The third was that this was a wave which the Liberal Party,
by its very nature, was unable to ride. Though this is less obvious,
and though Wells himself might have repudiated the suggestion if
it had been put to him, I think a fourth assumption can also be
detected between the lines. This is the assumption that the
fragmented and heterogeneous social interests which supported
the Liberal Party were, by virtue of their fragmentation and
heterogeneity, marginal or obsolescent; and that liberalism was
therefore doomed to be ground out between the upper and nether
millstones of organized capital and organized labour, the big and
disciplined interests which would shape the twentieth century, and
around the struggle between which its politics would revolve.
History, in short, was like the young man in the limerick who 'said
Damn / For I now perceive that I am / A creature that moves / In
determinate grooves, /In fact, not a bus but a tram'. And the tram-
lines were carrying it, inexorably and irresistibly, from the small to
the big: from the disorganized to the organized; from the uncoordi-
nated to the planned; from the mushy, wishy-washy, backward-
looking compromises of liberalism to the clear, harsh, unfudgeable
choice between right and left.

That view was not, of course, unique to Wells. It was widely
held in the stormy years before the First World War when *The New
Machiavelli* was published. By the inter-war period, it had become
commonplace – not only among Marxists and *marxisants*, for
whom it was almost self-evident, but even among neo-Fabians,

like the young Evan Durbin, and maverick Conservatives, like the young Harold Macmillan. After 1945, it was part of the mental furniture of the political left, while an only slightly different version of it was almost as prevalent on the political right. From it sprang a view of the history of non-Conservative Britain which the late Sir Denis Brogan once mocked as the 'mandate-of-heaven' theory. According to this theory, there was no puzzle about the vicissitudes of the British left in the first third of the twentieth century. Primacy in the anti-Conservative camp had passed inexorably from the Liberals to the Labour Party much as, in ancient China, the mandate of heaven used inexorably to pass from one dynasty to another – usually by way of a time of trouble, scarred by the strife of rival warlords. Labour had replaced the Liberals as the main anti-Conservative party in the state because it was bound to replace them: because the Liberals' mandate had run out; because liberalism could not satisfy the needs of a class society in a collectivist age whereas Labour could.

Parallel to the mandate-of-heaven theory ran a somewhat similar set of assumptions about the evolution of public policy. These assumptions too can be traced back to the period before the First World War. One revealing source for them is that masterpiece of lucid compression, *Liberalism*,[2] written by the New Liberal theorist, L. T. Hobhouse and published in the same year as *The New Machiavelli*. Liberalism, says Hobhouse, is about freedom. But the struggle for freedom has changed direction. In the old days, the enemy was authoritarian rule in church and state. Liberals fought for equality before the law, for representative government, for freedom of speech, belief and association. But these battles have now been won, or largely won. The goal now is more complex. Liberalism is now about positive freedom, or freedom *to*, rather than about negative freedom, or freedom *from*: its task is to liberate 'the self-directing power of personality', to enable men and women to realize themselves to the full; and in order to do that, state intervention must be used to guarantee to all individuals a share in the common stock large enough to ensure that their personalities can indeed flourish.

What Hobhouse advocated, later thinkers postulated. In his seminal essay, 'Citizenship and Social Class',[3] published in 1949 as the welfare legislation of the post-war Labour government was beginning to enter society's bloodstream, the sociologist T. H. Marshall put forward an essentially Hobhousian view of the way in which the concept of citizenship and of the rights of the citizen had evolved in practice. Citizenship, said Marshall, had three elements – civil, political and social; and over the preceding three centuries the struggle for citizenship rights had shifted from the first to the second, and then from the second to the third. Civil citizenship, manifested in equal civil rights, had been established in the eighteenth century, or at any rate in the 150 years between the Glorious Revolution and the first Reform Act. Political citizenship, equality of political rights, was largely the work of the nineteenth century. In the twentieth century, the focus had shifted to social citizenship, to the struggle for equal social rights. The real meaning of the post-war welfare state was that the principle of equal social rights was now enshrined in legislation.

A similar view was implicit in the writings of Anthony Crosland, the high priest of the Labour revisionism of the 1950s, whose *Future of Socialism*[4] was for many years my political bible and the bible of a large part of my political generation. Its central thesis was that socialism was about equality, not about public ownership; that the Keynesian revolution had rendered further nationalization unnecessary; and that, in present-day circumstances, the way to achieve greater equality was to combine rapid economic growth, high welfare spending and progressive taxation. But that was only the text. To use a jargon which was not then fashionable, there was also a subtext. And the subtext was Marshallian, indeed Hobhousian. It was that the primordial social-democratic ends of greater social and economic equality – in effect, the full realization of Marshall's vision of social citizenship – could perfectly well be achieved by and through the existing political system, since that system was already egalitarian: that, in this country, political citizenship and political rights were secure; and that, because they were secure, democratic socialists could concentrate on social reform and leave the policy to take care of itself.

And so I came, by a rather roundabout route, to my title. It seems to me that, in the early post-war period when Marshall and Crosland wrote, *bien pensant*, liberal-minded, broadly progressive opinion shared a view of twentieth-century British history – often without acknowledging or even realizing the fact, of course – which could fairly be described as partly Wellsian and partly Marshallian. History was seen as a great engine, proceeding gradually, inexorably, for the most part peacefully, always beneficently, along two parallel rails. One rail, the Wellsian rail, had to do with social structure, economic organization, political mobilization. The other, the Marshallian rail, had to do with policy, legislation, political objectives. The first ran, in the social and economic domain, from individualism to collectivism and, in the political, from declining liberalism to rising labour. The second ran from completed civil and political citizenship to a still expanding social citizenship. In short, the prevailing interpretation of modern British history – certainly on the left, but not only the left – was essentially Whig. Post-war history was seen as part of a long continuum of progress, going back well into the nineteenth century if not before, marked, above all, by the growth of the state, the coming of democracy, the rise of the working class and the extension of citizenship. Along those rails, moreover, History not only ran but would continue to run.

II

It is not difficult to see why that interpretation prevailed in the early post-war period. It may be that all politicians have to be Whigs in their approach to history, even if not in their politics. Only if they are sustained by the belief that they are working with the grain of the times – that they are travelling in history's direction and history in theirs – can they acquire a sense of purpose and direction, and avoid being overwhelmed by the pressures of the immediate. Be that as it may, the particular version of the Whig interpretation which I have tried to describe seemed, for a long time, to work. It enabled politicians, civil servants, pressure-group leaders and commentators to make sense of the era in which they lived; to locate themselves and their problems in time; in the simplest and most basic sense to know where they were going. The trouble, of course, is that after a while, it ceased to work. It made sense – or appeared to make sense – of the broadly social-liberal or social-democratic trajectory on which our society and politics seemed set in the 1940s, 1950s and early 1960s. It made no sense of the bewildering change of trajectory which took place in the 1970s; and which manifested itself most obviously in Mrs Thatcher's victory in 1979 and in her conduct thereafter. Suddenly, inexplicably, for no reason that the familiar, post-war interpretation could provide, history had left the Wellsian and Marshallian rails. The engine was no longer proceeding sedately towards ever more collectivism, an ever stronger Labour movement and ever wider citizenship rights. It lay helpless on the embankment, clouds of steam escaping from its cylinders, while the passengers clambered aboard a rival train, going in the opposite direction. For those of my political generation, who had been schooled so thoroughly in the post-war interpretation that they took it for granted, this state of affairs was, at one and the same time, extraordinary, outrageous and profoundly disorientating. It was as though history had turned traitor.

One common defence against a shock of this sort is to play down the events that caused it: to try to convince oneself that nothing much has happened and that life can go on as before. Another is to play them up: to depict oneself as the victim of an immeasurable disaster which no one could have prevented and for which no one is to blame. Both can be detected in the debate, now more than ten years old, over the meaning of the times through which we are now living. One school of thought questions whether the change of trajectory I have mentioned really took place at all. It holds that the Thatcher Revolution (or Counter-Revolution) has made only marginal differences to the real world; that 'Thatcherism' is a matter of style, personality and rhetoric, not of substance; that it is, in any event, an aberration which has now run its course; and that it always owed more to the contingencies of the moment than to any coherent ideology or political project. The other school argues that, on the contrary, the change of trajectory has been far more profound and all-encompassing than I have so far suggested: that it is the product of a sweeping, worldwide paradigm shift, extending from the process of production through the structure of industry and the organization of the economy to the shaping of social, political and even personal identities. Thatcherism, on this view, is merely the local, British froth on a mighty wave of change, sweeping through all industrial societies. Everywhere, 'organized capitalism' is giving way to 'disorganized'; government regulation to deregulation; what is sometimes called 'Fordist' mass production to flexible, small-scale 'post-Fordist' industrial processes; and planning, corporatism and state intervention to a new reliance on market forces.[5]

There are, I think, elements of truth in both these views. It is not difficult to show that, after a decade of Thatcherism, neither the market-liberal utopia envisaged in the writings of Friedrich von Hayek and Milton Friedman nor the 'enterprise culture' dreamed of by Lords Joseph and Young has come to pass. In ten years, the government's share of the gross domestic product has fallen only a trifle more than 3 per cent. The proportion of non-oil GDP taken by taxation and national insurance contributions is slightly higher than it was when Mrs Thatcher came to power. The economy is still dominated by large firms. Wage inflation has not been conquered. If survey data are anything to go by, the public remain obstinately attached to the Beveridgean welfare state and are willing to pay higher taxes to finance better public services.[6] By the same token, there is not much doubt that the contingencies of fate and accidents of personality have loomed as large in the life of this government as in that of all governments; or that Thatcherism, whether or not it can usefully be described as an 'ideology' and whether or not it has now run its course, has been far more flexible in practice than the demeanour of its chief progenitor is apt to suggest. Equally it is plain that at least some aspects of the Thatcher Revolution have their equivalents in other industrial countries; that what Samuel Beer once called 'hubristic Keynesianism'[7] is no longer in fashion anywhere; that the kind of planning successfully practised by Gaullist France and unsuccessfully copied by Wilsonian Britain has been abandoned almost everywhere; and that part of the explanation for all this lies in a complex, far-reaching set of technological, economic and social changes which have had a dramatic impact on the entire industrial world.

But when all the qualifications have been made, I remain convinced that a change of trajectory of some sort occurred at some stage in the last fifteen or twenty years; that the course our society and politics have taken in the final quarter of the post-war period has been significantly and importantly different from the course they were following in the first half of it; and that, to put it at its lowest, this change of course was connected with the change of regime which took place in 1979. I also remain convinced that, although the new trajectory has important features in common with the trajectories currently being followed by most other developed industrial societies, it has other features which are unique to Britain. Even if it be true that organized capitalism is everywhere giving way to disorganized capitalism, it does not follow that disorganized capitalism inevitably produces Thatcherism. As the current struggle over the Brussels Commission's Social Charter should have reminded us, it has not done so in the rest of the European Community. In short: something happened in 1979 or thereabouts; and the something was not worldwide.

What was it and why did it happen? Why did the historical engine, having puffed for so long under the Wellsian and

Marshallian rails, depart from them so disconcertingly? Why does the Whiggery of the post-war period, which seemed so plausible when I was growing up, now seem so antiquated? Why has the political climate of the last ten or fifteen years been so different from what most people, irrespective of their own wishes, would have expected in 1945, or 1955 or even, I dare say, in 1965? These questions provide, so to speak, the backdrop to the rest of my remarks. Almost self-evidently, I cannot hope to answer them. If I am even half-right, they are the central questions of post-war British history. The most I can do in the time remaining to me is to offer some tentative speculations as to where the answers may lie.

My first speculation is this. The switch of trajectory which we are discussing should be seen as a response to an interconnected set of changes – some technological, some economic, some social, some cultural – which gradually undermined the social-liberal or social-democratic settlement of the post-war period: the settlement to which Hobhouse had looked forward and which Marshall and Crosland both celebrated. The character and direction of the response have, however, been determined by deeply rooted national attitudes and structures, going back to earlier periods of British history. New forces have appeared on the scene, but they have been marshalled by old assumptions. The undoubted contrasts between the last quarter of the post-war period and the first half of it are, in part, the products of deeper continuities with earlier times. The politics of the last decade should be seen, at least in part, as a struggle to determine the direction which the new forces are to take. In Britain (but not in all countries) the political right has so far been more successful in that struggle than its rivals. The reason is that, in Britain, the right has been able to exploit enduring features of the political culture and the political tradition which have disadvantaged the left. To return for a moment to the language of my title, the reason why history left the rails is that it was never securely on them in the first place. The reason for that is that the rails themselves were never as firm as they looked.

That leads on to the second speculation. It might be entitled the paradox of Labourism, or why the New Machiavelli was wrong. Implicit in my H. G. Wells quotation, and implicit also in the mandate-of-heaven theory of non-Conservative politics, were the twin assumptions that, in the collectivist twentieth century, the prizes would go to the big, homogeneous blocks of organized capital and organized labour; and that liberalism was therefore doomed. And so, for a while, it seemed. The Liberal Party did cease to be a serious player in the political game. The Labour Party did replace it as the main anti-Conservative presence at the table. The trouble was that the prizes went to the right, not to the left. The two-party system which prevailed from 1868 to 1918, the system of Conservatives versus Liberals, produced a total of twenty-seven years of Conservative or Conservative-dominated Government against twenty-three of Liberal. The Conservative-versus-Labour system which succeeded it has produced a strikingly different pattern. Conservative or predominantly Conservative governments have been in office for slightly more than fifty of the seventy years since the Labour Party first became the official opposition in the House of Commons, and Labour governments for only twenty. Even if we look only at the sixty years since 1929, on the grounds that Labour had not fully replaced the Liberals until then, the score is still forty-one to nineteen in the Conservatives' favour. Most of the Labour governments concerned, moreover, have either been in a minority in the House of Commons or have commanded majorities too small to allow them to legislate as they wished. Only twice – in 1945 and 1966 – has Labour won a parliamentary majority in double figures. The governments at the head of those majorities held office for a total of only nine years. A thriving academic industry has grown up around the debate over Labour's so far unimpressive electoral performance in the age of Mrs Thatcher. The real question is why that performance was so unimpressive before Mrs Thatcher was heard of.

The answers are, of course, multifarious. Part of the answer, however, is that Wells's assumption that the future lay with disciplined, homogeneous, solidaristic blocks was not merely false, but in an important sense the reverse of the truth. He was, of course, right in thinking that the heterogeneity, variety and indiscipline of the diversified Liberal crowd he anathematized were political liabilities. He failed to realize that they were assets as well. The wide-ranging, ramshackle, almost octopoid pre-1914 Liberal coalition succeeded as well as it did partly because it was wide-ranging, ramshackle and octopoid. The Labour coalition which took its place has been less successful largely because it has been more homogeneous and less diverse: and because, as a result, its range has been narrower. For Labour's strength has also been its weakness. Its strength has lain in its position as the vehicle of the labour interest, which is immanent in the very structure of industrial society, and as the embodiment of the labour ethos, which gives texture and meaning to the labour interest. Because of that it was able to topple the Liberals from their perch: to that it owes its hold on the tribal loyalties of its core constituency in the unionized working class. But precisely because it has been the vehicle of the labour interest and embodiment of the labour ethos, it has never quite managed to transcend Labourism. Only on rare occasions – 1945, 1966, conceivably today – has it managed to speak as confidently and appeal as successfully to the intermediate groups and non-labour identities outside its core constituency as to the core constituency itself; to enrol under its banner the whole of the diversified crowd which once marched behind the Liberals' banner instead of only part of it. Partly as cause and partly as consequence, its relationship with the radical intelligentsia – the suppliers of political ideas, the setters of cultural trends, the shapers of public moods – has always been uneasy. Keynes's famous remark that, although he sympathized with many of Labour's social aspirations, the class war would find him on the side of the 'educated bourgeoisie'[8] could have been echoed by thousands of lesser figures. As a result, Labour's tenure of the crucial intellectual and moral high ground of politics was always uncertain. It was never as true as Labour people liked to think that the Tories were the stupid party. In the language of the New Left, Labour never successfully challenged the cultural hegemony of the right, at any rate in the richest and most popular parts of the country. One reason is that the culture of Labourism was too narrow, too inward-looking and too defensive to give it the intellectual and moral resources with which to do so.

My third speculation has to do with the Marshallian rail rather than with the Wellsian one. In a now famous study, Albert Hirschman suggested that there are two mechanisms with which consumers may control producers. One is Exit: taking one's custom elsewhere, ceasing to buy the product, the quintessential mechanism of the market. The other is Voice: nagging, argument, persuasion, complaint. That is quintessentially the mechanism of politics. And, says Hirschman, Voice goes with and depends upon Loyalty: upon ties of mutuality which endure through time. You will listen to me only if I am loyal to you. I will think it worth while to try to persuade you only if, in some sense or other, you are loyal to me. That insight, I believe, throws a vivid shaft of light – or, to put it more precisely, two shafts of light – on the matters I have been discussing.

The first is this. The growth of social citizenship – indeed, the very notion of social citizenship – implies a smaller role for the market and a greater role for government. Exit does less and Voice does more. The pioneers of social citizenship were well aware of this, of course, but they saw no problems in it. Indeed, they rejoiced in it. For, as I tried to show a few moments ago, they took it for granted that the new social citizenship was a supplement to the old political citizenship: that the struggle for political rights and political equality had been won: that democracy, having triumphed in the political sphere, should expand into the social sphere, where the battle was still going on. Because they took this for granted, they also took it for granted that the institutions and practices of the social-citizenship state would be subject to popular control: that Voice would not only have a larger role to play, but would in practice be able to play it. What Hirschman's insight leads one to ask is whether this assumption was true. Was Voice able to play the enhanced role assigned to it? Had the struggle for political rights been won? Were the institutions of social citizen-ship effectively subject to popular control? More important still, did the supposed social citizens themselves – the patients in the doctor's waiting room, the parents outside the school playground, the tenants on the council estate, the crowd waiting to approach the DHS counter – feel that they controlled the institutions which acted in their names? Or did they even feel themselves to be the subjects of a remote and sometimes even arbitrary authority? In the heyday of the post-war settlement, these questions were not asked, much less answered. But they were posed with increasing urgency and frequency in its twilight years – not least, by the advancing New Right. On the whole, the answers were just what the New Right wanted to hear. Voice, came the reply, was not working properly in the social sphere. The social citizens did not control the institutions which were supposed to serve their needs. The social-citizenship state was not really a citizenship state at all. It was a state of subjecthood.

As everyone knows, the New Right's conclusion was that, in this field at any rate, Voice cannot work and that the only solution is therefore to return to Exit; to abandon the whole project of social citizenship; and to rely as far as possible on the market or at least on a surrogate market. That was not, of course, the only possible conclusion. Another – and in my view, the correct one – was that Hobhouse, Marshall, Crosland and the rest had been dangerously over-optimistic: that they had tried to build the top floor of

citizenship before the first floor was in place: that the real problem
was that political citizenship, which was supposed to precede
social citizenship, had not been achieved after all: that, in the most
profound sense, Britain's (or, at least, England's) was not really a
civic culture. But, for the moment at any rate, it does not matter
which conclusion was right. What matters is that, in the Britain of
the late 1970s and most of the 1980s, the New Right's conclusion
struck a resounding chord. When they were told that Voice was
bound to fail, that they would never be able effectively to control
the institutions of social citizenship, that the social citizenship state
was bound to be bureaucratic, top-heavy and remote, and that
dignity, autonomy and choice could be enhanced only by giving
greater scope to the market, large numbers of people – including
large numbers of working-class people who had formerly voted
Labour – nodded in bemused agreement. Yet I am not convinced
that their nods implied agreement with the New Right's hostility
to the values of social citizenship. As I mentioned earlier, survey
data indicate that those values remain popular. They nodded, I
suspect, for two reasons. Experience had convinced them that
there was something in the New Right's critique of the way in
which the values were put into practice. And because their
assumptions had been shaped by a non-civic culture, by a subject
culture with little or no place for active and participatory citizenship, they could see no grounds on which to quarrel with the New
Right's conclusion. Exit won the argument – and anyone who
thinks Exit did not win the argument should look at the Labour
Party's policy review – because the culture provided too little
space for Voice. Social citizenship faltered because political citizenship was lacking. When Mrs Thatcher expressed her abhorrence of
the French Revolution – and by implication of the revolutionary
promise contained in the Declaration of the Rights of Man and the
Citizen – she was evoking one of the most powerful themes of our
subject culture. In doing so, she was going a long way towards
explaining the collapse of the post-war settlement and her own
accession to power.

III

My last speculation is the most speculative: so speculative, in fact,
that it is best introduced with a question. Of what are we citizens
– 'we' being inhabitants of this island rather than members of the

human race? The Declaration of the Rights of Man and the Citizen is couched in general terms, but it has a particular reference. The citizens of whom it speaks are not disembodied abstractions, inhabiting some bloodless philosophical empyrean. They are the citizens called to arms in the 'Marseillaise': *enfants de la patrie*: products of a particular culture and history, attached by unbreakable ties of memory and identity to a particular piece of territory. And since the French Revolution, at any rate, that culture and history have usually been assumed to be national rather than provincial or local or, for that matter, international. The notion of citizenship has been inextricably bound up with the notion of nationhood. Citizens have been citizens of states; states have embodied nations. But what does nationhood mean in this strange entity known as the United Kingdom of Great Britain and Northern Ireland? And if the answer to that question is confused or problematic, what can citizenship mean? I said a moment ago that, for Hirschman, Voice goes with Loyalty, with a sense of membership of a political community, bound together by ties of mutual obligation and enduring through time. Assuming he is right, what is the community to which British citizens might be expected to be loyal?

Questions like these are among the most resonant and explosive in the modern world. It is one of the clichés of our time that, in an age of international interdependence, of global markets, global companies, supranational institutions and transnational policies, national identities have stubbornly reasserted themselves against the tide of cultural homogenization. Some of these identities have been embodied in and expressed through states. Perhaps the activities of the French state under Charles de Gaulle provide the most obvious example. But, with or without states, sometimes intransigently and selfishly, sometimes constructively and co-operatively, nations, ethnicities, linguistic or cultural collectivities which feel themselves to have common identities, have been on the march. Catalans, Basques, Flemings; Estonians, Armenians, Lithuanians; Corsicans, Welshmen, Quebecois – the list is almost endless. Yet there is one ethnic group, quite well known and with quite a notable history behind it, whose name does not spring automatically to the lips as a candidate for membership of that list. I refer, of course, to the English.

Yet it is, I think, inconceivable that the forces which have made themselves felt in this way in so many other cultures should have had no impact on England. The reason the English do not

automatically appear to be candidates for the list is not that they
do not deserve to be on it. It is that civilized, cultured, progressive
British intellectuals – whether English or non-English by origin –
do not feel comfortable with English nationalism in the way they
feel comfortable with Welsh or Scottish nationalism, or for that
matter with the nationalisms of almost everyone else. There are, I
admit, some exceptions. George Orwell was probably the most
eloquent and most moving. In his strange, quirky, mischievous
way, A. J. P. Taylor was another. But these are exceptions that prove
the rule. The cultivated, educated, progressive intelligentsia – the
class that provided the intellectual foundations of the post-war
settlement and managed and celebrated it once it was in place –
has not known how to come to terms with English nationality. Two
consequences have followed. One is the curiously strangulated,
inarticulate and reactive (I almost said reactionary) character of
English nationalism. By and large, it has been a pre-, even anti-
Enlightenment, nationalism: the nationalism of the anti-Jacobin
mobs of the 1790s or the Powellite dockers of the 1960s: the
nationalism of subjects defiantly asserting their subjecthood rather
than, as in France or the United States, the nationalism of the
sovereign people. The second consequence is that it has provided
a formidable reservoir of support for the Thatcher revolution.

For Mrs Thatcher does not belong to the cultivated progressive
intelligentsia, and does not share its inhibitions. On the contrary,
she loathes and detests it – not least because it has the characteristics I tried to describe a moment ago. She has no problems with
her English identity and no qualms about asserting it. English
nationalism – above all, the ferocious nationalism of the English
south-east – is her stock-in-trade. She has mined the seam of
radical, populist, anti-Establishment, anti-continental English nationalism which Cobbett mined so effectively in the early nineteenth century, and which Orwell hoped the left would mine
during and after the Second World War. Her success in doing so
suggests, it seems to me, that the seam was always more important
than historians and political scientists have given it credit for
being; that one reason why post-war Whiggery went adrift a little
more than half-way through the period, and why it has little to tell
us about the route to 1979, is that it paid too much attention to the
solidarities of class and not enough to the solidarities of nation.

1990

CHAPTER NINE

The Enterprise Culture: Old Wine in New Bottles?

I

The enterprise culture has been variously seen – as a slogan, as an ideology, as a dream and as a nightmare. I shall treat it as an aspiration: as an aspiration implied (though not logically entailed) by an exceedingly complex – indeed, in some respects internally contradictory – exercise in *statecraft*, some elements of which are ideological in character while others are not. I shall argue that the aspiration is unlikely to be achieved in full. But I believe that it may be, indeed that it has already been, achieved in part. I also believe that, whether it is achieved or not, the attempt to achieve it is likely to have profound consequences for our political economy and our political, cultural and moral lives. I shall focus principally on the nature, antecedents, rationale and implications of the aspiration, but I also want to speculate a little on the possible consequences of pursuing it.

Unfortunately, this is easier said than done. The term is heavily loaded with emotion, both favourable and unfavourable; like many such terms, it is also swathed in confusion. Therefore, I shall begin by making certain distinctions. In the first place, I distinguish between an (or the) enterprise culture and the existence within a given society of enterprising people. This may seem an obvious distinction, but it is nevertheless an important one. Advocates of the enterprise culture often suggest that it is only in such a culture that enterprising people are to be found, or at any rate that such a culture is uniquely hospitable to enterprising people. Since most of us like to think we are enterprising, that suggestion is a powerful rhetorical weapon. But if the term is defined in such a way, it ceases to be of any analytical value, and there is no point in discussing it any further. Enterprising people exist and have existed in a huge range of societies; to judge by the decorations in the tombs of the Valley of the Kings, there were plenty of them in Pharaonic Egypt, and the most cursory reading of the *Iliad* shows that they were equally plentiful in Homeric Greece. But it would obviously be ludicrous to suggest that these were enterprise cultures.

Secondly, I distinguish between the enterprise culture and the competitive market. I do so because advocates of the enterprise culture often seem to take it for granted that it is an indispensable prerequisite of a market economy; indeed, they sometimes use the two terms almost interchangeably. This seems to me a very dangerous oversimplification. Whatever else it may or may not be, today's enterprise culture is plainly an echo or a replica of the early nineteenth-century 'entrepreneurial idea' which Harold Perkin so memorably described some years ago.[1] And, as Perkin has himself argued, markets antedated the entrepreneurial ideal by centuries, if not by millennia. But it is not necessary to go back to the dawn of human society to see that the bundle of ideas associated with the word 'market' and the bundle associated with the word 'enterprise' belong in two different compartments. In the mixed economies that have been characteristic of the developed western world since the Second World War, resources have been largely allocated by the market. But the mixed economies of the post-war period were not sustained by enterprise cultures, and in certain crucial respects the governing philosophies of those who managed them ran counter to the principles underlying what is now advocated as the enterprise culture. Indeed, advocates of the enterprise culture were (and are) fiercely critical of the mixed economy on precisely those grounds. To put the point at its simplest and crudest, while it may be true that an enterprise culture cannot exist without a market economy, the converse does not hold.

Thirdly, I distinguish between the enterprise culture and the wave of change that has swept through the world economy in the last fifteen or twenty years, and which, in the opinion of many observers, is replacing the 'organized capitalism' of the post-war period with a new kind of 'disorganized capitalism'. All over the western world, this school of thought argues, the last fifteen years have been marked by a switch from 'Fordist' to 'post-Fordist'. industrial processes; by the decline of traditional mass-production in favour of new forms of 'flexible specialization'; indeed, by the emergence of a new 'techno-economic paradigm' based on customized products made for specialized markets, small production runs, decentralized decision-making and a new kind of craftsmanship. At the same time, disillusion with 1960s-style 'heroic' planning has encouraged a shift away from the 'macro-corporatism' that often underpinned that form of planning. Irrespective of ideology, government after government has sought to give freer rein to market forces; everywhere 'deregulation' has been the order of the day.[2] British advocates of the enterprise culture have spotted these trends, and have sought to assimilate them into their argument. It is because Britain is moving towards an enterprise culture, they claim, that these changes have taken place; the fact that they are taking place proves that the enterprise culture runs with the grain of the times. Unfortunately for that argument, such changes have appeared throughout the western world; indeed, it is at least arguable that they have gone further in parts of continental Europe than they have here.[3] But it is only in the United Kingdom (and perhaps in the United States) that governments have also sought to create an enterprise culture.

Hence, to take one of the most obvious recent examples, consider the battle currently taking place over the so-called 'social dimension' of the European Community's 1992 project. As is well known, the 1992 project involves a massive exercise in deregulation, designed to set market forces free and, in doing so, to promote higher investment and more rapid growth. As such, it fits the paradigm of 'disorganized capitalism' rather well. In the view of the Brussels Commission and of most Community member governments, a necessary corollary is a social programme designed partly to ensure that deregulation does not lead to what the Germans call 'social dumping' or a 'race for the bottom', and partly to maintain a social and political consensus in favour of the project. Mrs Thatcher and her colleagues approved of deregulation, but they violently opposed the proposition that its effects should be mitigated by social policies at the European level. Indeed, they attacked the Commission's Social Charter as 'corporatist' and even as 'Marxist' – in other words, as incompatible with their version of the enterprise culture. But most continental governments (including the Christian Democratic government of West Germany) support it, because to them it is axiomatic that social partnership and a social consensus are prerequisites of a successful programme of deregulation and perhaps also of a successful market economy.

Behind this difference of opinion, there lies, I believe, a much more fundamental difference of approach, which in turn reflects an even deeper difference of culture and tradition. The British government, supported by British advocates of the enterprise culture *à l'anglaise* or *à l'américaine*, holds, in effect, that economic change and adjustment to economic change come and can only come through the market: in Albert Hirschman's suggestive language, through Exit and the threat of Exit.[4] The undistorted, competitive market rewards economic agents who adjust and punishes those who fail to adjust; thus, the enterprising and adaptable prosper, while the unenterprising and unadaptable fall by the wayside. Interference with market forces, whether by the state or by the intermediate voluntary associations of civil society, can only slow down the adjustment process. The continental tradition embodied in the Brussels Commission's Social Charter sees the processes of change and adjustment in a more complex way. It does not deny that Exit and the threat of Exit have a part to play. But it holds that Exit can and should be supplemented by what Hirschman called Voice: that economic agents are influenced not only by the hope of reward and the fear of punishment, but by persuasion, negotiation and mutual education.

Hand in hand with this difference goes a more subtle one. Economic change produces losers as well as gainers. Central to the politics of change is the question of how to deal with losers and potential losers. As John Zysman has argued, if change is to take place, losers and potential losers must either be bought off, or swept aside.[5] Implicit in the tradition of Anglo-Saxon economic liberalism is the assumption that losers must be swept aside – most obviously by the market, but also by the state, whose role is to ensure that market forces are not impeded and that market outcomes are not interfered with. In the continental tradition, losers are bought off (as, for example, in the Common Agricultural Policy): a degree of strict allocative economic efficiency is sacrificed for the sake of social peace and political consensus. Not the least of the implications of the Social Charter and the divergent responses to it is that these differences of tradition and assumption have survived the huge techno-economic shifts of the late twentieth century; that 'post-Fordist' 'disorganized capitalism' (if that is indeed what we are seeing) can perfectly well coexist with an economic culture quite different from the enterprise culture of present-day Britain and the United States.

Finally, I distinguish between the enterprise culture and what Samuel Beer has called the 'romantic revolt'.[6] By this, Beer meant the complex shift of mood and sensibility that seems to have taken place in many, if not all, advanced industrial societies in the 1960s and 1970s. Central to this shift, in Beer's view, was a new assertion of the 'romantic' values of authenticity, spontaneity and individuality and a corresponding rejection of hierarchy, bureaucracy and externally imposed classifications and identities. This 'romantic revolt', he thought, had undermined the collectivist policy of the post-war period, because it had facilitated class decomposition and eroded the authority both of corporatist producer groups and of the old, elitist political class. All this had made necessary a switch to a new populism reminiscent of that of the United States.

The extent – even the existence – of such a romantic revolt is clearly debatable. Personally, I think Beer spotted something. I also think there is a connection between his romantic revolt and the enterprise culture of the Thatcherites. In particular, I think that the rhetoric of the enterprise culture – the rhetoric of 'choice', 'freedom', 'individualism', 'initiative' and the rest – appeals because it strikes chords that the romantic revolt has brought into existence. In spite of all of this, however, I still believe that the enterprise culture and the romantic revolt must be distinguished from each other. In the first place, the range of identities legitimized by the enterprise culture is very limited. It gives increased scope for one's identity as a consumer, but not for other identities. Indeed, it is positively hostile to identity-choices that threaten the authority of the entrepreneur and the supremacy of entrepreneurial values. You can be a heretic ranging the supermarket shelves, but you must be a conformist everywhere else – necessarily, since it is of the essence of the enterprise culture that it gives pride of place to entrepreneurial values and to the entrepreneurial character type. (This is another reason why the enterprise culture should be distinguished from the market economy: the market is morally neutral, but the enterprise culture extols particular moral values at the expense of others.) More important still, the romantic revolt is essentially anti-hierarchical: the values of authenticity and individuality run against the values of order, discipline and obedience. Despite its individualistic rhetoric, however, the enterprise culture, at least as understood by its most enthusiastic advocates, is, in one crucially important respect, profoundly hierarchical. The modern free market, it is important to remember, is a place where hierarchically organized firms compete for custom: part of the point of the enterprise culture is to empower the consumer in the market, but part is to legitimize hierarchy in the firm.

II

Having spent some time discussing what the enterprise culture is not, I now want to discuss what it is, or at least what it may be. Here I agree with Harold Perkin. What is under discussion, it seems to me, is a latter-day version of the nineteenth-century entrepreneurial ideal: an attempt to realize Sir Keith Joseph's 1975 aim to resume 'the forward march of *embourgeoisement* which went so far in Victorian times'.[7] I also agree with Perkin that this involves a kind of historiographical conjuring trick, which it is important to see through. The trick, of course, is to equate the modern, bureaucratic, hierarchical, professionally managed firm with the individualistic owner-manager of early capitalism. Advocates of the enterprise culture seek to justify the power and rewards of private-sector corporate managers and of the outcomes of market competition between the corporations they manage, just as supporters of the nineteenth-century entrepreneurial ideal sought to justify the social claims of the individualistic owner-managers of that period. Moreover, the justification offered by the former is essentially the same as that once offered by the latter. Just as the nineteenth-century entrepreneurial ideal depicted the owner-manager as a Promethean hero who, by his abstinence, enterprise and willingness to take risks, created the wealth that the whole society enjoyed, so the advocates of the enterprise culture depict the professional managers of today's private-sector corporations as the wealth creators on whose enterprise and dedication the prosperity of the rest of us depends.[8] But there the similarity ends. Despite the obvious special pleading of its advocates, the entrepreneurial ideal of the nineteenth century referred to a recognizable social reality. The owner-manager it celebrated was not, of course, a Promethean hero to everyone – that depended on one's point of view – but he did at least exist and he was at least an entrepreneur. He did risk his own capital, and he did have to survive in a fiercely competitive market. However enterprising they may be in the ordinary sense of the word, today's corporate managers are not, in that sense, entrepreneurs. They risk other people's capital, not their own. And although the giant firms they run still compete with each other, the market in which they do so is a quite different creature from the atomistic market of 150 years ago.

This leads on to one of the most puzzling features of the whole subject. To put it simply, why should any justification be necessary? Supporters of the free market often imply that markets are in some profound sense natural and that institutions or practices that 'distort' it are in some sense unnatural. Then why not simply eliminate such 'distortions', accept market outcomes and leave morality out of it? On market-liberal assumptions, the rewards produced by the undistorted market are, by definition, just. If a successful corporate manager is worth $500,000 a year in the market place, and requires a battery of managerial powers and privileges to enable his firm to function successfully in the market place, then it is right for him to receive $500,000 a year and be given the powers and privileges he needs. Then why bother to legitimize them? Surely the market is itself the source of legitimacy?

The answer, I believe, is twofold: one, so to speak, internal to the enterprise-culture camp, and the other external to it. The 'internal' answer has been put best by F. A. Hayek in volume III of *Law, Legislation and Liberty*. In past times, he writes, the values that sustain a market order

> were inevitably learned by all the members of a population consisting chiefly of independent farmers, artisans and apprentices who shared the daily experiences of their masters. They held an ethos that esteemed the prudent man, the good husbandman and provider who looked after the future of his family and business by building up capital, guided less by the desire to consume much than by the wish to be regarded as successful by his fellows . . .
>
> At present, however, an ever-increasing part of the population of the Western world grow up as members of large organisations and thus as strangers to those rules of the market which have made the great society possible. To them, the market economy is largely incomprehensible; they have never practised the rules on which it rests and its results seem to them irrational and immoral.[9]

In short, a market order is possible only if the moral values appropriate to it prevail. At present they do not. In a market order, market outcomes and market power would, indeed, be *ipso facto* legitimate. Unfortunately, we do not yet live in such an order. Corrupted, late twentieth-century men and women, products of decades (perhaps even of a century) of creeping collectivism, do not 'understand' the moral requirements of a market order and are not ready for the dawn of market freedom. So before the dawn breaks – indeed, before it *can* break – they must be remade. And, for that, a cultural revolution is necessary. The enterprise culture is, at one and the same time, the revolutionaries' instrument and their destination. Just as the Bolsheviks discovered that the corrupt and backward-looking human material bequeathed to them by the tsars was not ready for a stateless Leninist utopia, and concluded that the long-suffering Russian *muzhik* must be remade into a new kind of Soviet Man before utopia could arrive, so the advocates of the enterprise culture have concluded that the feckless, enterprise-eschewing, market-distorting human material bequeathed to them by the post-war consensus and the long decades of compromise and appeasement that led up to it must be remade in the image of the entrepreneurial ideal before the market order they seek can come into being.

This leads on to the 'external' answer; the answer that might be expected to come from outside the enterprise-culture camp itself. (It may perhaps be the same answer in different words.) This is that the advocates of the enterprise culture are seeking, quite deliberately, to change the parameters within which arguments about the morality of the market may take place; that they hope to change the moral environment within which market power and market outcomes are judged. They want to do this because they know – who better? – that in the post-war mixed economy the market has had to function within fairly narrow moral limits and because they wish to widen these limits. They wish to widen the limits for a number of reasons, of course, but it seems to me that one reason stands out above all the others. The nineteenth-century entrepreneurial ideal has to do with authority as well as with freedom. Central to it was the assumption that the owner-manager had an absolute right to do what he wished with his own: that any interference with his authority over the labour he hired was an attack on the rights of property. In much the same way, part of the point of the twentieth-century enterprise culture is to restore authority, in the state, in the firm and, for that matter, in public-sector organizations as well. To return to Hirschman's vocabulary for a moment, the object of the exercise is to create a state of affairs in which adjustment by Voice is unnecessary because everyone accepts the consequences of adjustment by Exit: in which the tedious, time-consuming and (for some) humiliating process of consultation and negotiation that Voice entails can be short-circuited; and in which, in consequence, managers once again enjoy 'the right to manage', while governments have the right to govern. More simply, what is at stake is an attempt to legitimize a shift in the balance of social and economic power – a shift from the public sector to the private, as Harold Perkin has pointed out,[10] and in my view, much more important, a shift in both public and private sectors from those at the bottom of hierarchies to those at the top.

III

At this point, however, enter a huge and embarrassing paradox. A crucial part of the object of the Thatcherite project is to limit the role of the state. There are two important reasons for this. One is ideological. Neo-liberals hold that the market is the realm of freedom, and the state the realm of coercion: that it is one of the central premises of their whole creed. It follows that, as a matter of moral principle, the state's role should be limited. The second and more important reason is pragmatic. Neo-liberals also hold that the extension in the role of the state, which took place in the 1960s and 1970s, led to a vicious circle of overload and ungovernability. The state's reach came to exceed its grasp: the more it promised, the less it could perform; and the wider the gap between promise and performance, the more its authority declined. The obvious moral is that the state's role must be pruned back – not in order to weaken it, but on the contrary, to strengthen it.

This is where statecraft – the 'old wine' of my title – comes into the story. As James Bulpitt has suggested, the Tory tradition is of a strong and authoritative state, which concentrates on what he calls 'high politics' while leaving 'low politics' to other agencies – to local government and to intermediate associations of all kinds.[11] Macmillan in the early 1960s, and still more Heath in the early 1970s, departed from this tradition. Both embarked on interventionist economic policies, which dragged the state into the sphere of 'low politics' and which, at least potentially, also threatened its monopoly of 'high politics'. In both cases, the result was a demoralizing electoral defeat: in Heath's case, in circumstances that made the Conservative Party's survival as a governing party appear problematical. Mrs Thatcher's real attraction did not lie in her new-fangled 'monetarist' economics: it was that economic liberalism provided a route by which her party could rescue the state from the toils of 'low politics' and, in doing so, return to the exceedingly old-fangled tradition of Tory statecraft.

Herein lies the paradox. The cultural revolution implied by the project of creating an enterprise culture can be carried out only by a strong and, above all, intrusive state, which intervenes incessantly in 'low politics'. Only the state can change the mix of incentives and disincentives that traps fallen late twentieth-century men and women in the dependency culture of bloated public provision and attenuated private enterprise; only the state can humble or disarm the vast range of intermediate institutions that embody and transmit corrupting, anti-entrepreneurial values. If an enterprise culture is to come into existence, universities must be much more tightly curtailed, the self-governing professions must be remodelled, the freedom of action of local authorities must be 'marketized' and the trade unions must lose power. But all this runs counter both to traditional Tory statecraft and to neo-liberal ideology. The central theme of the politics of the 1980s was to be found in the working-out of that paradox – in the oscillation between the twin poles of the 'free economy' and the 'strong state': between the need to enhance the *power* of the state in order to create an enterprise culture and the need to diminish the *role* of the state in order to ensure that the enterprise culture is truly 'enterprising'.

At this point, some questions may be in order. How successful has this project been, and how successful is it likely to be? On one level, of course, it is bound to fail. It is plainly impossible, in the closing years of the twentieth century, to re-create the kind of enterprise culture that existed in the early nineteenth century. But failure will not necessarily undermine the legitimacy or the appeal of the project. The examples of the Church Militant and of the Communist Party of the Soviet Union show only too clearly that a millenarian ideal can often be rather like the carrot placed just in front of the proverbial donkey. The fact that the donkey never catches up with the carrot only leads him to redouble his efforts. The fact that the ideal is never realized only reinforces the faithful in their zeal, giving them an ever-growing list of obstacles to be overcome and of enemies to defeat. And, even if the enterprise culture is never attained, the attempt to attain it may have other important consequences. In particular, it may block off other possible courses. One of Hirschman's most fruitful insights was that Voice – his alternative to Exit – depends upon Loyalty; that the processes of negotiation, discussion and mutual education upon which adjustment through Voice depends are likely to produce results only if those who engage in them are held together by ties of mutual obligation which endure through time. If, by strengthening Exit, Loyalty is eroded, if market forces attenuate the ties of community, the chances of returning to Voice at some time in the future are likely to diminish. Negotiated adjustment – the kind of adjustment implied by the European Commission's Social Charter – depends upon a communitarian ethic. Such an ethic may well be a casualty of current attempts to create an enterprise culture, even if they are not wholly successful. And in that case, there would be no other hole to go to.

1992

CHAPTER TEN

Henry Dubb versus Sceptred Awe

I

'I have changed everything', Mrs Thatcher is supposed to have said in 1976.[1] For long her claim was taken at face value, by outraged opponents no less than by eager supporters. Her fall, and the tribulations of her successor, have brought a new perspective. Post-Thatcher Britain is beginning to look suspiciously like pre-Thatcher Britain; the supposedly transformed state of the revolutionaries like the unregenerate state of the *ancien régime*. In this essay, I explore a possible reason for this curious state of affairs. I suggest that the key to the story may lie in the interplay between three visions or myths of the British state, all of which have deep roots in British history, but all of which have been emptied by the upheavals of the last twenty years or so. I conclude with the hope – for it is only a hope – that a fourth and more promising vision, equally venerable, but in this century less influential, is about to replace them.

I begin, like a barrister introducing a case, with three exhibits. Each exhibit is a quotation. Each quotation seems to me to represent a particular vision, or understanding, or perhaps myth of the British state. I shall suggest that the interplay between these three visions or myths holds a key – *a* key, not *the* key – to the history of the British state over the last fifty years or so. I shall argue that, for a variety of reasons, each of these visions has lost or is losing its persuasive power and moral authority. Finally, I shall speculate whether the British political tradition has the intellectual and moral resources to inspire an alternative vision closer to the realities of the modern world.

Exhibit A is a quotation from a speech to the House of Commons, made by Winston Churchill on 15 May 1945. Note the date. It was one week after the broken German armies had surrendered unconditionally to the Allies: one week after the most spectacular triumph in the whole history of the British state. Churchill was moving a Humble Address to the Sovereign, congratulating him on the successful conclusion of the war in Europe. In the circumstances, a certain vainglory might have been forgivable. There was none: or, if there was, it was not a military vainglory. Churchill began by pointing out that the British sovereign embodied 'a multiple kingship unique in the world of today and so far as I know in the history of the past'. Then he went on:

> Of this multiple kingship we in these islands are but a single member, but it is a kingship to which all the other Governments of the Empire feel an equal allegiance and an equal right. It is the golden circle of the Crown which alone embraces the loyalties of so many states and races all over the world ...
>
> ... We are fortunate indeed that an office of such extraordinary significance should be held by one who combines with an intense love of our country and all his people a thorough comprehension of our Parliamentary and democratic constitution. Well may it be said, well was it said, that the prerogatives of the Crown have become the privileges of the people ...
>
> ... If it be true, as has been said, that every country gets the form of government it deserves, we may certainly flatter ourselves. The wisdom of our ancestors has led us to an envied and enviable situation. We have the strongest Parliament in the world. We have the oldest, the most famous, the most secure, the most serviceable monarchy in the world. King and Parliament both rest safely and solidly upon the will of the people expressed by free and fair election on the basis of universal suffrage. Thus this system has long worked harmoniously, both in peace and war.[2]

Exhibit B is less dramatic, both in language and occasion. Its author was a still unknown young Irishman called George Bernard Shaw. It comes from an essay entitled 'The Transition to Social Democracy', which Shaw contributed to the *Fabian Essays* of 1889. Shaw's purpose was to persuade his fellow socialists – many of whom then disagreed with him – that the appropriate vehicle for their project was the state. At the beginning of the century, he conceded, it would not have been. In those days of jobbery and bribery, before the three great Reform Acts, 'incompetence and corruption' were 'inherent state qualities, like the acidity of lemons'. But, says Shaw, no longer.

> Make the passing of a sufficient examination an indispensable prelimi-
> nary to entering the executive; make the executive responsible to the
> government and the government responsible to the people; and State
> departments will be provided with all the guarantees for integrity and
> efficiency that private money-hunting pretends to. Thus the old bugbear
> of State imbecility did not terrify the Socialist; it only made him a
> Democrat. But to call himself so simply, would have had the effect of
> classing him with the ordinary destructive politician who is a Democrat
> without ulterior views for the sake of formal Democracy – one whose
> notion of Radicalism is the pulling up of aristocratic institutions by the
> roots – who is, briefly, a sort of Universal Abolitionist. Consequently, we
> have the distinctive term Social Democrat, indicating the man or
> woman who desires through Democracy to gather the whole people
> into the State, so that the State may be trusted with the rent of the
> country, and finally with the land, the capital and the organization of
> the national industry – with all the sources of production, in short,
> which are now abandoned to the cupidity of irresponsible private
> individuals.[3]

Exhibit C, by contrast, is very dramatic indeed. It comes from an address delivered to the St George's Society on St George's Day, 1968. The author was Enoch Powell, in those days still a prominent Conservative politician. His theme was the rediscovery of England and the English identity which, in his view, had to follow the end of empire. This is how he begins.

> Herodotus relates how the Athenians, returning to their city after it had
> been sacked and burnt by Xerxes and the Persian army, were astonished
> to find, alive and flourishing in the midst of the blackened ruins, the
> sacred olive tree, the native symbol of their country. So we today, at the
> heart of a vanished empire, amid the fragments of a demolished glory,
> seem to find, like one of her own oak trees, standing and growing, the
> sap still rising from her ancient roots to meet the Spring, England
> herself.

The present generation of the English, Powell continues, has come 'home again from years of distant wandering'. Having returned, it has discovered an unexpected affinity with earlier generations, generations before 'the expansion of England', generations whose inscrutable effigies are to be found in England's country churches. Suppose they could talk to us, he asks, what would they say? This is his answer:

> One thing above all they assuredly would not forget, Lancastrian or
> Yorkist, squire or lord, priest or layman; they would point to the

kingship of England and its symbols everywhere visible. The immemorial arms, gules, three leopards or, though quartered of late with France,
azure, three fleurs de lis, argent; and older still the Crown itself and that
sceptred awe in which Saint Edward the Englishman still seemed to sit
in his own chair to claim the allegiance of all the English. Symbol yet
source of power, person of flesh and blood, yet incarnation of an idea;
the kingship would have seemed to them as it seems to us, to embrace
and express the qualities that are peculiarly England's: the unity of
England, effortless and unconstrained, which accepts the unlimited
supremacy of Crown in Parliament so naturally as not to be aware of
it.[4]

So: 'the golden circle of the Crown', whose prerogatives have
been mysteriously transmuted into 'the privileges of the people'.
State departments equipped with all necessary 'guarantees of
integrity and efficiency'. The 'sceptred awe' of Saint Edward the
Englishman recalling the 'sacred olive tree' of the Athenians. What
do these images imply?

II

Exhibit A, Churchill's victory speech, I take to represent a vision of
the state which I shall call 'Whig imperialist'. Central to that vision
is a notion of balance – of balance between freedom and order,
rulers and ruled, progress and stability. Central also are the notions
of peaceful adaptation, timely accommodation, responsive evolution. In Harold Nicolson's marvellous political novel *Public Faces*, a
pompous Foreign Office official called Arthur Peabody, and known
to his staff as 'old Peabottle', meditates on the nature of foreign
policy. He likens it to 'a majestic river, flowing in a uniform
direction, requiring only, at moments of crisis, a glib, but scrupu-
lous, rectification of the banks'.[5] That is Whig imperialist statecraft
in a nutshell. Civil society is a majestic river, flowing in a uniform
direction. The role of the state is to administer the occasional glib
rectification of the banks. Statecraft – politics – is, in R. A. Butler's
phrase, 'the art of the possible': an art 'responsive to the demands
of each new age, empirical as to method, resourceful in expressing
itself in popular idiom'.[6]

Constitutional rigidity, born of fixed principles, is to be avoided
at all costs. It is impossible to lay down in advance what the role of
the state should be. As John Maynard Keynes put it in his essay,

'The End of Laisser-Faire', the Agenda and Non-Agenda of Government, as he called them, cribbing from Bentham, cannot be determined 'on abstract grounds'. The question of what the state should do and what it should leave to private individuals can be answered only 'on its merits in detail'.[7] By the same token, it is foolish and dangerous to try to protect civil rights or liberties through some formal code. Their true protection lies – can only lie – in the informal conventions, particular enactments and tacit understandings of a liberty-loving political class. And the reason why Britain's situation is uniquely 'envied and enviable' is that her rulers have learned the mysteries of this kind of statecraft: that they mastered what we might call the Peabottle principle: that they have known instinctively when to resist and when to accommodate; when to administer the appropriate rectification to the banks and when to leave the river alone.

Exhibit B, my quotation from Shaw, represents a vision which, following one of its most eminent exponents, Sidney Webb, I shall call 'democratic collectivist'. Like the Whig imperialist vision, it is, in a profound sense, teleological. It too sees the history of modern Britain as a long continuum of peaceful progress. But the differences are as significant as the similarities. For democratic collectivists, political authority is rational and secular in character, not sacral: they have no time for immemorial custom or golden circles. Where Whig imperialist statecraft is reactive, democratic collectivist statecraft is proactive. The democratic collectivist state does not wait to rectify the banks of the social river; it digs a new channel through which the waters have to flow. Where Whig imperialists appeal to judgement, experience, the intuitive wisdom of an ancient political class, democratic collectivists appeal to science, reason, professional expertise. Both speak of democracy, but they understand it in different ways. The Whig imperialist state is democratic because it responds to popular demands. The democratic collectivist state is democratic because it is subject to popular control.

Two implications follow. Because the democratic collectivist state is rational, it has both the capacity and the duty to replace the irrational higgling of the market place with rational co-ordination and direction. And because it is democratic, further instalments of Shaw's 'formal democracy' – attempts to pull up aristocratic institutions by the roots of the sort that 'Universal Abolitionists' engage in – are pointless distractions from the path ahead. The task for democratic collectivists is to take control of the existing institutions of the state, and to use them to make society more rational and more just. Anything else is a frivolous luxury.

The vision represented by exhibit C, my quotation from Enoch Powell, is harder to label. I suppose one possibility might be Tory nationalist. I prefer a label stolen from the historian, Jonathan Clark, who uses it to describe his own position.[8] I shall call it 'authoritarian individualist'.

It too is similar in some ways to the Whig imperialist vision. There is the same emphasis on immemorial custom. For it, too, political authority is sacral, not rational. As Michael Oakeshott, that most subtle of authoritarian individualists, put it, the 'intimations of government' are to be found in 'ritual'. But there are marked differences as well. The authoritarian individualist vision is much bleaker. Change is as likely to be for the worse as for the better. The role of the state is bleaker too. It has to police the passions which would otherwise tear society apart: to guarantee order and discipline against the disorder and indiscipline inherent in fallen human nature. It also has to guarantee property rights, social hierarchy, individual liberty against the forces of envy and folly which continually threaten them. To do all this, it must be strong and authoritative. '[W]e do not ask for a feeble state', said Mrs Thatcher in her famous Airey Neave lecture, soon after taking office. 'On the contrary we need a strong state to preserve both liberty and order.'[9] And to be strong, the state must speak to the heart as well as to the head. It is not, said the great Lord Salisbury more than a century ago, a 'mere joint stock company', as individualistic radicals imagine. It needs 'poetical trappings':[10] majesty, dignity, glory. To strip these away would be at once impious and dangerous.

But there is an ambivalence at the heart of authoritarian individualist statecraft. For the state is dangerous as well as necessary: a looming enemy as well as an indispensable friend. In the wrong hands, it may invade spheres which it has no business to enter: encroach on the liberties which it exists to secure. Authoritarian individualists therefore view the responsive, adaptive Whig imperialist state with a jaundiced eye. Suppose it responds to the wrong pressures? Suppose it adapts in the wrong way? Suppose that under the cloak of genial and accommodating Whiggery it turns into the impious and destructive democratic collectivist state? What then?

III

So far I have looked at the implications of my three visions for statecraft: for the art of government; for rulers and those seeking to rule. They also have implications for two other crucial dimensions of statehood. One is sovereignty; the other is identity or nationality. The sovereignty story is full of complexities, but the essentials are starkly clear. For different reasons and by way of different paths, all three visions converge on the same destination: on Enoch Powell's 'unlimited supremacy of Crown in Parliament'. To put it more precisely, all three take for granted the doctrine which the great Victorian jurist, A. V. Dicey, called 'the keystone of the Constitution': the doctrine of, in his words, the 'absolute legislative sovereignty or despotism of the King in Parliament'. For all three, in short, the sovereignty of the Crown in Parliament is inherently unshareable and inalienable; for all three, the engine of concentrated executive power which Dicey's doctrine celebrates and legitimizes must be left intact.

It is not difficult to see why Whig imperialists and authoritarian individualists should converge on this end point. This is the mystery enshrined in the immemorial customs they celebrate: the sacral source of political authority they both presuppose. But why should democratic collectivists join them? The democratic collectivist vision is rational, utilitarian, instrumental. Why, then, have democratic collectivists failed to challenge the Dicey doctrine? The answer, I believe, is twofold. Part of it is to be found in an autobiographical fragment in Aneurin Bevan's *In Place of Fear*, published just after his resignation from the Attlee government. 'A young miner in a South Wales colliery', Bevan wrote, 'my concern was with the one practical question: Where does power lie in this particular state of Great Britain, and how can it be attained by the workers?' His answer was Parliament: 'a sword pointed at the heart of property-power'.[11]

Dicey's engine of concentrated power, in other words, offers the one hope of toppling the privileged and emancipating the dispossessed. State power is the answer – the only conceivable answer – to market power. And if, in Britain, state power happens to be founded on medieval mumbo-jumbo, then so be it. That leads on to the second part of the answer. The powers of the Crown in Parliament, say the democratic collectivists, are exercised by ministers: ministers come by definition, from the majority party in the House of Commons: the majority party in the House of Commons has, by definition, been given its majority by the people. Whatever constitutional laywers may say, the powers of the Crown in Parliament are *de facto* the people's powers. The body of democracy has been inserted into the skin of Westminster absolutism. To damage the skin would be to damage the body.

The identity story is also rather complicated, but in a different way. There is no doubt about the Whig imperialist vision of British identity. The British state is, in a unique and special sense, an imperial state: inescapably the hinge of Churchill's worldwide multiple kingship. By the same token, the British nation is a uniquely imperial nation: constituted as a nation by its decision to seek an oceanic and imperial destiny rather than a merely continental, European one. Thus, for Churchill, British history is only part of the history of the 'English-speaking peoples' which he wrote in four substantial volumes. And thus, for G. M. Trevelyan, the loss of Calais under Mary Tudor was 'pure gain' because it taught the Elizabethans to 'look westwards for new lands'.[12]

The authoritarian individualist vision of nationhood and identity is as deeply felt, as passionately evoked, as the Whig imperialist. But it is an English vision, not a British one: post-imperial, not imperial. Of course, authoritarian individualist politicians, obliged to woo voters in the non-English nations of the island speak, when they remember to, of Britain. But you do not need to have mastered the subtleties of deconstruction to see that when 'Britain' is said, 'England' is generally meant. The myths, the symbols, the iconography are English. One example will have to stand for many. In May 1982, at the height of the Falklands War, Mrs Thatcher addressed the Conservative Women's Conference. First, she referred to 'we'. Then 'we' became 'we British'. But the final peroration gave the game away: 'And let our nation, as it has so often in the past, remind itself and the world: "Naught shall make us rue / If England to herself do rest but true."'[13] Is it altogether surprising that, under her leadership, the Conservative Party did not fare as well north of the Border as it used to do?

But what of democratic collectivism? What is the democratic collectivist vision of identity and nationhood? The answer is that there isn't one. The 'poetical trappings' with which democratic collectivists have been comfortable, the solidarities they have sought to evoke have been those of class, not those of nation. I can think of one giant exception, Bernard Crick's hero, George Orwell.

In his wartime writings, Orwell tried to find a distinctive democratic collectivist idiom of nationhood. The result was some of the
most haunting polemical prose in the English language. But the
point about Orwell's achievement is that it stands almost alone. In
general, democratic collectivists have been forced back on the
Whig imperialist language of nationhood and identity, for want of
a language of their own. When Hugh Gaitskell appealed to '1,000
years of history' in his great speech opposing British membership
of a European Union, it was Whig imperialist history that he had
in mind. And when, in the first Commons debate on the Falklands
War, Michael Foot accused the Government of 'betraying' the
Falkland Islanders, it was a Whig imperialist chord that he hoped
to strike.

IV

These, then, are the visions of the state which my three exhibits
were chosen to represent. Of course, they were never the only
ones. Of course, they were often less coherent, more inchoate, less
sharply differentiated from each other than I have depicted them
as being. But, for all that, they have been the dominant visions of
the British state for most of the post-war period. And because they
have been so dominant for so long, it is extraordinarily difficult to
throw them off. Even now, I suspect, Old Peabottle's majestic Whig
river still flows through the collective subconscious of the Athe-
naeum and the Cabinet Office mess. Even now, if you 'scratch
someone on the left – even a congenital milk-and-water Menshevik
like me – you will find at least a vestige of Shaw's disdain for the
anarchic waste of private money-hunting. And I am sure that,
south of the Border and east of the Severn, millions of people,
including millions of Labour voters, have at least a corner in their
hearts for Powell's English oak trees. But, in spite of this lingering
afterglow, I believe that all three visions are now exhausted.

The fate of the Whig imperialist vision is brutally plain. You
can't be an imperialist if you have no empire. The golden circle of
the Crown still keeps its old magic. But the unravelling of Britain's
world role, decolonization in Asia and Africa, the search by the old
white dominions for new roles and, not least, entry into the
European Community have destroyed the unique and mysterious
multiple kingship it once encompassed. In doing so, they have also
destroyed the identity and undermined the statecraft that went

with the multiple kingship. The democratic collectivist vision has fared no better. Whatever may be true of left-of-centre hearts, whose head still accepts the Shavian presupposition that the rational and democratic state is, by definition, more efficient than the higgling of the market? Social welfare, yes. Managed capitalism, certainly. A symbiosis between public and private power, some of us hope so. But state ownership? State planning? Even state direction? Those primordial ingredients of the democratic collectivist vision perished during the upheavals that swept the world economy in the 1970s.

That leaves the authoritarian individualist vision. Here matters are more complicated. The exhaustion of the Whig imperialist and democratic collectivist visions in the 1960s and 1970s created a vacuum – a vacuum of understanding; a vacuum of sentiment; above all, a vacuum of language and of rhetoric. Into that vacuum rushed authoritarian individualism. Its bleak, late nineteenth-century statecraft was more congruent – or rather less incongruent – with the diverse, disorganized capitalism of the late twentieth century than either relaxed, accommodating Whiggery or directive democratic collectivism. Above all, it and it alone had an identity to which it could speak, tribal loyalties which it could mobilize.

But there was a contradiction between that identity and the state which the authoritarian individualists aspired to rule. The state was Britain. The identity was English. For a while, the contradiction went unnoticed. Authoritarian individualist statecraft swept all before it. Tribal loyalties were mobilized to such effect that, in the last general election, the principal working-class party in the south of England was Mrs Thatcher's. But the better authoritarian individualism played in Penge, the worse it played in Peebles: the more loudly it was cheered in England, and particularly in southern England, the more it grated on everyone else. The results are manifest – the Scottish Claim of Right; the Scottish Constitutional Convention; the commitment by all the Scottish political parties save the Unionists to one form or other of a Scottish Parliament. No one knows what the consequences will be, but one point is clear. Britain is, and always has been, a multinational state, not a national one. The Scottish nation was incorporated into that state through negotiation, not through conquest. All the signs are that Scotland now wishes to renegotiate the settlement that led to her incorporation. She may opt for separate statehood within the European Community. She may prefer internal autonomy within a more or less federal United

Kingdom. The first would mean the disappearance of the British state. The second would transform it beyond recognition. Neither outcome is tolerable from an authoritarian individualist perspective. Yet authoritarian individualist statecraft has helped to force both onto the agenda.

A deeper contradiction haunts it as well. As my quotation from Enoch Powell showed, the Dicey doctrine of the absolute and inalienable sovereignty of the Crown in Parliament is even more fundamental to the authoritarian individualist vision than to the others. But we live in a world in which the notion of absolute sovereignty – whether of the Crown in Parliament or of anyone else – has ceased to chime with economic and social reality. In this world, the search for absolute sovereignty is the pursuit of the infeasible by the incorrigible. Government, public power still have important roles. But the sovereign nation-state – the state which Thomas Hobbes called 'that great Leviathan, that mortal God' – has become an anachronism, above all in its European birthplace. No member state of the European Community is still sovereign in the old way. The Community is built on power-sharing. It has to be, because power-sharing among polities is the necessary response to the interdependence of economies; and economic interdependence is the Community's hallmark. Indeed, economic interdependence is not only the Community's hallmark: it is the inevitable consequence of the deregulation and liberalization which are fundamental to the individualist dimension of the authoritarian individualist vision. But power-sharing is ruled out by the Dicey doctrine. It is therefore anathema to authoritarian individualist statecraft – as, of course, to any other statecraft based on that doctrine. Authoritarian individualists cannot draw the obvious conclusion and secede from the Community. They wish to maximize the influence of the British state, and they know that it would have less influence outside than within. But they also cannot accept the power-sharing logic of Community membership. On that contradiction, Mrs Thatcher was impaled. Thanks to it, she fell. Who can doubt that it remains to plague her successors?

Is there a way out? It is not difficult to see where it would lead. We would have to master a politics of power-sharing, negotiation, discussion, coalition-building – both in Britain and in the European Community. We would have to reconstruct the British state in a fashion that would facilitate such a politics, with guarantees of human rights; constitutional checks and balances; above all, an effectively federal distribution of power. We would have to accept, and rejoice in accepting, that political identities can be plural as well as singular: that if Catalans can say, 'I am Catalan; I am Spanish; I am European', we ought to be able to say, 'I am English, or Welsh, or Scots, or, who knows, a Northumbrian or a Yorkshireman; I am also British; and I am European.' And, in order to do all this, we would have to turn our backs on Enoch Powell's 'sceptred awe'; on Aneurin Bevan's sword; and on Churchill's golden circle.

V

That is the direction in which an alternative vision of the state would have to point. The question is whether such an alternative exists or could exist. I cannot know the answer, but I offer a thought. My title is 'Henry Dubb versus Sceptred Awe'. The meaning of 'sceptred awe' should, by now, be clear. What do I mean by Henry Dubb? Who *was* Henry Dubb? The answer, of course, is that he wasn't. He was an invention of the great economic historian and socialist thinker, R. H. Tawney. He was Tawney's ordinary citizen – down-to-earth, sober, unromantic; but still a citizen, imbued with the instincts of citizenship and stubbornly attached to its values. I see him as a symbol of a tradition – elusive, fugitive, often half-forgotten, but never quite abandoned – of which Tawney was one of the chief exponents in the twentieth century. It is a difficult tradition to distil in a phrase. Tawney caught the essence when he wrote that Britain had accepted democracy

> as a convenience, like an improved system of telephones; she did not dedicate herself to it as the expression of a moral ideal of comradeship and equality, the avowal of which would leave nothing the same. She changed her political garments, but not her heart. She carried into the democratic era, not only the institutions, but the social habits and mentality of the oldest and toughest plutocracy in the world ... She went to the ballot box touching her hat.[14]

What he meant was that the teleologies underpinning both the Whig imperialist and the democratic collectivist visions of the state were false; that Britain was not really a democracy after all; that the prerogatives of the Crown had not been mysteriously transmuted into the privileges of the people, or that if they had been, such a transmutation was not to the point; that democratic citizenship must be active, not passive; and that ours was not. To put the point in another way, the Tawneian tradition has insisted that democratic institutions without a democratic culture are like clothes without a body. I do not suggest that that tradition is bound to generate reconstituted identities and a refashioned state on the lines I sketched out a moment ago. Democratic citizenship is a perilous adventure, not a panacea. I do suggest that the Tawneian tradition is the only one that offers the possibility of refashioning the state and reconstituting identities through negotiation and debate rather than through manipulation or force; and that if this cannot be done through negotiation and debate, it is not worth doing at all.

For most of the twentieth century, the Tawneian tradition has been submerged. It is, of course, a highly subversive tradition – as subversive of the progressive mandarinate which set the tone of British public policy in the post-war period as of the defiantly reactionary neo-liberals who followed them. The values it bears run directly counter to the values implied by the notion of an absolute and indefeasible Crown in Parliament. As such, it also runs counter, not just to the Whig imperialist and authoritarian individualist visions of the British state, but to the democratic collectivist vision, many of whose exponents thought of themselves as followers of Tawney. Yet it is part of our history. I suspect it can be traced back to the civic humanists of the seventeenth and eighteenth centuries. There are echoes of it in some, though by no means all, of the liberal thinkers of the nineteenth, and in rather more of the popular radicals of the same period. It surfaced in the early labour movement, notably in the ILP. Oddly enough, there were echoes of it in the robust anti-Establishment rhetoric of Mrs Thatcher – not the least of the sources of her appeal to middle England. Now there are signs that it is beginning to re-emerge. They include the current citizenship debate, which now engages supporters of all three United Kingdom political parties, as well as the cross-party pressure group, Charter 88; draft written constitutions proffered by figures as diverse as Tony Benn and the Institute of Economic Affairs; and opinion surveys recording substantial majorities in favour of constitutional change. So I end with a question. Is stolid old Henry Dubb at last on the march? If he is, as I suspect he may be, he may yet astonish us all.

1993

• CHAPTER ELEVEN •

Collaborative Capitalism and Constitutional Reform

I

Few would dispute that the character of an economy depends in part on the character, conduct and culture of the state. Even those who believe that the competitive free market is bound, by definition, to allocate resources more efficiently than any other mechanism, and that public intervention in the economy does more harm than good, accept that governments can affect economic behaviour for good or ill – for good, by removing barriers to free competition, and for ill by erecting or maintaining them. Other schools of thought hold that, at least in principle, state intervention can either improve economic performance, or at least facilitate its improvement.

Except in very broad terms, however, the nature of the connection is far from clear. Early nineteenth-century Britain, late nineteenth-century Germany and present-day Japan have all been economic success stories, but their political institutions differed sharply from each other. There is not much doubt that, over the long haul and in time of peace, capitalist market economies perform better than socialist command economies (though it is worth remembering that the forced industrialization of Stalin's Soviet Union created one of the most impressive war machines in the history of the world), but capitalist market economies come in a variety of forms, and so do the regimes that correspond to them. The widely held notion that there is a necessary connection between capitalism, the free market and democracy is an illusion.

Pinochet's Chile had a capitalist free market, but it was not a democracy. The economy of Hitler's Germany was unmistakably capitalist, but only dubiously free-market.

By the same token, it is impossible to establish a clear connection between economic performance and any particular set of constitutional arrangements. The constitution of the United States has altered very little in the last 100 years. A century ago, the American economy was, by most indices, the most successful in the world. In the last thirty years or so, it has been one of the least successful. Gaullist France and pre-unification Federal Germany were both democracies, but their versions of democracy could scarcely have been more different. Both were hugely successful in economic terms. (Whether post-unification Germany will be equally successful remains to be seen.) Much the same applies in reverse. In the 1970s, it was widely believed that Britain's relative economic decline could be attributed to the sharp oscillations of policy produced by 'adversary politics'; and that electoral reform would produce the policy continuity needed to put things right.[1] The 1980s saw a long period of policy continuity, albeit in a still adversarial system, but relative decline continued.

Yet it would be wrong to end the story there. The connections between the character and conduct of the state, the rules set out in its constitution, the understandings and codes of behaviour encapsulated in those rules and the performance of the economy are complex, subtle and poorly understood, but that does not mean that there is no connection. Constitutions, after all, define the terms on which public power is distributed and on which it can legitimately be exercised. Only on the heroic, and surely absurd, assumption that public power can have no influence whatever on economic performance could that definition be economically irrelevant. On a deeper, and perhaps more important, level, a constitution is a kind of distillation of a political community's view of its better self; an embodiment of its conception of the nature of politics, of the sources of political authority and ultimately of the good society; a mirror reflecting its public philosophy and most cherished values. And, in mirroring values, constitutions also reinforce them. They help to tell the members of a political community who they are and how they ought to behave. Since the members of a political community are also actors in an economy, the message has an economic dimension as well as a political one.

II

Looked at against that background, the debate over constitutional reform in contemporary Britain takes on a new significance. As everyone knows, the British constitution is uncodified, a jumble of sometimes ambiguous precedents, not a document which any citizen can obtain and read. But its message is no less insistent for that. At its core lies the ancient doctrine of the absolute sovereignty of the Crown-in-Parliament; and the values which that doctrine mirrors and reinforces are only too clear. They are hierarchical, not participatory; monist, not pluralist; in a profound sense, pre-democratic, not democratic. The vision of the good society which they encapsulate and underpin is one in which the rulers rule and the ruled know their place: in which legitimate power flows from the top down, not from the bottom up; in which public policy is the property of the rulers, not of the ruled; and in which decisions are made in the south-eastern core, not in the periphery. In our time, the powers of the absolutely sovereign Crown-in-Parliament have, of course, been at the disposal of the victors in a democratic election. The democratic radicals of the nineteenth century did not win all their battles, but they did win some of them. Because their victory was incomplete, however, democracy came to this country as a thief in the night rather than as a conqueror at the gates. Our *ancien régime* withstood the great revolutions of eighteenth-century America and France, which served as the crucibles for the modern ideal of equal citizenship; it beat off the Napoleonic revolution on horseback; and it remained untouched by the upheavals of 1848. Though it expired in the end, it stamped its quasi-democratic successor with its impress. New men, new groups and even the occasional new woman were admitted into the political Establishment. But it changed them more than they changed it. It was still the same old Establishment, its values and assumptions were still hierarchical and the powers it exercised were still the Crown's and not the people's.

It would be absurd to suggest that these values are directly responsible for Britain's relative economic decline, but there is growing evidence that they, and the public philosophy with which they are associated, stand in the way of the changes of culture and practice which are the prerequisites of economic success in our time. As the French economist Michel Albert has brilliantly argued,[2] there are at least two models of capitalism, not one. One is what he calls the 'neo-American' model, found in its most developed form in Britain and the United States, and based on individual success and short-term profit. The other is the 'Rhenish' model of Switzerland, Germany, the Low Countries, Scandinavia and, with some variations, Japan. Its central elements are consensus, collective success and concern for the long-term. By almost any index, the 'Rhenish' model has been triumphantly successful; in our time, the 'neo-American' model has been a dismal failure. The question is, why?

Both are capitalist. In both, the means of production are largely in private hands; in both, resources are allocated largely through the market; both are dominated by private, profit-seeking firms which compete for custom and stand or fall by their ability to pass the tests of the market-place. In a struggle between capitalism and socialism, both are therefore on the same side. But it is only because that struggle has loomed so large for so long that we have failed to see that, in most other respects, the 'neo-American' and 'Rhenish' models are profoundly different, perhaps even antagonistic. 'Rhenish' capitalism is, of course, competitive. The yardstick of profitability has to be satisfied. But it is also collaborative. It depends on a subtle symbiosis of competition and co-operation, underpinned by corporatist or quasi-corporatist institutions and practices which the neo-classical economic doctrines of the Anglo-American tradition would condemn as protectionist and therefore inefficient. In short, its market is not the famous 'undistorted' market of the Anglo-American economics profession and the Anglo-American political class. What the Anglo-American tradition sees as distortions, impeding free competition, it sees as the necessary conditions of competitive success.

Success has been forthcoming – and on a scale which would have seemed inconceivable as recently as a generation ago. The reasons are complex. The notion of the 'social market', which British politicians often trot out as an explanation, merely confuses the issue. The 'social market', as understood in Britain, is an Anglo-American-style free market, mitigated by a rather offensive kind of 'compassion'. But the point about 'Rhenish' capitalism is that the market does not operate on Anglo-American lines; that it is not driven by individual self-interest and the search for profit in the short term; that market forces are constrained by dense and complex networks of intersecting interests, held together by solidaristic values and co-operative habits.

Because of all this, market actors are able to take a long view – above all, in respect of human capital. The system as a whole trades off losses in the short-term efficiency on which the Anglo-American tradition focuses against gains in the public goods of consensual adaptation and social peace. It owes its extraordinary success to its capacity to make that trade-off. For, in a sophisticated economy, human capital holds the key to competitive power, with the result that consensual adaptation and social peace become ever more valuable. By the same token, the possessive, inevitably short-term, individualism that drives the neo-American model becomes self-stultifying. Against that background, the precipitate relative decline of the British economy over the last fifty years, and of the American over the last thirty, ceases·to be a matter for surprise.

Unfortunately, however, 'Rhenish' capitalism is poorly understood – above all, of course, in English-speaking economic cultures, saturated with the presuppositions of mainstream Anglo-American economics. For it has no ideology. It is a practice, not a doctrine. It has grown up higgledy-piggledy, through trial and error, negotiation and compromise; and it has never been theorized. Its exponents have no texts, no sacred books, no simple cries. All they can do is to point to a complex and messy reality which takes time and hard work to understand. Its delicate symbiosis between competition and collaboration, the networks of intersecting interests and co-operative practices on which it depends, depend on tacit understandings and uncodified assumptions which are almost incomprehensible to those brought up in the Anglo-American tradition.

That does not mean, however, that there is nothing more to be said. In an important study, Jonathan Boswell argues that the key to the success of the 'Rhenish' model (not that he uses the term) lies in a notion of economic community 'fundamentally opposed' both to the liberal individualism which lies at the heart of mainstream Anglo-American economics, and to conventional collectivism.[3] An economic community would be

> a complex of connecting cells whose mutual sensitivities represent a vital force ... The economic organisations themselves are to be associates or social partners ...
> Neither intimacy nor a constant huddling together is envisaged, let alone unanimity. The social partners are to be strung together by elastic bands, not cords or chains. On the other hand, analogies from conventional political understandings, international relations or the sports field are too slack. Economic community involves a lot more

than, say, common membership of a nation state, non-belligerent co-existence or joint involvement in a competitive game . . .
The whole network is to be interwoven by mutual responsibilities. No 'invisible hand' is expected to harmonise the different parts. Mere balance or competition among the separate interests contributes little to, may often detract from, the common good. Nor is obedience to the state and the law to be loaded with the inordinate burden of producing that common good . . . Rather, public responsibilities as well as powers are to be widely diffused among economic agents.[4]

This is plainly a world away from individualistic economic liberalism and collectivist state socialism. Less obviously, it is equally far removed from the British version of the post-war mixed economy: from the system described by Andrew Shonfield, celebrated by Anthony Crosland and managed, with diminishing success, by the governments of the 1950s, 1960s and 1970s. For that system never got beyond 'belligerent co-existence'. A jealous political class, imbued with the preconceptions of parliamentary absolutism, refused to diffuse public responsibilities and powers among economic agents, while an archaic economic culture, suffused with the assumptions of possessive individualism, failed to adapt to technological change. The great economic organizations never became social partners. There was no network of mutual responsibilities. Hence, the Hobbesian *sauve qui peut* which overwhelmed the governments of the 1970s and which paved the way for the renaissance of individualistic economic liberalism in the 1980s.

III

Plainly, there is no simple short cut to a Boswellian economic community. No conceivable set of constitutional changes could, of themselves, transplant the 'Rhenish' model to British soil. As plainly, however, the values and practices transmitted and legitimized by the British doctrine of absolute parliamentary sovereignty are incompatible with it. As Boswell points out, the delicate symbiosis between competition and collaboration which he anatomizes depends on four crucial factors. There must be reasonable continuity in the membership and direction of the organizations whose co-operation is the prerequisite of a co-operative economy. They must not be so small or so numerous that they have no concern for the public interest, or so big and so few that they dwarf the political authorities. Their activities must be sufficiently transparent to be monitored by those they affect, and – even more importantly – by the wider society. There must be forums in which they learn the norms of co-operation. Above all, the public philosophy of the society in which they act must give a high place to the values of fraternity, association and participation. Current British constitutional doctrine – and, still more, the values and presuppositions embedded in it – bars the way to all of these.

That, however, is only the beginning of the story. At the heart of Albert's 'Rhenish' capitalism and of Boswell's 'economic community' lies a conception of the individual, and of the proper relationship between the individual and the community, which is alien, not just to British constitutional doctrine, but to the entire British political tradition. Lockean liberalism is no more congruent with it than is Hobbesian absolutism; Fabian social democrats are as remote from it as is the Hayekian New Right and the Bennite New Left. But most British constitutional reformers are, at heart, Lockean liberals. They base their case against Westminster absolutism, implicitly or explicitly, on a demand for, and an assertion of, individual rights; behind that demand lies the assumption that, in some profound sense, the individual is prior to the community. The notions that rights imply duties, that individuals are shaped by a community which is more than the sum of its parts, and realize themselves fully only by discharging their obligations to it, make them uneasy. Yet notions of this sort are part of the soil in which 'Rhenish' capitalism has grown. A Lockean constitution, based on the notion of citizenship rights, would, in practice, devolve power, encourage transparency and facilitate pluralism. As such, it would be a great advance on the Hobbesian constitution we now know. But it would not, in itself, procure the changes of culture and assumption which a transition to collaborative capitalism would make necessary. In this perspective, at any rate, constitutional reform is not a solution but a catalyst, not a destination but a starting-point.

1993

• CHAPTER TWELVE •

Travails of an *Ancien Régime*

His first impression is that he is in church. The vaulted roofs and stained-glass windows, the rows of statues of great statesmen of the past, the echoing halls, the soft-footed attendants and the whispered conversation, contrast depressingly with the crowded meetings and the clang and clash of hot opinions he has just left behind in his election campaign. Here he is, a tribune of the people, coming to make his voice heard in the seats of power. Instead, it seems he is expected to worship; and the most conservative of all religions – ancestor worship. (Aneurin Bevan on a new MP's debut in the House of Commons)[1]

I

In this century, public controversy about the British state has followed a roundabout path. For a generation before the First World War, the form, structure and role of the state; its relationship with the nation or nations it was supposed to embody; its place in the global political economy; and, on a deeper level, the very idea of the state were all in contest. The battles over Irish Home Rule, Tariff Reform, extensions of the suffrage, the powers of the House of Lords and the social reforms of 1906–14 raised profound questions about statehood as well as about statecraft – questions of which the more thoughtful of the protagonists were themselves aware. For the 'state' was the terrain on which rival political traditions battled with each other and defined themselves.[2]

After 1918, these fires burned low. The economic and social responsibilities of the state were still in contention. But controversy about its relationship with the nation or nations of Britain died down after its rulers conceded self-government to southern

Ireland. The Parliament Act of 1911 and the Representation of the People Act of 1918 ended the pre-war battle over its form and structure, while the abandonment of the gold standard in 1931 and the coming of imperial preference in 1932 ended the turn-of-the-century debate over its place in the global political economy. And through all the upheavals of the next thirty years statehood was the dog which did not bark in the night. There were plenty of disputes about what the state should do. Virtually no one asked what it should be.

Now the wheel has come full circle. The rise of the New Right, the breakdown of the post-war settlement and the 'hollowing out' of the state under the Thatcher and Major governments[3] have called its structure and role into question, in a fashion not seen since the First World War. The debates of the 1970s and 1980s over the IMF loan, the Thatcherites' Medium Term Financial Strategy and membership of the ERM have gone to the heart of the British state's place in the global political economy. The troubles in Northern Ireland, the demand for devolution in Scotland and Wales and, most of all, membership of the European Union have posed profoundly divisive questions about its relationship with the nation or nations over which it presides. The position of the monarchy – the paramount symbol of British statehood – is more uncertain than ever before in the century, while opinion surveys reveal growing signs of public disaffection with the political system.[4] Partly because of all this, both opposition parties are committed to a series of constitutional changes which, if implemented, would transform the form, structure and constitutive understandings of the British state more comprehensively than at any time since its birth in 1707.

The world of reflection and ideas has moved in parallel to the world of action and decision. The late nineteenth and early twentieth centuries saw an intense theoretical debate between Hegelian Idealists, for whom the state was the benign embodiment of the social whole, and traditional individualists, for whom it was a potential threat to personal freedom.[5] In the half-century after the First World War, academic interest in the state died down except among Marxists, and even for them its nature and functions were rarely problematic. Here too the turn-of-the-century dog has woken up again. New Right theorists have depicted the Keynesian welfare state of the post-war period as a monstrous Leviathan, bound by the logic of collective action to push its frontiers further and further forward unless and until an alarmed society calls a halt. Commentators in the Marxist tradition have rediscovered Gramsci's notion of hegemony, with its implication that control of the state may be a crucial ingredient in ideological dominance. Social democrats, trying to make sense of their downfall in the 1980s, have started to question their old indifference to the form and structure of the state. The result of all this has been a vigorous, sometimes passionate, occasionally anguished debate about the role, nature, purposes, values, structure and boundaries of the state – issues which the post-war generation had thought settled.[6]

II

The academic rediscovery of the state is not, of course, confined to Britain. Nor are the pressures emanating from a proto-federal European Union, the challenge which the renaissance of non-metropolitan ethnicities offers to the central state or the threat which global competition poses to the welfare entitlements which the states of western Europe guaranteed in the post-war era. Yet in certain crucial respects, Britain's experience has been unique; and it is in the causes and nature of its uniqueness that we shall find the key to the situation described above.

Two periods deserve attention. On the European continent, the inter-war period saw convulsive regime transformations in Germany and Italy and debilitating political instability in France. Even in the United States, the New Deal is best seen as a transformation of the regime, albeit procured by very different political and social forces. In Britain, by contrast, the form and structure of the state were in less contention than before 1914, while the available evidence suggests that it rested on a firmer basis of popular support. Since the 1970s, however, British exceptionalism has taken a bleaker form. No other west European country has seen as divisive an attack on the post-war Keynesian welfare state and on the public philosophy that legitimized it. In no other west European country, with the possible exception of Spain, is the relationship between the central state and the nation or nations it claims to embody in such contention. No other member state of the European Union has found it so difficult to adapt to membership. Above all, as Alan Milward suggests, the post-war trajectory of the British state has gone down while those of the other great states of western Europe have gone up.[7]

European integration was designed to reconstruct the nation-state, not to diminish it; and, in the case of its two chief movers, that is what it has done. By any reckoning, the French and German states are more efficacious, more legitimate and more confident in 1995 than they were in 1955. By any reckoning, the British state is less so.

The question is, why? Few would dispute that there is a connection between the downward trajectory of the post-war British state, the confusion surrounding its place in the global political economy, the exceptional virulence of the New Right attack on the British version of the post-war Keynesian welfare state and the controversies over the relationship between the British state and the nation or nations it purports to embody. Many would agree that there is also a connection between all of these and the extraordinary durability of that same state in the past. But it is not so clear what the connections are. I shall argue that the key to them lies in the special peculiarities of what is still, in critically important respects, an *ancien régime*: that the confusion and disarray I described above are symptoms of a profound challenge to the British state; and that the challenge is all the more disorientating because Britain's *ancien régime* has successfully fended off so many previous challenges. And I shall suggest that this challenge has four dimensions – global; national; economic; and constitutional – each corresponding to a crucial aspect of the *ancien régime* itself.

III

This is where Aneurin Bevan's mordant description of ancestor worship in the House of Commons comes into the argument. There is no doubt that the Westminster air resounds with ancestral voices. It is not so clear what the voices are trying to say. When Bevan wrote, the prevailing interpretation was Whig-liberal, sometimes with a social-democratic gloss. For Whig-liberals and social democrats the history of the British state was a history of successful modernization, adaptive evolution, responsive accommodation. Britain was the pioneer of parliamentary government, of the rule of law and of the quintessentially modern separation of state from civil society; and because she had made an exceptionally early passage to modernity she had also made an exceptionally painless passage to democracy.

This Whig-liberal interpretation was challenged by an orthodox Marxist interpretation, for which the essence of British exceptionalism lay in the fact that Britain was the first country in the world to undergo a bourgeois revolution and to make the transition from feudalism to capitalism. But in spite of their differences, the Whig and Marxist interpretations mirrored each other. For both, such manifestly non-bourgeois, pre-modern features of the British state as the monarchy, the House of Lords and the established Church – indeed, all the elaborate archaisms of form and ritual that tell Britain's rulers and would-be rulers who they are and how they ought to behave – were either decorative survivals without operational significance, or Bagehotian devices to mobilize consent for the sober reality of modern governance.[8] What counted, to use Bagehot's language, was the 'efficient' part of the constitution, not the 'dignified' part; and the former was as modern as the latter was antiquated. Indeed, for many commentators, antiquity was the vehicle of modernity. One of the commonplaces of the political science of the early post-war period was that the key to Britain's uniquely happy passage to the modern world lay in what Richard Rose termed the 'traditionally modern' character of her political culture;[9] that the tradition of autonomous executive power which the British state had inherited from its medieval precursors was better suited to twentieth-century realities than were the transitory fancies of nineteenth-century liberalism.[10]

In the last thirty years, this comforting amalgam of Whiggery, social democracy and classical Marxism has been comprehensively subverted. The first significant challenge to it came from the Gramscian New Left of the 1960s.[11] For writers in this school Britain's undoubted exceptionalism had a much more disturbing meaning.[12] Britain was exceptional, not in experiencing the first bourgeois revolution in history, but in experiencing the least bourgeois of the great bourgeois revolutions; not in making an exceptionally early and uniquely happy passage to modernity, but in making an incomplete and ultimately unsuccessful one. The pre-modern, pre-capitalist, non-bourgeois features of the British state and British political economy were not mere icing on an essentially modern cake. They were an integral part of the cake itself.

More recently, the Gramscian critique of the old Whig and Marxist orthodoxies has been reinforced by a still more subversive High Tory critique, springing from a radically different conception of politics and political man, but pointing in a remarkably similar direction. For High Tory historians, there was no bourgeois revolution at all. The Civil War was a rebellion, not a revolution; the Glorious Revolution, a restoration. The eighteenth-century British state was an *ancien régime*, like the *ancien régimes* of the European mainland.[13] It too was a confessional state in which the dominant church was part of an elaborate structure of power, authority and social control. In Britain, as on the other side of the Channel, the values of the elite – which enjoyed hegemony in the society at large – were aristocratic, not bourgeois; hierarchical, not individualistic. J. C. D. Clark, the most systematic and subtle exponent of this view of the eighteenth century, thinks the 1832 Reform Act marked the end of the British *ancien régime*, but the High Tory historiography of the nineteenth and twentieth centuries points a different moral. Though the British state was modified in the nineteenth and twentieth centuries, it suggests, its essential nature remained unchanged.[14] In spite of successive extensions of the suffrage, the invention of the mass party and the growth of the state, a small and homogeneous elite still presided over the same old structure of power and authority, still played the great game of high politics by the old rules and still derived its legitimacy from the old doctrine of the absolute sovereignty of the Crown-in-Parliament.

J. G. A. Pocock, though no High Tory, reaches a similar destination by a different route.[15] He shows that a republican, neo-Machiavellian vision of politics, going back to Renaissance Italy, played a central part in the political struggles of the late seventeenth and eighteenth centuries. At the heart of this vision lay an antithesis between active civic virtue and the dependent passivity induced by a corrupt and corrupting Court. According to Pocock, the Country ideology, with its emphasis on participation and civic duty, was successfully countered by a Court ideology which emphasized the need for a strong central executive; it was the American colonists, not the British, who eventually rejected parliamentary monarchy and sought to realize the civic vision in a republic. Though democracy came to Britain in the end, its coming owed little to the republican ideal. It was procured by 'the medieval technique of expanding the king-in-parliament to include new categories of counsellors and representatives'.[16] What was exceptional about Britain was belated medievalism, not precocious modernity.

IV

Where the *ancien régime* discourse challenges the Whig view of the British state, a more complex discourse, focusing on the relationship between state and nation, challenges the whig conception of an unproblematic British identity.[17] Writers as diverse as J. C. D. Clark and the Gramscian nationalist, Tom Nairn, have pointed out that the British state is a multinational state, like Austria-Hungary, not a nation-state like France. This is so in the obvious sense that its borders encompass four nationalities (five if the Protestant community of Northern Ireland is counted as a nation). It is also so in the less obvious sense that the British state came into existence in the first place only because the hitherto separate nation-states of Scotland and England agreed to set it up. The seventeenth-century union between the Scottish and English Crowns was not a union of states, and was not bound to lead to one. The union of states which eventually came into being, moreover, was a union of a very odd kind. It was not a federation, with a separation of powers between different tiers of government. According to English jurisprudence, at any rate, the absolutely sovereign Crown-in-Parliament of England was transmuted into the absolutely sovereign Crown-in-Parliament of Great Britain. But Scotland was not incorporated in the English state, as Wales had been. She retained two vital attributes of statehood – her own established Church and her own legal system – which have provided rallying points for a distinct Scottish identity ever since.

That leads on to a more subtle point. The 'Britain' which came into existence in 1707 was a factitious construct, not an irresistible emanation of national feeling. The memories and loyalties that eventually came to sustain it were created by it, not it by them. The British identity, which Whig and conventional Marxist historiography presupposed, enabled Scots and English alike to transcend old national animosities in a blaze of glory. In doing so, it gave the new British state – a much more fragile creature, it should be remembered, than it looks in retrospect – a new and special legitimacy. But it did not emerge spontaneously of its own accord. It was made, not born. And what has been made can be remade, perhaps even unmade.

A further point follows as well. This new 'British' identity was necessarily imperial, not national. It was forged in the eighteenth-century race for empire with Bourbon France and in the long revolutionary and Napoleonic wars that followed.[18] For, in its precarious early years, the British state depended on success. Its justification was that it was a better predator than other states; that the pickings of its empire were richer; that the blaze of glory that surrounded it was brighter. Later, when success had bred more success, when the global pre-eminence of the British state seemed beyond challenge, a more relaxed tone came to predominate. Now its justification was the *pax Britannica*: its role as the guarantor and linch-pin of the world market glowingly described in *The Communist Manifesto*; its ability to police the world's sea lanes with its navy and to underpin the world's payments system with its currency. In its relaxed later stages as much as in its tense early ones, however, the grandeurs and servitudes of empire were of its very essence; and the same grandeurs and servitudes inevitably shaped the identity it claimed to embody.

V

On one level, that is scarcely a new discovery. The old Whig historians would not have been surprised to hear that empire was a *leitmotiv* of British history. But for them, empire was a function of evolutionary success. Recent scholarship, by contrast, tells the story of a Faustian bargain, in which the price of successful adaptation in one era turns out to be maladaptation in the next. Thus, for Eric Hobsbawm, control over the 'satellite world' of empire helped to transform late nineteenth-century Britain from a competitive into a parasitic economy, with malign results later on.[19] For Andrew Gamble, Britain's nineteenth-century glory as 'world island' – creator and pivot of the first truly global political economy in history – locked her into a structure of values, institutions, operational codes and comparative advantages which has been a barrier to modernization ever since.[20] For Paul Kennedy, empire was a source of 'overstretch', cutting into the economic base which had made imperial expansion possible in the first place.[21]

More recently, P. J. Cain and A. G. Hopkins have offered a more nuanced synthesis, pushing the debate into new territory,[22] while David Edgerton has thrown new light on the relationship between the military dimension of empire and the state's role in the economy.[23] For Cain and Hopkins, the Glorious Revolution was a watershed, but not as pictured in old Whig or marxist historiography. Its significance lay in the fact that it made possible the emergence of a predatory 'military-fiscal state', marvellously equipped for the struggle for empire. This 'military-fiscal state' was underpinned by an alliance between the landed magnates, who dominated parliament and owned most of the nation's wealth, and the burgeoning service sector of the south-east, headed by the financial magnates of the City of London. The decisive institutional innovations which ushered it in were the creation of the Bank of England and the National Debt. These enabled the emergent British state to mobilize credit on a scale its continental rivals could not equal. But it could mobilize credit only because it was creditworthy; because service-sector lenders could trust it with their money. In the nineteenth century, it experienced a kind of mutation. Under the aegis of a distinctive 'gentlemanly capitalism', it banished 'Old Corruption'; replaced protection with free trade; and substituted Gladstonian economy for fiscal laxity. The gentlemanly-capitalist state of the nineteenth century was more ambitious than the military-fiscal state of the eighteenth. It sought to make the world safe for gentlemanly capitalism, not just to acquire booty. But it was as militaristic as its coarser eighteenth-century predecessor, developing a characteristic 'British way in warfare' focused on a high-tech (and high-cost) navy.[24] Above all, the nexus, financial services/creditworthiness/imperial expansion/aristocratic leadership, remained in being; and the values and assumptions that underpinned it still shaped the statecraft of the political elite.

It shaped domestic statecraft as well as imperial. Indeed, the two were – had to be – different sides of the same coin. The formal empire of bases, trading posts, self-governing colonies, directly ruled territories and variegated dependencies was only part of a bigger informal empire of capital movements and trading relationships. Capital poured out from London to investment-hungry territories in distant places, some of them parts of the formal empire and others not. In combination with the invisible earnings of British banks, British insurers and British shipping, the income from these investments more than covered Britain's deficit on visible trade. Meanwhile, her stubborn adherence to free trade ensured that her debtors could earn the wherewithal to service their debts. In Susan Strange's language, sterling became the world's first 'Top Currency',[25] the dominant reserve and trading medium, further enhancing the supremacy of British financial services in the world at large and making it even more essential to pursue domestic policies that would preserve that supremacy and, in doing so, fortify the supremacy of the financial-service sector in the British economy.

For the overriding purpose of the gentlemanly-capitalist state was to make sure that the rules of the global order were observed. That imperative applied as much to Birmingham as to Buenos Aires or Bombay. Everywhere, markets had to be open; debts had to be paid; and the canons of fiscal orthodoxy had to be observed. Above all, sterling, the linchpin of the system, had to be freely convertible into gold, and the British Treasury and Bank of England had to frame their policies accordingly. The fiscal constitution of which they were the custodians – free trade, balanced budgets and the gold standard – was the hinge on which the global order turned. The central state's attitude to the British provinces, and to the industrial economy of the provinces, was stamped by the same imperatives. It had a monopoly of the high politics on which its global role depended, and managed the provinces through a tacit form of indirect rule, reminiscent of colonial governance, that left local affairs to local elites.[26] But the crucial clause in this unwritten territorial constitution was that the interests of provincial Britain came second to the requirements of the global system.

VI

Against that background, the complex and contested interrelationships between the British state and the British economy begin to fall into place. As Ronald Dore pointed out some time ago, the growth of the British state since the heyday of *laissez-faire* has followed an aberrant path. Like most other western states, it became first a regulatory state and later a welfare state. Unlike its most successful competitors in East Asia and on the European mainland, however, it did not become a developmental state – a state that uses public power, in Dore's words, 'explicitly to promote the competitiveness of the nation seen as one actor in a cut-throat world economy'.[27] One of the central questions of twentieth-century British history is why successive attempts to steer it in that direction all failed.[28] In the perspective offered by Cain and Hopkins on the one hand, and by Edgerton on the other, that question becomes much more complex. For there is a sense in which the 'gentlemanly capitalist' state *was* a developmental state after all, albeit of a highly eccentric kind. Though it did not acknowledge the fact explicitly, it *did* use public power to promote international competitiveness and even technological innovation. It used it, however, on behalf of the 'gentlemanly-capitalist' service sector in its south-eastern heartland and of the technology-hungry defence establishment. Unless they were fortunate enough to be part of the military-industrial complex, the 'ungentlemanly capitalist' manufacturers in the provinces had to fend for themselves.

Free trade, defence of the gold standard and adherence to the canons of fiscal orthodoxy should not be seen as irrational impediments to national development and nothing more. They may have impeded the development of the national economy as a whole, but they fostered development in its dominant sector. They were the instruments of an entirely rational economic strategy, dictated by the needs of the financial-service sector and by the interwoven imperatives of imperial power and Top Currency management. In essence, two rationalities were in conflict: the rationality of the global system and the rationality of domestic industry. Given its inescapably, necessarily imperial vocation, the *ancien régime* was bound to privilege the former over the latter. This process, moreover, was cumulative. The more the British state gave priority to the demands of global gentlemanly capitalism to the detriment of domestic ungentlemanly capitalism, the stronger were the pressures upon it to continue to do so. As time went on, the structure of comparative advantage within which the managers of the British economy had to operate was tilted further and further towards the financial-service sector; and it became more and more difficult to break out of it. To that extent, W. D. Rubinstein is right in arguing that occasional post-war attempts to overcome the gap between the relatively impoverished industrial north and the prosperous, service-dominated south-east ran counter to economic and social realities.[29] But the structure of comparative advantage reflected in these realities owed more to the priorities of the British state in earlier periods than to the workings of divine providence.

Much the same applies to Michel Albert's suggestive contrast between the individualistic, finance-dominated, stock-market-driven 'neo-American' capitalism of Britain and the United States and the collaborative, 'Rhenish' model of central Europe, Scandinavia and Japan.[30] Few would dispute that present-day British capitalism is quintessentially 'neo-American' in Albert's sense. Yet, as Colin Crouch, Jonathan Zeitlin and Will Hutton have pointed out, important elements of his 'Rhenish' alternative were present in the industrial provinces of the nineteenth century[31] – not least among the Sheffield cutlers described by Alfred Marshall.[32] But to sustain them, Britain's political and monetary authorities would have had to follow a developmental strategy of the sort followed in imperial Germany. To do that, they would have had to defy the imperatives of Top Currency management. And, for gentlemanly capitalists, that was unthinkable.

VII

As all this implies, the outstanding characteristic of Britain's *ancien régime* has been its resilience and longevity. Both were as marked in the early post-war period as they had been before 1939. Like its continental equivalents, the political and social settlement hammered out in the late 1940s and early 1950s was the product of 'second-best compromises', not conscious intent.[33] But the compromises were not accidental. They were stamped through and through by the inherited reflexes, assumptions and operational codes of the *ancien régime* – albeit as mediated by the pressures of the post-war world, by the preferences of the state's new managers, by the demands of their constituents and by the theories of Keynes.

In spite of obvious changes, the most striking feature of the post-war settlement was its continuity with the past. The 'developmental' interventionism implied by Labour's 1945 commitment to planning was abandoned in favour of Keynesian demand management – a new variation on the familiar theme of indirect rule.[34] Nationalization, originally seen as a prerequisite of a planned economy, produced a series of half-autonomous industrial satrapies, only a little easier to control than large private firms. The international record is more complicated, but it exhibits essentially the same pattern. At first the Labour government flirted with a 'two-worlds' strategy, combining leadership of an autarkic sterling bloc with leadership of non-Communist Europe. In the end, however, it opted for subaltern status in the American-centred global system which became the successor to the nineteenth-century *pax Britannica*.[35] It did so for a variety of reasons. But there is not much doubt that the chief reason was that, of the options on offer, the role of chief lieutenant to a hegemonic United States was the most congruent with the interests of the financial-service sector and with the operational codes developed during 250 years of 'world island' statecraft.

Above all, the form and structure of the state and the patterns of authority and consent that underpinned it were left unchanged. The absolutely sovereign Crown-in-Parliament remained absolutely sovereign; the localities were still viewed as colonies, to be managed through indirect rule; leaders still led and followers still followed. The strangulated, almost furtive, quasi-corporatism of the interwar period extended its scope; state institutions were closely intermeshed with the great producer groups of organized labour and organized capital;[36] in the most sensitive areas, at any rate, welfare policy was hammered out in negotiations with the most powerful of the professional groups involved.[37] But open power-sharing on Scandinavian or central European lines was conspicuous by its absence. The participatory productivism of the wartime shop-stewards movement dribbled away;[38] there was no *Mittbestimmung*, either within industry or between industry and the state. In both private and public spheres, Leo Amery's subtle rephrasing of Lincoln – 'government of the people, for the people, with but not by the people'[39] – continued to epitomize the governance of Britain. We should not belittle the Attlee government. It did more good to more people than any other government in twentieth-century British history. But in the perspective of the *longue durée* of British statehood, it was a government of renewal, not of transformation. And, partly because of this, the settlement which gradually took shape while it was in power was unstable, fluctuating and subject to continual attempts to reconstruct it.

Now the renewed *ancien régime* has started to wear out. Since the late 1960s, four interconnected sets of changes have called its presuppositions into question and eroded its legitimacy. In the first place, a radical mutation of the global political economy has made it impossible to practise the 'world-island' statecraft of the post-war period, confronting the political class with a dilemma to which past history offers no guide. The role of chief subaltern to a hegemonic United States is no longer available: the United States is no longer a hegemon. The loss of the Vietnam War, the toppling of the dollar, the end of the Bretton Woods exchange-rate system, the globalization of capital markets, the end of the cold war and the growing competitive power of East Asia have, between them, destroyed the American-centred global system in which post-war

British governments found their special niche. In logic, there are two possible successors, each involving a painful and disorientating break with the traditions of the *ancien régime*.

The first is to become the Hong Kong of Europe; the second is to become a whole-hearted member of an increasingly proto-federal European Union. The first entails rolling with the punch of the global market place – sticking vigorously to the orthodoxies of free trade; attracting mobile international capital through deregulation, a flexible labour market and a regressive tax regime; exploiting the comparative advantages conferred by the English language, by the City of London and by propinquity to the European mainland; but refusing any form of European integration that goes beyond freeing trade and capital movements. The second entails embracing a European rather than a global vocation; sharing power with the Union's institutions and its other member states; recognizing that the fundamental purpose of the European project is, in the words of the Rome Treaty, to create an 'ever-closer Union'; and, at least in principle, accepting the need for further transfers of competence and authority from the national to the supranational level.

Both options run against the grain of British statehood, at least potentially. Power-sharing and coalition-building are, and always have been, fundamental to the European project. But power-sharing and coalition-building are logically incompatible with the parliamentary absolutism which lies at the heart of the *ancien régime*. Yet if the European option is, in the long run, incompatible with British statehood, so too is the Hong Kong option. Influence in world affairs has always been the lifeblood of the British state; as Europe's Hong Kong, outside the proto-federation across the Channel, Britain could not expect to be more than a minor player on the world stage. Confronted with these dilemmas, the British political class has been consumed by an agony of confusion and prevarication. In the early 1970s, the Heath government plumped for the European option. New Right logic points unmistakably towards the Hong Kong option, but, in this field at least, the Thatcher and Major governments never quite relinquished their Heathite legacy. As a result, the European question has been a grumbling appendix in the entrails of the British state. It has never been excised, but the pain has never gone away.

Part of the explanation lies in the second set of changes. Together with the loss of empire and a Europe-wide renaissance of non-metropolitan ethnicities, entry into the European Community challenged – perhaps even made nonsense of – the imperial 'British' identity constructed in the eighteenth and nineteenth centuries. All identities, even the most benign, presuppose an 'other' with a different identity. Almost by definition, *ancien-régime* Britain's 'other' was continental Europe. The British were the people – free, oceanic, globe-girdling, discoverers of the secrets of parliamentary government and civil liberty – who had made themselves by shaking off continental entanglements and resisting continental despots. Shorn of empire, and locked into an integrating Europe, the purpose of which was to build an 'ever-closer union' among its peoples, they would not – indeed, could not – be such a people any longer. Nor, however, could they be anyone else. Imperial Britain was not one among several possible Britains, in the way that republican France is – or, at least, used to be – one among several possible Frances. Imperial Britain was Britain. The iconography, the myths, the rituals in which Britishness was embodied were, of necessity, imperial, oceanic, extra-European: they could not be anything else. Empire was not an optional extra for the British; it was their reason for being British as opposed to English or Scots or Welsh. Deprived of empire and plunged into Europe, 'Britain' had no meaning. What had meaning were either the separate nations of the British Isles or Tom Nairn's bloodless, historyless, affectless 'Ukania'.[40]

Meanwhile, the smaller peoples of the British Isles have reasserted their own, pre-British identities in a fashion reminiscent of the Flemings, the Catalans, the Basques and the Corsicans, to say nothing of a long line of Slavic peoples in eastern and central Europe. The result has been a vigorous, sometimes passionate (and, in the case of Northern Ireland, bloody) debate about the meaning of nationality and its relationship with the British state. The logical response would be to reconstruct the notions of 'Britain' and 'Britishness' around a reconstructed union, based on federalist power-sharing, and looking forward to a possible 'Europe des régions' in the twenty-first century. In Scotland, and to a lesser extent in Wales, that response appears to be widely shared. The identities implicit in the Scottish and Welsh demands for home rule are plural, not singular; they would be realized by reconstructing the multinational British state and anchoring it in a supranational European Union, not by abolishing it. But federalism within Britain would be no more tolerable to the *ancien régime* than is membership of a federalizing Europe.

The third set of changes has been the most painful, or at any rate the most obtrusive. By the mid-1970s, a combination of continuing relative economic decline and global transformation had produced a crisis in the relationship between the British state and the British economy. It was no longer possible to combine overt quasi-Keynesianism, furtive quasi-corporatism and membership of a broadly liberal, open international economy in the way that the post-war settlement had combined them. The attempt to do so produced mounting inflation, deepening currency depreciation, bruising battles between the state and organized labour and what seemed to the political class to be a threat of ungovernability. In principle, at any rate, the state and its managers had to choose between three possible paths. The first was the renascent economic liberalism of the New Right. The second was the 'Alternative Strategy' of the Labour left – a combination of state-led national development and anti-capitalist gestures behind a wall of import controls. The third was never articulated in so many words, but it was nevertheless immanent in the situation in which British policy-makers found themselves. It was (or perhaps it would be better to say it would have been) a 'European', part-Christian and part-social-democratic strategy, combining unequivocal commitment to the European Community with an explicit, perhaps legally entrenched, form of corporatist power-sharing and an attempt to reorientate British capitalism along broadly Rhenish lines.

As everyone knows, state and people chose the first – not least because it seemed to be the most congruent with the traditions and operational codes of the *ancien régime*, as well as with the existing character of British capitalism and the structure of comparative advantage it had created. The second and third paths would both have entailed a sharp break with the past, a new aproach to the economy, a new kind of state and a new vision of Britain. Though the first came to be presented as a revolution, its real attraction was that it seemed to be the least revolutionary of the three.

This leads on to the fourth and least obvious set of changes. It has slowly become clear that there was a paradox in the congruence between New Right ideology and *ancien régime* tradition. New Right economics were compatible with that tradition. Indeed, the forms and structures in which it was embodied were indispensable to the achievement of New Right objectives: parliamentary absolutism and executive autonomy were the midwives of neo-liberalism. Without the concentration of power which they made possible, the Thatcher and Major governments could not have marginalized the trade unions, curbed the local authorities, privatized most of the nationalized industries or imposed market norms on the remaining public sector. But forms and structures are one thing; tacit understandings another. And in at least two respects, the neo-liberal project ran against the grain of the tacit understandings of the *ancien régime*. In the first place, its understandings were responsive, not proactive; permissive, not coercive. Indirect rule was of its essence; its motto was 'live and let live'. Concentrated executive power was always there in reserve, but with the unspoken proviso that it should be kept in reserve as much as possible. The old Whig historians were not wrong in depicting Britain as the pioneer of civil society; and it is not a paradox that the intermediate institutions that make up a civil society flourished more under her *ancien régime* than under the modernizing regimes of mainland Europe. Secondly, and in some ways even more importantly, the operational codes of the central state were shaped by a professional ethic, dating from the administrative reforms of the nineteenth century, which drew a clear line between the public domain and the domain of the market place.[41]

With these tacit understandings, New Right economics were soon at war. When the Thatcher and Major governments used the formidable battery of powers available to the central state to reconstruct civil society in the image of an 'enterprise culture', they were true to New Right teaching. But they were using the forms of the *ancien régime* to snuff out its spirit. The same was true of their attempt to blur the old distinction between state institutions, animated by a public-service ethic, and market institutions, driven by the profit motive. Hayekian neo-liberalism, in short, has turned out to require as fundamental a reconstruction of the state as would Rhenish social democracy or isolationist national development – albeit a reconstruction of understanding and conduct rather than of structure.

The implications go deeper than appears at first sight. The forms of the *ancien régime* survive, but fifteen years of New Right rule have almost killed its spirit. As some High Tories are beginning to realize, its spirit can be resuscitated only by abandoning its forms: its old tolerance of diversity only by introducing checks and balances to limit the parliamentary absolutism which has been part of it since the Reformation statutes of Henry VIII.[42] Meanwhile, the identity it used to embody has evaporated, while the place it used to occupy in the global political economy has disappeared. Reconstruction of some sort seems inevitable. The questions are how and when, not whether.

1995

Notes

Chapter 1 Journey to an Unknown Destination

1 The term is Eric Hobsbawm's, in his *Age of Extremes*, part II, *The Short Twentieth Century 1914–1991*, Michael Joseph, London, 1994.

2 For the role of the Marshall Plan as the vehicle through which the Americans tried to export the social compromises embodied in the New Deal to Europe see M. J. Hogan, *The Marshall Plan: America, Britain and the Reconstruction of Western Europe, 1947–1952*, Cambridge University Press, Cambridge, 1987.

3 For an illuminating description of the accommodation between revisionist social democracy and free-market ideology see Donald Sassoon, *One Hundred Years of Socialism: The West European Left in the Twentieth Century*, I. B. Tauris, London and New York, 1996, pp. 730–77.

4 Michel Albert, *Capitalism against Capitalism*, Whurr Publishers, London, 1993; Harold Perkin, *The Third Revolution: Professional Elites in the Modern World*, Routledge, London, 1996.

5 Simon Head, 'The New, Ruthless Economy', *New York Review of Books*, 29 February 1996, pp. 47–52.

6 The Commission on Social Justice, *The Justice Gap*, IPPR, London, 1993, pp. 44–5.

7 Head, 'The New, Ruthless Economy', p. 47.

8 Harold Perkin, *The Rise of Professional Society: England since 1880*, Routledge, London, 1989.

9 For illuminating discussions of the role of trust in market economies see Francis Fukuyama, *Trust: The Social Virtues and the Creation of Prosperity*, Hamish Hamilton, London, 1995; John Kay, *The Foundations of Corporate Success: How Business Strategies Add Value*, Oxford University Press, Oxford, 1993; and Michel Albert and Rauf Gonenc, 'The Future of Rhenish Capitalism', *The Political Quarterly*, July–September 1996, pp. 184–93.

10 Andrew Shonfield, *Europe: Journey to an Unknown Destination*, Allen Lane/Penguin, London, 1973.

11 David Marquand, 'The Secret People of Oxford', *New Statesman*, 13 July 1957.

12 A. J. P. Taylor, 'Tory History', in his *Rumours of Wars*, Hamish Hamilton, London, 1952, pp. 14–18.

13 Ernest Gellner, *Words and Things: A Critical Account of Linguistic Philosophy and A Study in Ideology*, Victor Gollancz, London, 1959.

14 Raymond Plant, 'Social Democracy', in David Marquand and Anthony Seldon, *The Ideas that Shaped Post-War Britain*, Fontana Press, London, 1996.

15 John P. Mackintosh, *The British Cabinet*, Stevens, London, 1962, p. 546.

16 Andrew Shonfield, *Modern Capitalism: The Changing Balance of Public and Private Power*, Oxford University Press, London, 1965.

17 David Marquand, 'Controlling the Controllers', *Interplay*, December 1967.

18 For which see Perry Anderson, 'Origins of the Present Crisis', originally published in the *New Left Review* in 1964 and reprinted in Perry Anderson, *English Questions*, Verso, London, 1992, pp. 15–47.

19 C. A. R. Crosland, *The Conservative Enemy: A Programme of Radical Reform for the 1960s*, Jonathan Cape, London, 1962.

20 David Marquand, *Ramsay MacDonald*, Jonathan Cape, London, 1977, p. 3.

21 Crosland, *The Conservative Enemy*, p. 8.

22 David Marquand, 'Europe' in Ben Whitaker (ed.), *A Radical Future*, Jonathan Cape, London, 1967.

23 Illuminating examples include Kathleen Burke and Alec Cairncross, *'Goodbye Great Britain': The 1976 IMF Crisis*, Yale University Press, New Haven and London, 1992; David Coates, *Labour in Power: A Study of the Labour Government 1974–1979*, Longman, London, 1980; and Edmund Dell, *A Hard Pounding: Politics and Economic Crisis 1974–76*, Oxford University Press, Oxford, 1991.

24 Sir Keith Joseph, *Reversing the Trend: A Critical Reappraisal of Conservative Economic and Social Policies*, Barry Rose, Chichester and London, 1975; and *Stranded on the Middle Ground*, Centre for Policy Studies, London, 1976; Stuart Holland, *The Socialist Challenge*, Quartet Books, London, 1975.

25 David Marquand, 'A Social Democratic View', in Insitute of Economic Affairs, *The Dilemmas of Government Expenditure: Essays in Political Economy by Economists and Parliamentarians*, IEA Readings 15, London, 1976.

26 David Marquand to John Horam, 10 September 1976.

27 Notebook, October 1977.

28 David Marquand, *Parliament for Europe*, Jonathan Cape, London, 1979.

29 Mancur Olson, *The Rise and Decline of Nations*, Yale University Press, New Haven and London, 1982.

30 Anthony Lester, 'Fundamental Rights in the United Kingdom: The Law and the British Constitution', *University of Pennsylvania Law Review*, 125, no. 2.

31 Peter Clarke, *Liberals and Social Democrats*, Cambridge University Press, Cambridge, 1978.

32 Michael Stewart, *The Jekyll and Hyde Years: Politics and Economic Policy Since 1964*, J. M. Dent, London, 1977.

33 David Marquand, 'Has Social Democracy a Future?', *The Spectator*, 29 September 1979.

34 David Marquand, 'Taming Leviathan: Social Democracy and Decentralisation', Eighth Rita Hinden Memorial Lecture, Socialist Commentary Publications Ltd, London, 1980.
35 David Marquand, 'The Politics of Nostalgia', University of Salford, 1979.
36 Albert O. Hirschman, *Exit, Voice and Loyalty: Responses to Decline in Firms, Organisations and States*, Harvard University Press, Cambridge, Mass., 1970.
37 David Marquand, 'Inquest on a Movement', *Encounter*, July 1979.
38 David Marquand, *The Unprincipled Society: New Demands and Old Politics*, Jonathan Cape, London, 1988.
39 Charles E. Lindblom, *Politics and Markets: The World's Political-Economic Systems*, Basic Books, New York, 1977; John Zysman, *Governments, Markets and Growth: Financial Systems and the Politics of Industrial Change*, Cornell University Press, Ithaca and London, 1983; Ronald Dore, 'Industrial Policy and How the Japanese Do It', *Catalyst*, Spring 1986, pp. 45–58 and *British Factory – Japanese Factory: The Origins of National Diversity in Industrial Relations*, University of California Press, Berkeley and Los Angeles, 1973; Andrew Gamble, *Britain in Decline: Economic Policy, Political Strategy and the British State*, Papermac, London, 1981; Philippe C. Schmitter and Gerhard Lehmbruch (eds), *Patterns of Corporatist Policy Making*, Sage Publications, London and Beverly Hills, 1982; Keith Middlemas, *Politics in Industrial Society: The Experience of the British System since 1911*, André Deutsch, London, 1979; Harold Perkin, *The Origins of Modern English Society 1780–1880*, paperback edn, Routledge and Kegan Paul, London, 1972; Alasdair Macintyre, *After Virtue: A Study in Moral Theory*, Duckworth, London, second edn, 1985; Mary Midgeley, *Beasts and Men: The Roots of Human Nature*, Methuen, London, 1980.
40 Brian Lee Crowley, 'The Limitations of Liberalism: The Self, the Individual and the Community in Modern Political Thought with special reference to F. A. Hayek and Sidney and Beatrice Webb', London University Ph.D., 1985, p. 14.
41 Marquand, *The Unprincipled Society*, pp. 232 and 246.
42 See in particular Adrian Oldfield, *Citizenship and Community: Civic Republicanism and the Modern World*, Routledge, London, 1990, and Michael J. Sandel, *Democracy's Discontents: America in Search of a Public Philosophy*, Belknap Press, Cambridge, Mass., 1996.
43 Albert, *Capitalism against Capitalism*; Colin Crouch and David Marquand, *Ethics and Markets: Co-operation and Collaboration within Capitalist Economies*, Blackwell, Oxford, 1993; Jonathan Boswell, *Community and the Economy: The Theory of Public Co-operation*, Routledge, London, 1990; Perkin, *The Third Revolution*; Kay, *The Foundations of Corporate Success*.
44 David Marquand, *The Progressive Dilemma: From Lloyd George to Kinnock*, Heinemann, London, 1991.
45 Karl Polanyi, *The Great Transformation: The Political and Economic Origins of Our Time*, Beacon Press, Boston, 1957, originally published in 1944 as *The Political and Economic Origins of our Time*.

46 Ibid, pp. 140–1.
47 Robert Skidelsky, 'Thatcher's Unfinished Business', *Prospect*, January 1996, pp. 38–45.

Chapter 2   Reinventing Civic Republicanism

1 Vaclav Havel (ed. Jan Vladislav), *Living in Truth*, paperback edn, Faber, London, 1989.
2 Douglas Hurd, 'Citizenship in the Tory Democracy', *New Statesman*, 29 April 1988.
3 Raymond Plant, 'Citizenship, Empowerment and Welfare' and Julian Le Grand, 'Re-thinking Welfare: A Case for Quasi-Markets?' in Ben Pimlott, Anthony Wright and Tony Flower (eds), *The Alternative*, W. H. Allen, London, 1990.
4 HMSO, *Encouraging Citizenship: Report of the Commission on Citizenship*, London, 1990.
5 *Talking About Commitment: The Views of Young People on Citizenship and Volunteering*, The Princes Trust, Commission on Citizenship and Social and Community Planning Research, London, 1990.
6 Raymond Plant, 'Citizenship', pp. 39–40.
7 T. H. Marshall, *Citizenship and Social Class and other Essays*, Cambridge University Press, Cambridge, 1950.
8 C. A. R. Crosland, *The Future of Socialism*, Jonathan Cape, London, 1956.
9 See, in particular, Vivien Hart, *Distrust and Democracy: Political Distrust in Britain and America*, Cambridge University Press, Cambridge, 1978; Denis Kavanagh, 'Political Culture in Great Britain: The Decline of the Civic Culture' in Gabriel A. Almond and Sidney Verba, *The Civic Culture Revisited*, Little, Brown, Boston, 1980; Alan Marsh, *Protest and Political Consciousness*, Sage Publications, London and Beverly Hills, 1977.
10 F. A. Hayek, *Law, Legislation and Liberty*, vol. III, *The Political Order of a Free People*, Routledge and Kegan Paul, London, 1979.
11 Andrew Gamble, *The Free Economy and the Strong State: The Politics of Thatcherism*, Macmillan, London, 1988.
12 Ralf Dahrendorf, *The Modern Social Conflict: An Essay on the Politics of Liberty*, Weidenfeld and Nicolson, London, 1988.
13 Colin Crouch, 'Citizenship and Community', in Colin Crouch and Anthony Heath (eds), *Social Research and Social Reform: Essays in Honour of A. H. Halsey*, Clarendon Press, Oxford, 1992, pp. 81–3.
14 Harold Perkin, *The Origins of Modern English Society 1780–1880*, paperback edn, Routledge and Kegan Paul, London, 1972.
15 For this distinction see Adrian Oldfield, *Citizenship and Community: Civic Republicanism and the Modern World*, Routledge, London, 1990.
16 Ibid., p. 5.
17 Robert M. Bellah, Richard Madsden, William M. Sullivan, Anne Swidler and Steven M. Tipton, *Habits of the Heart: Individualism and Commitment in*

American Life, University of California Press, Berkeley and Los Angeles, 1985.
18 Hurd, 'Citizenship'.
19 Oldfield, *Citizenship and Community*, p. 6.
20 Ibid., p. 173.
21 Bellah et al., *Habits of the Heart*, pp. 295–6.

Chapter 3   After Socialism

1 A. J. P. Taylor, 'The European Revolution', *The Listener*, 22 November, 1945, p. 576, quoted in Charles S. Maier, *In Search of Stability: Explorations in Historical Political Economy*, Cambridge University Press, Cambridge, 1987, p. 153.
2 For these second-best compromises see Philippe Schmitter, 'Neo-Corporatism and the State', in Wyn Grant (ed.), *The Political Economy of Corporatism*, Macmillan, London, 1985, p. 37.
3 Joseph Schumpeter, *Capitalism, Socialism and Democracy*, George Allen and Unwin, London, 1976 edn, especially pp. 131–42.
4 L. S. Amery, *Thoughts on the Constitution*, Oxford University Press, Oxford, 1947, pp. 14–18.
5 Harold Macmillan, *The Middle Way: A Study of Economic and Social Progress in a Free and Democratic Society*, Macmillan, London, 1966 edn, p. 190.
6 For a powerful alternative reading, arguing that the upheavals in eastern Europe should be seen as proletarian revolutions against state capitalism, see Alex Callinicos, *The Revenge of History: Marxism and the East European Revolutions*, Polity Press, Cambridge, 1991.
7 Francis Fukuyama, *The End of History and the Last Man*, Penguin, London, 1993.
8 Geoff Mulgan, 'Reticulated Organisations: The Birth and Death of the Mixed Economy', in Colin Crouch and David Marquand, *Ethics and Markets: Co-operation and Competition within Market Economies*, Basil Blackwell, Oxford, 1993.
9 Martin J. Bull, 'Doing A Bad Godesberg: The Italian Communist Party and the Democratic Party of the Left', paper presented at the Political Studies Association Annual Conference, 7–9 April 1992.
10 Robert Elgie, 'Doing a "Bad Godesberg": Radical Transformations of Parties of the Left in Comparative and Historical Perspective. The French Socialist Party', paper presented at the Political Studies Association Annual Conference, 7–9 April 1992; Edmund Dell, 'A World of Care', *The Political Quarterly*, October–December, 1992, p. 377.
11 The Labour Party, *Meet the Challenge, Make the Change: A New Agenda for Britain*, Labour Party, London, 1991.
12 *Labour's Election Manifesto: It's Time to Get Britain Working Again*, Labour Party, London, 1992, p. 7.

13 For a masterly account of the irrationality of Soviet central planning and its relationship with Marxist theory, see Alec Nove, *The Economics of Feasible Socialism*, George Allen and Unwin, London, 1983; for a vigorous attack on Nove, see Callinicos, *The Revenge of History*.

14 Václav Havel has painted the most vivid picture of this mixture of compliance and cynicism known to me. See Václav Havel, essays, *Living in Truth* (ed. Jan Vladislav), paperback edition, Faber, London, 1989.

15 See, in particular, his description of the aristocracy and the monarchy on the eve of revolution: 'the dynasty becomes isolated; the circle of people loyal to the death narrows down; their level sinks lower; meanwhile the dangers grow; new forces are pushing up; the monarchy loses its capacity for any kind of creative initiative; it defends itself, it strikes back, it retreats; its activities acquire the automatism of mere reflexes.' Leon Trotsky, *The History of the Russian Revolution*, Victor Gollancz, London, 1934, p. 118.

16 For an optimistic recent assessment of their prospects see Perry Anderson, *English Questions*, Verso, London, 1992, pp. 314–23.

17 For a sympathetic account of the Wilson project see Ben Pimlott, *Harold Wilson*, HarperCollins, London, 1992, ch. 13.

18 Fritz W. Scharpf, *Crisis and Choice in European Social Democracy*, Cornell University Press, Ithaca and London, 1991, pp. 274–5.

19 For the critical role of the last see Harold Perkin, *The Rise of Professional Society: England since 1880*, Routledge, London, 1989.

20 Leszek Kolakowksi, 'Introduction' in Kolakowski and Stuart Hampshire (eds), *The Socialist Idea: A Reappraisal*, Quartet Books, London, 1977, p. 15.

21 Michael Walzer, *Spheres of Justice: A Defence of Pluralism and Equality*, Basic Books, New York, 1983, pp. 119–20.

22 Ibid., p. 95.

23 Albert O. Hirschman, *Exit, Voice and Loyalty: Responses to Decline in Firms, Organizations and States,* Harvard University Press, Cambridge, Mass., 1970.

24 Brian Barry, 'The Continuing Relevance of Socialism', in Robert Skidelsky (ed.), *Thatcherism*, Chatto and Windus, London, 1988, p. 146.

25 Roy Hattersley, *Choose Freedom*, Penguin, London, 1987; Bryan Gould, *A Future for Socialism*, Jonathan Cape, London, 1989.

26 Quoted in Norman Denis and A. H. Halsey, *English Ethical Socialism: Thomas More to R. H. Tawney*, Clarendon Press, Oxford, 1988, p. 213.

27 Karl Marx, 'Marginal Notes to the Program of the German Workers' Party', Karl Marx and Friedrich Engels, *Selected Works*, Foreign Languages Publishing House, Moscow, 1951, vol. II, p. 23.

28 Robert Blatchford, *Merrie England*, Clarion Newspaper Company, London, 1895, p. 43.

29 Friedrich Engels, *Anti-Dühring: Herr Eugen Dühring's Revolution in Science*, Foreign Languages Publishing House, Moscow, 1954, p. 391.

30 Preface to vol. II of *Capital*, Foreign Languages Publishing House, Moscow, 1961, p. 15; 'Speech at the Graveside of Karl Marx', Karl Marx and Friedrich Engels, *Selected Works*, Foreign Languages Publishing House, Moscow, 1951, vol. II, p. 153.

31 For the details of this transaction see my *Ramsay MacDonald*, Jonathan Cape, London, 1977, pp. 41–3.

32 Alan Bullock, *The Life and Times of Ernest Bevin*, vol. II, *Minister of Labour 1940–1945*, Heinemann, London, 1967, p. 381.

33 Quoted in Leszek Kolakowski, *Main Currents of Marxism*, vol. II, *The Golden Age*, Clarendon Press, Oxford, 1978, p. 387.

34 For their effect on the British Labour movement see Henry Drucker, *Doctrine and Ethos in the Labour Party*, George Allen and Unwin, London, 1979.

35 For the importance of these co-operative understandings, see Jonathan Boswell, *Community and the Economy: The Theory of Public Co-operation*, Routledge, London, 1990.

36 Sometimes more than prophets. After being howled down at an anti-war meeting in his constituency in August 1914, Keir Hardie told a friend, 'I now understand the sufferings of Christ at Gethsemane.' K. O. Morgan, *Keir Hardie, Radical and Socialist*, Weidenfeld and Nicolson, London, 1975, p. 226.

37 For two vivid examples, see Caroline Benn, *Keir Hardie*, Hutchinson, London, 1992, pp. 351–2, and Jean Lacouture, *Léon Blum*, Seuil, Paris, 1977, pp. 556–7.

38 Mulgan, 'Reticulated Organisations'.

39 For the notion of the developmental state see Ronald Dore, 'Industrial Policy and How the Japanese Do It', *Catalyst*, Spring 1986, pp. 45–58.

40 Alasdair MacIntyre, *After Virtue: A Study in Moral Theory*, second edn, Duckworth, London, 1985, p. 105.

41 Albert O. Hirschman, *Shifting Involvements: Private Interest and Public Action*, Martin Robertson, Oxford, 1982.

42 Quoted in Peter Stansky, *William Morris*, Oxford University Press, Oxford, 1983, p. 64.

Chapter 4   Liberalism's Revenge? Resolving the Progressive Dilemma

1 Isaiah Berlin, 'Fathers and Children', in Isaiah Berlin (ed. Henry Hardy and Aileen Kelly), *Russian Thinkers*, Penguin, London, 1979, pp. 296–7.

2 For a more extensive discussion see my *Progressive Dilemma*, Heinemann, London, 1991.

3 Alec Cairncross, *Years of Recovery: British Economic Policy 1945–51*, Methuen, London, 1985, p. 303.

4 Michael Freeden, *Ideologies and Political Theory: A Conceptual Approach*, Clarendon Press, Oxford, 1996, p. 33.

5 John Stuart Mill, *Utilitarianism, Liberty and Representative Government*, Everyman Library edn, J. M. Dent, London, 1910, p. 239.
6 Donald Sassoon, *One Hundred Years of Socialism: The West European Left in the Twentieth Century*, I. B. Tauris, London, 1996, pp. 734–5.
7 John Keane (ed.) *Civil Society and the State*, Verso, London, 1988.
8 For a fuller account see my 'Half-Way to Citizenship? The Labour Party and Constitutional Reform', in Martin J. Smith and Joanna Spear (eds), *The Changing Labour Party*, Routledge, London, 1992.
9 Colin Crouch, 'Italy since the 1996 Elections: A Special Case with General Lessons', *The Political Quarterly*, January–March 1997, pp. 23–30.
10 Albert O. Hirschman, *The Rhetoric of Reaction: Perversity, Futility, Jeopardy*, Harvard University Press, Cambridge, Mass., 1991.
11 Paul Hirst and Grahame Thompson, *Globalization in Question: The International Economy and the Possibilities of Governance*, Polity Press, Cambridge, 1996.
12 Crouch, 'Italy since the 1996 Elections', p. 27.
13 Stefan Collini, *Public Moralists, Political Thought and Intellectual Life in Britain 1850–1930*, Clarendon Press, Oxford, 1991.
14 Harold Perkin, *The Rise of Professional Society: England since 1880*, Routledge, London, 1989.
15 The phrase is Eric Hobsbawm's, *The Age of Extremes*, part II, *The Short Twentieth Century 1914–1991*, Michael Joseph, London, 1994, p. 330.
16 Benjamin R. Barber, *Jihad vs McWorld*, Times Books, New York, 1995.
17 Michael Sandel, *Democracy's Discontents: America in Search of a Public Philosophy*, Belknap Press, Cambridge, Mass., 1996. Michael Walzer, *Spheres of Justice: A Defence of Pluralism and Equality*, Basic Books, New York, 1983.
18 John Kay, *Foundations for Corporate Success: How Business Strategies Add Value*, Oxford, Oxford University Press, 1993.
19 For which see Michael Thompson, Richard Ellis and Aaron Wildavsky, *Cultural Theory*, Westview Press, Boulder, San Francisco and Oxford, 1990.

Chapter 5   The Politics of Monetary Union

1 Commission of the European Communities, 'Report to the Council and the Commission on the Realisation by Stages of Economic and Monetary Union in the Community' (Werner Report), *Bulletin of the European Communities*, vol. 3, no. 11 (supplement), 1970.
2 Roy Jenkins, 'European Monetary Union', Lloyd's Bank Review, no. 127 (the text of the Jean Monnet Lecture delivered at the European University Institute, Florence, on 27 October 1977).
3 Roy Jenkins, speech to the European Parliament, Official Journal of the European Communities, *Debates of the European Parliament*, no. 225.

4 Commission of the European Communities, 'Report of the Study Group on Economic and European Monetary Union, 1980' (Marjolin Report), *Bulletin of the European Communities*, 1975.

5 Commission of the European Communities, 'Report of the Study Group on the Role of Public Finance in European Integration' (MacDougall Report), *Bulletin of the European Communities*, April 1977, vol. II, pp. 564–72.

6 Walter Hallstein, *Europe in the Making*, George Allen and Unwin, London, 1972.

7 House of Lords, *Second Report by the Select Committee on Procedures for Scrutiny of Proposals for European Instruments* (Maybury-King Report), HMSO, London, 1973.

8 David Marquand, *Parliament for Europe*, Jonathan Cape, London, 1979.

9 House of Lords, *Relations between the United Kingdom Parliament and the European Parliament after Direct Elections* (44th Report of the Select Committee on the European Communities), HMSO, London, 1978.

10 John Fitzmaurice, 'National Parliaments and European Policy Making: The Case of Denmark', *Parliamentary Affairs*, vol. 29.

Chapter 6   The New Medievalism

1 Karl Marx, *New York Daily Tribune*, 25 June 1853, quoted in Leszek Kolakowski, *Main Currents of Marxism*, vol. I, *The Founders*, Clarendon Press, Oxford, 1978, p. 348.

2 Karl Marx and Friedrich Engels, *Selected Works*, vol. I, Foreign Languages Publishing House, Moscow, 1951, pp. 36–7.

3 Quoted in Kolakowski, *Main Currents of Marxism*, vol. II, p. 400.

4 Quoted in Anthony H. Birch, *Nationalism and National Integration*, Unwin Hyman, London, 1989, p. 39.

5 Adam Smith, *An Inquiry into the Nature and Causes of the Wealth of Nations*, University of Chicago Press, Chicago, 1976, vol. I, p. 520.

6 Quoted in Asa Briggs, *Victorian People*, Odhams Press, London, 1954, p. 225.

7 For a fuller discussion of the contrast between British and continental European experience in this field see Colin Crouch and David Marquand (eds), *The New Centralism: Britain out of Step in Europe?* Blackwell, Oxford, 1989.

8 Eugen Weber, *Peasants into Frenchmen: The Modernization of Rural France 1870–1914*, Chatto and Windus, London, 1966, contains the best account I know of the way in which the French state tried systematically to obliterate older territorial identities in order to create a French 'nation'.

9 For flexible specialization and disorganized capitalism see, in particular, Michael J. Piore and Charles Sabel, *The Second Industrial Divide: Possibilities for Prosperity*, Basic Books, New York, 1984, and Scott Lash and John Urry, *The End of Organized Capitalism*, Polity Press, Cambridge, 1987.

10 For a fuller discussion of this point, see Judith Marquand, *Autonomy and Change: The Sources of Economic Growth*, Harvester Wheatsheaf, Hemel Hempstead, 1989, pp. 154–72.

11 Samuel H. Beer, *Britain against Itself: The Contradictions of Collectivism*, Faber, London, 1982, pp. 107–208.

12 Ronald Inglehart, *The Silent Revolution: Changing Values and Political Styles among Western Publics*, Princeton University Press, Princeton, 1977.

Chapter 7   Reinventing Federalism

1 Massimo Cingolani, 'Disparités régionales de produit par tête dans la Communauté européenne', *EIB Papers*, no. 19, March 1993, European Investment Bank, Luxemburg.

2 *Report of the Study Group on the Role of Public Finance in European Integration*, Commission of the European Communities, April 1977, vol. I.

3 Alan S. Milward, *The European Rescue of the Nation-State*, Routledge, London, 1992.

Chapter 8   History Derailed?

1 H. G. Wells, *The New Machiavelli*, John Lane, the Bodley Head, London, 1991, pp. 325–6.

2 L. T. Hobhouse, *Liberalism*, Williams and Norgate, London, 1911.

3 T. H. Marshall, *Citizenship and Social Class and other Essays*, Cambridge University Press, Cambridge, 1950.

4 C. A. R. Crosland, *The Future of Socialism*, Jonathan Cape, London, 1956.

5 For a brilliant exposition of the first view see Hugo Young, *One of Us: A Biography of Margaret Thatcher*, Macmillan, London, 1989. The second view is particularly associated with the journal *Marxism Today*. For 'Fordism' and 'post-Fordism' see Michael Piore and Charles Sabel, *The Second Industrial Divide: Possibilities for Prosperity*, Basic Books, New York, 1984. For organized and disorganized capitalism see Scott Lash and John Urry, *The End of Organized Capitalism*, Polity Press, Cambridge, 1987.

6 The evidence is summarized in John Rentoul, *Me and Mine: The Triumph of the New Individualism*, Unwin Hyman, London, 1989 and Ivor Crewe, 'Has the Electorate become Thatcherite? in Robert Skidelsky (ed.), *Thatcherism*, Chatto and Windus, London, 1988.

7 Samuel H. Beer, *Britain against Itself: The Political Contradictions of Collectivism*, Faber, London, 1982.

8 Quoted in R. J. Skidelsky, 'Keynes's Political Legacy', in Alastair Kilmarnock (ed.), *The Radical Challenge: The Response of Social Democracy*, André Deutsch, London, 1987, p. 87.

Chapter 9   The Enterprise Culture: Old Wine in New Bottles?

1 Harold Perkin, *The Origins of Modern English Society*, Routledge and Kegan Paul, London, 1972.
2 See Scott Lash and John Urry, *The End of Organized Capitalism*, Polity Press, Cambridge, 1987.
3 P. Hirst and J. Zeitlin, *Reversing Industrial Decline?* Berg, Oxford, 1989.
4 See Albert Hirschman, *Exit, Voice and Loyalty: Responses to Decline in Firms, Organizations and States*, Harvard University Press, Cambridge, Mass., 1979.
5 In John Zysman, *Governments, Markets and Growth: Financial Systems and the Politics of Industrial Change*, Cornell University Press, Ithaca and London, 1983.
6 In Samuel H. Beer, *Britain against Itself: The Political Contradictions of Collectivism*, Faber, London, 1982.
7 Sir Keith Joseph, *Reversing the Trend: A Critical Appraisal of Conservative Economic and Social Policies*, Barry Rose, London and Chichester, 1975, p. 57.
8 Peter Morgan, Address to the Annual Convention of the Institute of Directors, London, 1990.
9 Friedrich Hayek, *Law, Legislation and Liberty: The Political Order of a Free People*, Routledge and Kegan Paul, London, 1979, vol. III, pp. 111–27.
10 In Harold Perkin, *The Rise of Professional Society: England since 1880*, Routledge, London, 1989.
11 James Bulpitt, 'The Discipline of a New Democracy: Mrs Thatcher's Domestic Statecraft', *Political Studies*, 34, 1 (1985), pp. 19–39.

Chapter 10   Henry Dubb versus Sceptred Awe

1 Patrick Cosgrave, *Margaret Thatcher: Prime Minister*, Arrow Books, London, 1979.
2 HC Debates, Fifth Series, vol. 410, 15 May 1945, cols 2305–7.
3 George Bernard Shaw, 'The Transition to Social Democracy', in Asa Briggs (ed.), *Fabian Essays*, George Allen and Unwin, London, 1962 edn, p. 216.
4 J. Enoch Powell, *Freedom and Reality* (ed. John Wood), Elliott Rightway Books, paperback edn, Kingswood, Surrey, 1969, pp. 338–9.
5 Harold Nicolson, *Public Faces*, Constable, London, 1932, p. 2.
6 Lord Butler, *The Art of the Possible*, Hamish Hamilton, London, p. 28.
7 J. M. Keynes, 'The End of Laisser-Faire', in his *Essays in Persuasion*, W. W. Norton, New York and London, 1963, pp. 312–13.
8 J. C. D. Clark, 'The History of Britain: A Composite State in a Europe des Patries', in J. C. D. Clark (ed.), *Ideas and Politics in Modern Britain*, Macmillan Press, Basingstoke and London, 1990, pp. 39–44.
9 Margaret Thatcher, *In Defence of Freedom: Speeches on Britain's Relations with the World 1976–1986*, Aurum Press, London, 1986, p. 63.
10 Quoted in Philip Buck, *How Conservatives Think*, Penguin, London, 1975, p. 113.

11 Aneurin Bevan, *In Place of Fear*, republished by EP Publishing, Wakefield, 1976, pp. 21 and 25.
12 G. M. Trevelyan, *History of England*, Longmans,. London, 1956 edn, p. 232.
13 Thatcher, *In Defence of Freedom*, pp. 72–9.
14 Quoted in Ross Terrill, *R. H. Tawney and His Times: Socialism as Fellowship*, André Deutsch, London, 1974, p. 173.

Chapter 11   Collaborative Capitalism and Constitutional Reform

1 See, in particular, S. E. Finer (ed.), *Adversary Politics and Electoral Reform*, Wigram, London, 1975. For a powerful critique see A. M. Gamble and S. A. Walkland, *The British Party System and Economic Policy 1945–1983: Studies in Adversary Politics*, Clarendon Press, Oxford, 1984.
2 Michel Albert, *Capitalisme contre capitalisme*, Seuil, Paris, 1991.
3 Jonathan Boswell, *Community and the Economy: The Theory of Public Co-operation*, Routledge, London, 1990.
4 Ibid., p. 54.

Chapter 12   Travails of an *Ancien Régime*

1 A. Bevan, *In Place of Fear*, EP Publishing, Wakefield, 1976, p. 26.
2 J. Meadowcroft, 'Conceptions of the State in British Political Thought', Oxford University D.Phil. thesis, 1990.
3 R. A. W. Rhodes, 'The Hollowing Out of the State: The Changing Nature of the Public Service in Britain', *The Political Quarterly*, April–June, 1994, pp. 138–51.
4 For the role of the monarchy see T. Nairn, *The Enchanted Glass: Britain and its Monarchy*, Radius, London, 1988; for public disaffection see Joseph Rowntree Reform Trust Ltd, *The State of the Nation 1991*, 24 April 1991.
5 For this theoretical debate see Meadowcroft, 'Conceptions of the State' and K. Dyson, *The State Tradition in Western Europe: A Study of an Idea and an Institution*, Martin Robertson, Oxford, 1980.
6 For an excellent summary of this debate see P. Dunleavy and B. O'Leary, *Theories of the State: The Politics of Liberal Democracy*, Macmillan, London, 1987.
7 A. Milward, *The European Rescue of the Nation State*, Routledge, London, 1992.
8 W. Bagehot, *The English Constitution*, Chapman and Hall, London, 1867, pp. 51–6.
9 R. Rose, *Politics in England: An Interpretation*, Little Brown, Boston and Toronto, 1964.
10 L. S. Amery, *Thoughts on the Constitution*, Oxford University Press, Oxford, 1947.

11 A. Gamble, 'The British Ancien Régime', in Hans Kastendiek and Richard Stinshoff (eds), *Changing Conceptions of Constitutional Government: Developments in British Politics and the Constitutional Debate since the 1960s*, Universitäts Verlag Dr. N. Brockmeyer, Bochum, 1994.

12 The *locus classicus* is Perry Anderson, 'Origins of the Present Crisis', originally published in the *New Left Review* in 1964 and reprinted in P. Anderson, *English Questions*, Verso, London, 1992, pp. 15–47.

13 The key formulations are in J. C. D. Clark, *English Society 1688–1832: Ideology, Social Structure and Political Practice During the Ancien Régime*, Cambridge University Press, Cambridge, 1985; *Revolution and Rebellion: State and Society in England in the Seventeenth and Eighteenth Centuries*, Cambridge, 1986; and 'The History of Britain: A Composite State in a Europe des Patries?' in *idem, Ideas and Politics in Modern Britain*, Macmillan, London, 1990, pp. 32–49.

14 See in particular A. B. Cooke and J. Vincent, *The Governing Passion: Government and Party Politics in Britain 1885–86*, Harvester Press, Brighton, 1974; and M. Cowling, *The Impact of Labour 1920–1924: The Beginning of Modern British Politics*, Cambrige University Press, Cambridge, 1971.

15 J. G. A. Pocock, *The Machiavellian Moment: Florentine Political Thought and the Atlantic Republican Tradition*, Princeton University Press, Princeton, 1975.

16 Ibid., p. 547.

17 For this discourse see T. Nairn, *The Break-Up of Britain: Crisis and Neo-Nationalism*, NLB, London, 1977; B. Levack, *The Formation of the British State: England, Scotland and the Union*, Clarendon Press, Oxford, 1987; and H. Kearney, *The British Isles: A History of Four Nations*, Cambridge University Press, Cambridge, 1989.

18 L. Colley, *Britons: Forging the Nation 1707–1837*, Yale University Press, London, 1992.

19 E. Hobsbawm, *Industry and Empire: From 1750 to the Present Day*, Penguin, London, 1990 edn, pp. 191–2.

20 A. Gamble, *Britain in Decline: Economic Policy, Political Strategy and the British State*, Macmillan, London, 1981.

21 P. Kennedy, *The Rise and Fall of the Great Powers: Economic Change and Military Conflict from 1500 to 2000*, Unwin Hyman, London, 1988.

22 P. J. Cain and A. G. Hopkins, *British Imperialism: Innovation and Expansion 1688–1914*, Longman, London and New York, 1993.

23 David Edgerton, 'Liberal Militarism and the British State', *New Left Review*, January–February 1991, pp. 138–69.

24 Edgerton, 'Liberal Militarism'.

25 S. Strange, *Sterling and British Policy: A Political Study of an International Currency in Decline*, Oxford University Press, London, 1971.

26 J. Bulpitt, *Territory and Power in the United Kingdom: An Interpretation*, Manchester University Press, Manchester, 1983.

27 R. Dore, 'Industrial Policy and How the Japanese Do It', *Catalyst*, Spring 1986, pp. 45–8.

28 For my earlier attempt to find the answer see D. Marquand, *The Unprincipled Society: New Demands and Old Politics,* Jonathan Cape, London, 1988.

29 W. D. Rubinstein, *Capitalism, Culture and Decline in Britain, 1750–1990,* Routledge, London, 1993, pp. 36–7.

30 M. Albert, *Capitalisme contre capitalisme,* Éditions du Seuil, Paris, 1991.

31 C. Crouch, 'Co-operation and Competition in Germany', in C. Crouch and D. Marquand, *Ethics and Markets: Co-operation and Competition within Capitalist Economies,* Blackwell, Oxford, 1993, pp. 94–5; W. Hutton, *The State We're In,* Jonathan Cape, London, 1995, ch. 5; Jonathan Zeitlin, 'Why are there No Industrial Districts in the United Kingdom?' paper prepared for the conference on 'Les Petites et Moyennes Entreprises', Observatoire du Changement Social en Europe Occidentale, Poitiers, 22–24 April, 1993.

32 A. Marshall, *Principles of Economics,* Macmillan, London, 1910 edn, p. 296.

33 P. Schmitter, 'Neo-Corporatism and the State', in W. Grant (ed.), *The Political Economy of Corporatism,* Macmillan, London, 1985, p. 37.

34 A. Cairncross, *Years of Recovery: British Economic Policy 1945–51,* Methuen, London, 1985, pp. 299–332; A. Booth, *British Economic Policy, 1931–49: Was There a Keynesian Revolution?* Harvester Wheatsheaf, London, 1989.

35 Public Record Office, EPC (49) 73, Note by Sir Stafford Cripps, 4 July, 1949.

36 K. Middlemas, *Politics in Industrial Society: The Experience of the British System since 1911,* André Deutsch, London, 1979, and *Power, Competition and the State,* vol. I, *Britain in Search of Balance,* Macmillan, Basingstoke, 1986.

37 R. Klein, *The Politics of the National Health Service,* Longman, London, 1989.

38 J. Hinton, *Shop Floor Citizens: Engineering Democracy in 1940s Britain,* Edward Elgar, Aldershot, 1994.

39 For a searching examination of the implications of Amery's formulation see S. H. Beer, 'Reform of the Constitution: An American View', *The Political Quarterly,* April–June, 1993, pp. 198–209.

40 T. Nairn, *The Enchanted Glass,* p. 88.

41 R. Chapman, *Ethics in the British Civil Service,* Routledge, London, 1988.

42 F. Mount, *The British Constitution Now: Recovery or Decline?* Heinemann, London, 1992.

Index